the worry free *Life*

TAKE CONTROL OF YOUR THOUGHT LIFE BY
weeding out the bad and nurturing the good!

*CLINICALLY PROVEN AND FAITH-BASED

TERENCE J. SANDBEK, PH.D.
PATRICK W. PHILBRICK

The Worry Free Life: *Take Control of You Thought Life by Weeding Out the Bad and Nurturing the Good*
Terence J. Sandbek Ph.D. & Patrick W. Philbrick

Copyright © 2008 Green Valley Publishing L.L.C.:

Green Valley Publishing LLC
4300 Auburn Bl, Ste 206
Sacramento, Ca 95841
(530) 621-3098

Find us on the Web at: *www.TheWorryFreeLife.com*
Books may be ordered from: *Orders@TheWorryFreeLife.com*
Readers may contact the authors by email: *Support@TheWorryFreeLife.com*

Chief Editor: Letha Scanzoni
Cover Design and Layout: Libby Nicholson, gocreativeonline.com

Unattributed quotations are by Terence J. Sandbek, Ph.D.
and Patrick W. Philbrick

ISBN, printed. 978-1-59971-931-3
Library of Congress 2007906642

Printed and bound in the United States of America

Table of Contents

In Appreciation

Writing a book is like teaching because it implies expertise on the part of the writer or the teacher. As authors we have learned that the "expert" is one who is continually learning from the readers and the students. Our students and the readers of the manuscript have given us invaluable and insightful feedback for this project. We are indebted to the many people who have contributed knowingly or unknowingly to the book you now have in your hands. Nevertheless, we take full responsibility for the end product.

We want to thank the staff and volunteers at Green Valley Community Church in Placerville, California who God so graciously put in our path to make this program possible: Pastors Ken Burkey and Scott Sinner, Life Skills Director Cindi Ehrghott, Tina Pearson, Janet Wilkes, Joni Rice, and Mike Dennis. In fact, there are far too many to name but we fully appreciate even those that have not been named.

The following people kindly and graciously read the manuscript in the early stages and gave us feedback that greatly enhanced the contents: Jennifer Franz, Veronica Manderson, Alice Parente, Trish Parker, and Julie Swain.

We were fortunate to have two excellent copy editors. Laura Moretti's keen eye thankfully eliminated many errors in the early days of the manuscript. She helped give shape to the written word while finding sentences that were not sentences, grammar that didn't grammar, and punctuation that didn't punctuate. Our final copy editor, Dave Cassafer, found still further errors that had slipped by many critical eyes. While the people before him make significant macro changes, Dave was a master at micro errors.

Author Letha Scanzoni spent countless hours doing the substantive editing that made a good manuscript into an excellent book. She continually amazed us by the pages of comments we incorporated into the pages of this book. She injected graciousness, wit, and intelligence into the many significant changes. Letha also encouraged us in this project be more aware of what we were trying to say and how to say it. She kept us focused on the book while simultaneously helping us to understand this was more than a mere book.

We want to dedicate this book to all the people who have read it in the past, the present, and will read it in the future. We hope that what they have found or will find between the covers of this book will enrich their lives through learning the skills for becoming all that God has intended them to be.

Credits
Bible Versions

Scripture quotations identified as NLT are from the New Living Translation, © 1966. Used by permission of Tyndale House Publishers, Inc., Wheaton, IL 60189. All rights reserved.

Scripture quotations identified as CEV are from the Contemporary English Version, © American Bible Society, 1995, 1999.

Scripture quotations identified as NIV are from the New International Version, 1973 by the New York Bible Society International. Published by Zondervan.

Scripture quotations identified as TEV are from Today's English Version (sometimes called the Good News Bible), © American Bible Society, 1966, 1971, 1976.

Scripture quotations identified as TNIV are from the Today's New International Version, © 2001 by the International Bible Society. Published by Zondervan.

Scripture quotations identified as KJV are from the authorized King James Version of the Holy Bible, 1611.

Scripture quotations identified as GNT are from the Good News Testament (formerly, [GNB] Good News Bible and [TEV] Today's English Version) © American Bible Society, 1976, 1992.

Scripture quotations identified as WEB are from the World English Bible (a modern update of the American Standard Version of 1901).

Scripture quotations identified as NCV are from the New Century Version © 1992 Word Publishing.

Preface

As a cognitive psychologist, I (Dr. Terry Sandbek) have spent about thirty years helping people change their negative, worrisome thoughts. This concentration on thought-changing is crucial for life changes because our emotions are driven by our thoughts, beliefs, attitudes, assumptions, expectations and all other manner of brain activity. In turn, our behavior is highly influenced by our emotional state.

Humans are capable of changing their beliefs through many different avenues. Sometimes we can make drastic changes just through talking aloud what we are thinking about. Having someone just listen to us nonjudgmentally can be an effective catalyst for mental change. Sometimes we can change our thinking patterns by quiet meditation and rumination. Psychologists also know there are instances where change occurs immediately and quickly, as may happen when a person says, "That's it. I am going to stop smoking," throws out his or her cigarettes, and never smokes again. One of the major focuses of education is to change our magical thinking of childhood to the rational thought processes of adulthood.

Development of Psychotherapy

When the profession of psychotherapy began, therapists used basic methods such as listening empathically, encouraging self-reflection, and strengthening resolve to help their clients. Since these are ways that people have demonstrated change in the outside world, most of these strategies were also effective inside the therapy office. Around the middle of the twentieth century, psychology began to become a science more than an art. The process of therapy was studied to find out what parts of it were the most effective for change. We eventually learned that although mere insight into *why* a person struggled with life was sometimes effective, for very many people, it wasn't effective at all. When it was effective, the procedure was time consuming and costly.

The first truly scientific approach to developing change strategies focused on *external behavior* and ignored, for the most part, internal processes such as emotions and thoughts. This approach brought about stunning results with problems such as fears, compulsions, and undesirable habits. Eventually, research psychologists began to apply the same scientific methodology to thoughts and emotions, referring to them as *internal behaviors*.

Out of this line of research came cognitive therapy — technically called cognitive-behavior therapy (CBT). Of the many therapies that exist in mental health (there are over five hundred), cognitive therapy has exploded to the top of the recommended therapy list. Its popularity is not due to a majority vote by psychologists but because of the overwhelming amount of research that confirms its effectiveness in helping to change people's lives.

Development of the Method Used in this Book

When I finished graduate school, CBT was in its infancy and was one of several different choices I had to use with my clients. I found that the more I used it, the more effective I became as a therapist. I also found that most, but not all, of my clients did not want to just talk. They wanted me to show them how to gain more control over their thoughts, feelings, and behavior. My initial clientele were people with panic disorders and people who had eating disorders (I eventually wrote a self-help book for people with eating disorders called, *The Deadly Diet*). Today, I use CBT with almost any problem people bring to my office.

One day, twenty years ago, a client of mine asked, "Let me get this right. You are trying to get me to change my mind—which is filled with negative thoughts—to get rid of all the negative thoughts in my mind?" I was taken aback because it appeared as if I were teaching this person how to make progress by running in a circle.

Within the same week, another client said to me in a fit of frustration, "Dr. Sandbek, there is a voice in my head talking to me." She immediately was afraid she had stepped over the line. She feared that if she was hearing voices, she would now be deemed crazy. Instead, the two situations sparked an idea in *my* head that I might use with other clients. After considerable thought, I began to introduce the idea to other clients.

I found that putting the worry and negative thinking outside of oneself appeared to have several advantages. The first would be to put "distance" between the client and the mental negativity. We know that babies' brains are not capable of worry in the way adults experience it. Nobody wants to worry. Many people see worry as one of the most debilitating of all human experiences. Putting the worry outside let my clients give up taking "responsibility" for hosting the negativity and worry inside their heads. Instead, they could take responsibility for doing something about it. By attributing the worry to something outside of themselves, my clients could avoid self-condemnation, judgment, and labels. We assigned ownership of this negativity to an outside source— a source we called the Voice.

As the years went by, I found that this strategy became a powerful therapeutic tool. I developed "Voice Awareness Training" to help people identify, analyze, and change the influence of the Voice in their lives. Along the way, many religious people asked if the Voice could really be Satan. Others said the Voice sounded very much like an emotionally abusive parent. For still others, a boss or a former girlfriend or boyfriend was identified as the source from which the Voice derived. Some people drew pictures of the Voice and gave it a name.

Within our church classes we (Pat and Terry) have found that calling the Voice the "Enemy" has been quite successful because many churches use that terminology to describe the darker side of human nature. In this book, we use the generic term "Voice" but urge you to substitute your own language if you find that to be easier and more convincing. Other names that people have suggested are: the Spoiler, the Nasty One, the Accuser, and the Adversary. If you would rather use one of these or some other name for what we call the "Voice," please do so. Whatever name you choose, your progress in learning these skills will be amplified by making the Voice as "real" as possible, even though it is simply a metaphor for that side of us that we would do better without.

Our Method at a Glance

You may wonder why we even introduce this concept of the Voice. As described above, cognitive psychology has convincingly shown that our thoughts and beliefs have a powerful effect on our emotions and behavior—whether for good or ill. By externalizing our unrealistic thoughts, we can more easily identify and change these destructive thought patterns.

Metaphors as Aids to Understanding

In the Introduction and chapter 1, we lay the groundwork by telling the story behind the book and describe how the material will be presented through the use of metaphors. We begin by speaking of your life as a journey and as a metaphorical garden over which you have stewardship. The Voice wants you to carry heavy old baggage on your journey (Metaphor 1). And the Voice also wants to enter your garden (Metaphor 2) in the form of pests and vermin in order to destroy your walk with God. A third metaphor, dominoes will also be introduced in chapter 2.

Two Kinds of Happiness

Jesus has told us he has left his peace for us to experience as his followers (John 14:27). This peace is a special kind of happiness that we talk about in chapter 2. Many people spend a large part of their lives trying to find happiness and inner peace. In chapter 2, we help you to make a distinction between transitory happiness and the type of happiness that lasts forever.

Understanding Emotions

Emotions can be enjoyable or personally destructive. If you wonder about the difference between healthy emotional pain and unhealthy emotional pain, then chapter 3 will help you to discover the difference. Knowing this difference is crucial to personal well-being because you need to use different tools to manage them. We spell this out in chapter 3.

Destructive Thinking Styles: Bugs in the Garden

Psychologists have developed an extensive catalog of destructive thinking styles that keep us from living life fully. These thoughts (often called "worry") can prevent us from reaching our personal spiritual goals. In chapter 4, we list twenty-one different thinking patterns (we call them "bugs" in your garden) which can lead us down the wrong path. They are often so common that we do not realize their existence. This chapter will help you become more aware of these thoughts so that you can use the tools in the following chapters to exterminate the bugs.

Identifying the Greatest Sources of Damage and Destruction

Far more troublesome than garden bugs are the vermin the Voice sends into your garden. These destructive varmints are the source of guilt, resentment, irrational fear, helplessness, worthlessness (depression) and unhealthy anxiety. Chapter 6 will help you to identify these vermin in the many nooks and crannies of your mind. You will learn a shortcut method for finding them (Keywords) and why they are so deadly.

Cognitive Restructuring: Special Tools for Fighting Back

When you have completed these chapters you will be ready to exterminate the bugs and vermin from your garden because you will learn the tools for doing this in chapter 7. These tools are not magic bullets even though they are extremely effective for taking your life back from the Voice. Psychologists call this strategy "cognitive restructuring." After you have begun using these tools on a regular basis, you begin to find those experiences that have often been missing from your life—experiences such as peace, joy and contentment.

Christian Affirmations to Help Your Inner Garden Grow

As any good gardener knows, it is not enough to remove weeds, bugs and vermin from your garden. Once the garden has been rid of noxious, life-destroying elements, the gardener needs to nurture and replant the garden. Chapter 8 begins this process for you by showing how to put enough mental nutrients in your garden so that the pests and vermin have difficulty returning. Christian affirmations will help you to fill those mental spaces as the Voice begins to recede from your life.

Weeding Out Illusions and Replanting

Replanting will begin in Chapter 9 as we show you the importance of Christian Rights, Positive Self-Care, Personal Responsibility, Social Responsibility, and Forgiveness . Even though you have learned by this chapter how to weaken the Voice, it will always try to regain a foothold in your life. You will plant these five strong trees that have the quality of being toxic to the Voice.

Putting Mental and Emotional Changes into Action

Since any mental and emotional changes we make must eventually be converted to action, we show you in Chapter 10 how to motivate yourself to make behavioral changes in your life. We have all known people who profess profound changes in their lives but continue to display behavior patterns which contradict these self-professed internal changes. Even after you have eliminated the Voice as a major obstacle in your life, old behavior patterns might remain. Changing habits can be difficult. These tools will help you begin the behavioral journey that will rid your life of bad habits and replace them with good habits.

Happiness Is . . .

Psychologists have discovered that we do not need to spend most of our time focusing on keeping our garden from going bad. Once we have neutralized the bad elements, we need to spend the majority of our time continually making it better. Chapter 11 will introduce you to some of the research in happiness that psychologists have conducted within the last several decades. The field of psychology that grew out of this research is called *positive psychology*. Rather than focus on why some people are unhappy, positive psychologists study why some people are happy and what can be learned from them. Drawing on such findings, you will be shown how to increase your subjective well-being, improve your emotional intelligence, strengthen your social relationships, experience more hope, and learn happiness-building skills such as the Gratitude Visit and Signature Strengths.

In Sum

This book and the accompanying classes are based on the integration of cognitive psychology and positive psychology. These two fields, relatively new in the history of psychology, have excellent research evidence attesting to their ability to offer effective skills for people who desire to change. Actually, this book is built upon *three* foundations: the Bible, cognitive psychology, and positive psychology. In the introduction that follows, you will read the authors' personal accounts of this book's origins.

Introduction

A Personal Word from Pat

This book is the product of two profound periods of growth in my life. Before I became a practicing Christian, I was very involved in the sport of Soaring. I had learned to fly sailplanes at the age of 12 and soloed at 14. I went on to become a flight instructor and the manager of a glider port when I was 23. Racing was always an ambition and becoming a national champion was a lifetime dream. By my late thirties I had acquired a state-of-the-art racing sailplane and was actively pursuing my dream. But I paid a price. It cost me everything I had and left no time for my wife, children or anybody else. My only goal was to be the best in the nation.

I did reasonably well in regional competitions, winning my share of races and gaining a reputation as one of the better pilots around. When I competed nationally, however, I always managed to sabotage myself by doing something too aggressive, sending my score tumbling down to the bottom of the list. I had everything invested in my championship aspirations: all my disposable income, all my free time, my image of myself, and the belief that my self-worth was dependent upon my achievements. Winning a race would leave me feeling great for about 24 hours. Losing a race would leave me depressed for months. I had a great career, a beautiful wife, good friends, but none of that satisfied me. I had to win the national title; there was no other choice. Life was just too meaningless and unbearable without that goal to pursue.

So, in an act of desperation one day, after recovering from a couple months of depression, I opened the phone book to psychologists and found an ad mentioning "Sport Psychology." I had been watching the

Olympics that year and learned that most of the Olympic teams were using psychologists. That is how I met Dr. Terry Sandbek.

Terry began to teach me the skills of cognitive behavioral psychology. His techniques were based on 25 years of clinical research using proven clinical therapies. These techniques have been shown to help with depression, anxiety, anger, eating disorders, phobias, as well as performance enhancement in sports and high performance business and sales techniques. The basic premise has been around for centuries: How you think determines how you feel, which in turn leads to corresponding behaviors and consequences. Jesus knew exactly how our minds work when he remarked: "It is the thought life that defiles you." Carrying a tape recorder with me in the cockpit, I spent countless hours recording and writing about my thoughts and emotions while flying and racing. I began to learn what made me "tick." Some of the revelations were so absurd that I would laugh out loud when I would play back the tapes and hear what had been going through my mind during critical stress situations. I began to learn that I was quite a different person in my thought life than I was on the surface.

The results were phenomenal. Not only did I begin flying better but also I began enjoying it more. I was much more relaxed, more in control. The temptation to "react" was tempered by a more contemplative and consequence oriented type of thinking. I was on my way to winning the nationals—or so I thought.

It was becoming apparent to me that these tools had great potential to help people in all kinds of situations: relationships, work, addictions, behavioral problems, anxiety and depression. It was also at this time that I discovered Terry had a second graduate degree from Fuller Theological Seminary in Pasadena, California. He began to share his faith with me, even encouraging me to read a couple of books by C. S. Lewis. It all sounded very interesting but I never applied any of it to my personal life, nor could I bring myself to go to church. I was still "holding it together" and didn't feel the need to do any of that kind of work in my personal life. I could not have been more wrong.

In 1994, I was "flying" high! I felt more in control of my life than I ever had. But I had no moral compass to guide me with my newly found power. I had a divorce that was so costly that it seriously hampered my ability to race—the one thing I really lived for. I began drinking more than was good for me. I tried to escape my inner pain with tobacco, booze, TV, and other distractions. I was really trying to escape the haunting emptiness inside. I hastily remarried and had a child on the way by 1995. By 1998, I had two wonderful baby boys, and I was a WRECK, heading rapidly into a death spiral. My marriage was horrible. We had little or no nurturing communication. There was a lot of screaming, a lot of drinking, and an ever-increasing sense of hopelessness. I saw my sons facing a future in a broken home, living out the same dysfunctional patterns I had suffered. I had visions of their poor little lives being condemned to the same bondage that was shackling me.

I will never forget the morning my wife approached me and decisively told me it was over. I cannot adequately describe the sense of horror that overtook me. I felt abandoned, rejected, unlovable, unforgivable, hopeless and very, very alone!

I was in Hell. My second marriage was now a shipwreck. I couldn't even allow myself to drink or escape in any of the old familiar ways. I knew that my drinking days were over for good, but I could not find a way out of this terrible abyss. After six months with no relief in sight, and out of sheer desperation, I began to pray the only prayer I knew: the Lord's Prayer.

Slowly things began to change. After a couple of months, I mustered up the courage to walk into church. Except for weddings and funerals, I hadn't been to a church service in decades. Even as I parked my car that day, I had doubts as to whether or not this was a good idea. Would it turn out to be just as dead to me as the church I remembered as a little boy? How had it come to this? Maybe I wasn't good enough to be one of these people. They will see right through me. What the hell was I thinking?

During that first service, I couldn't hold back the pain any longer, and I cried deeply for the first time ever. I felt as though loving arms were being thrown around me and a warm blanket of peace and comfort seemed to be draped around my shoulders. I also felt the kind of approval and love I had always longed for from my own father, a love he had never been able to provide. I realized that God had always been there and was just waiting for me to accept him into my life. I was loved the way I always thought love should be. There was no judgment nor guilt, nor condemnation; in fact, it was just the opposite. I felt as if someone in heaven was actually throwing a party celebrating my return home. On the drive home that day, the world was very, different. Colors were brighter, the horizon was wider, and I felt a sense of belonging and being loved. I felt hopeful and excited. I felt worthy! That was the first day of my life in Christ, a spiritual journey which has given me a great new life. That big old empty hole in my soul was now filled back up with love.

I began attending a recovery group at a local church. It wasn't the usual AA twelve-step program. They used the twelve steps but with a decidedly different twist. The facilitators insisted that each week we "step" a topic that had been bugging us that week. We were prodded into going as deeply as possible into what we were actually thinking and feeling when the event took place. It was then I realized that they were doing a form of the cognitive psychology that Dr. Sandbek had taught me ten years before. I refreshed myself in his principles and practices, bringing them into that small group. The rapid pace of my spiritual, emotional, and character growth was phenomenal. I began to feel hopeful, joyful, strong, and faithful. Life was a wonderful adventure again, full of limitless possibilities. Best of all, I fell more deeply in love with God than I could ever have imagined was possible. Anxiety, depression, a sense of worthlessness, all became virtually unfamiliar in my life. Old resentments were replaced with forgiveness and love. I replaced guilt with self-forgiveness and a hunger to learn as much as I could by taking on newer and more exciting challenges and risks.

As I read through Terry's material again, I realized that what he had taught me dovetailed perfectly with the Scriptures. In fact, the principles seemed to come right out of Scripture. To this day, I think he subconsciously developed his techniques because of his faith and his life-long love for God, even though on the surface his techniques were secular.

A Personal Word from Terry

Soon after Pat began teaching his new life skills class in the church, he asked me if I would be willing to help him put together the materials I taught him when we were working on his flying problem. We gathered all the handouts, worksheets, and extra materials together to design a ten-week course. After adding projector slides for each lesson, Pat began introducing the material.

The response was overwhelming. When word got out about this new class, the class size tripled. Class members found that this class was not one where they were expected to just attend, sit, listen, speak and go home. The material emphasized skills that the class members were expected to practice during the following week. Near the end of each class, the group was broken down into small groups with facilitators chosen and trained by Pat. This was the time to share the previous week's homework and prepare for the new material for the coming week.

Not only did the class participants enjoy this new approach to a small group, they began to report unexpected changes in their lives. One class member was so depressed, that prior to taking the class, he could not summon the energy to complete his resume and look for a job. Halfway through the class, he reported he had been looking actively for a job the entire week. His depression had begun to lift because of the skills he was learning.

Another class member talked about the success she was having with her teenage daughter. Their communication had improved dramatically since she began implementing her new-found skills. Each week more people would share success stories of how God was now able to work more effectively in their lives because the emotional and mental roadblocks were being removed that had stood between them and God.

For a year and a half, each new class was filled to capacity. Word began to circulate around the church that this class was life saving and life giving. People were discovering that the class taught them how to change their lived Christianity. People told us that sermons and Bible reading had helped them to know *what* to do to improve their walk with God. The class showed them *how* to do it.

After several series of classes, Pat mentioned to me that we should put this material into a book so that more people could have access to the material. The stunning life changes we had been seeing made this a reasonable idea. Since I was already gathering material for a new edition of my book, *The Deadly Diet*, and was writing the outline for a new book on worry, this suggestion fit my mental state.

The further we proceeded in writing this book, the more excited I became that we were creating a resource for Christians desiring to further their walk with God. A psychologist professor of mine told me that many people struggle with their faith because they have personal issues blocking their access to God's grace. The ministry of psychology is to help people identify and remove these internal obstructions.

In addition to the many fine Christian books already written, this book offers specific skills to guide people in tearing these obstructions down in order to experience the abundant life. My hope and prayer for each of you reading this book is that the Holy Spirit will help you access the power in these spiritual tools that have rejuvenated the Christian walk that many before you have traveled.

By beginning this book, you are starting a new life's journey. You'll be traveling to places known only in your dreams up until now. Maybe you dream of living a happier life. Perhaps you want a life in which you can deal more successfully with all the trials that have blocked your path. Possibly, you watch and envy others who appear to handle difficulties better than you. As you stand at the station watching others go by into distant lands you might believe these wondrous destinations are forbidden to you. There remains a desperate ache deep within you wondering where God's grace is for you.

You can read many excellent Christian books (see the References section at the end of the book for suggestions). Many of them describe the details and glories of the destination. For some readers, just knowing where to go is enough because their instincts tell them how to get there. However, many readers yearn to reach this destination but don't have the skills to begin or continue the journey. They need a road map.

A Road Map

This book provides such a map. Since simply knowing where to go is not enough, we show you how to get there. As we have already mentioned, the marriage of Christianity and psychology drives this book. The Bible teaches us *what to do* with our lives while psychology shows us *how to do it*.

This journey involves two parts: Learning how to get rid of the old baggage and then replacing it with something new. Your old baggage includes worry, destructive emotional pain and counterproductive behaviors. Another word for this old baggage is "habit." You may have learned many of your old maladaptive habits in childhood because they were functional—they worked for you in that time and place. These early ways of coping made you feel safe; they were the best you could do as a child. Even now, as an adult, your mind may throw you into automatic pilot so that you react according to childhood patterns without realizing it. Christian maturity is about learning to use new skills that provide more effective ways of handling life.

Your Personal Traveling Kit

These skills are not magic. They give you new options for creating a life of joy and peace. They will not solve all your problems—they are a set of tools in your personal travel kit. Life does not always cooperate with your journey. Sometimes the process of change is very slow. Patience is critical. Change does not happen like a light bulb going on. Ask others who care about you to help you be patient.

Often during the change process, people come to the conclusion, "I must have something personally wrong with me." Just because you need this book to help you change your life does not mean that you are emotionally or morally defective. We all need to learn how to live better. As with anything else in life, some people learn quickly and easily, others more slowly and with more difficulty. You may have competencies in other areas that other people do not have. You are now going to learn an additional way of being competent.

Avoiding self judgment is an important waypoint in your life journey. God has filled your core being with essential goodness. This core self might be difficult to reach because of your historical baggage. The trip is easier if you leave your historical baggage behind.

Another comment we hear often is how alone people feel with relation to a specific personal problem. Chances are that many people struggle with the same problems that plague your life. We give many examples in this book of real people who have conquered the very same difficulty you might now think insurmountable. Reading about these people will help you feel less alone.

Losing Your Old Baggage

When you begin to move toward your new life, you may have some uncomfortable feelings about your progress. For instance, you may be overcome with sadness. This makes sense. Loss of the old baggage is a common experience for the many people who have taken this journey ahead of you, and any kind of loss can bring sorrow. Mourning the loss of your old life style is okay. You are leaving what seems like a familiar friend because these habits were always there to comfort you. Many of us have had friends during our lifetime who were not good for us. They may have eroded our sense of self, discouraged positive personal growth, or even urged us to go down the wrong life path. Feeling sadness over the loss of something familiar is perfectly normal even when it's necessary. You might even need to spend time grieving over this loss. This can be a healthy activity because grieving helps you move forward by healing the pain.

Moving forward, rather than backwards or sideways, gives you more opportunity to invest your time and energy in God's grace. Shedding your old ways of thinking, feeling, and behaving precedes replacing them with more constructive ways for coping with life. This involves three agendas: switching from worry to concern; moving from unhealthy emotional pain to healthy emotional pain; and substituting healthy behaviors for old destructive behaviors.

Continuing to engage life in automatic pilot mode slows new learning. Almost everyone we work with has to confront their habits continually when learning new life skills. Falling back into old habits whenever you feel uncomfortable is normal. Discomfort prompts the brain to find the quickest and easiest solution for feeling better. Your old habits fill this need quite nicely. Lots of practice is necessary to learn how to use your new skills. Unfortunately new skills do not make you feel better as quickly as your old habits do. Repetition helps to overcome this problem. The more you practice your new skills—especially when you have no need to do so—the more you speed up your progress.

Your goal is not to eliminate all the uncomfortable feelings in your life. Even if you could do this, it would not be good for you. We all need to learn how to live with healthy discomfort. God has built this into your brain to notify you that you need to make some kind of change in your life. When you follow this lead, you are going to find that you have taken another step toward more grace. If you never felt healthy pain, then something would be drastically wrong with your life.

Resiliency

The first part of the book explains that eliminating your life problems is not what brings you peace of mind—it is how you handle these problems. Psychologists call this ability to respond to overwhelming life events by the term "resiliency."[1]

We want to help increase your resiliency to life's dilemmas and traumas. Research has shown very convincingly (with a few narrow exceptions) that your life circumstances do not bring you personal joy and inner peace. This holds true across all cultures. It is not what happens to you on the outside but how you respond to it on the inside that can make all the difference.

Of course, developing resiliency takes time. How long depends on the temperament you were born with and your willingness to practice your new skills. Practice does not require that you succeed every time. Practice involves many trial and error ventures. You can always practice too little, but never too much.

You are on a mission to dump the old habits and to become proficient in as many new habits as you can. That is an incredibly powerful notion for experiencing the joy of Christ. Remember: It is not simple. It is not easy. But it is possible.

Using A Grace Partner

The most successful way to use this book is to read it and do the assignments with another person. We call this person your Grace Partner. Having a Grace Partner increases the effectiveness of your learning by many degrees. This person can read the book and do the exercises with you. Our experience is that both of you will grow in your respective faith journeys. You can help each other with questions that arise. You can offer each other moral support when life gets rough. Reminding each other about what you have learned helps to hone the new skills you are learning. No one intends the Christian walk to be a solitary one. It is with other people

---

1 Shatte. A. & Reivich, K. (2002). *The resilience factor: 7 essential skills for overcoming life's inevitable obstacles*. New York: Broadway.

that we practice and live our faith. It is where we meet God in the most profound depths of our existence. Grace Partners help to share your most profound and intimate moments. This is a way for both of you to be in God's presence. The Bible tells us that we only need one other person to come face to face with God.[2] One of life's greatest moments is experiencing the joy of helping another person grow in the grace of Christ.

2 Warren, R. (2002). *The Purpose Driven Life*. Grand Rapids, MI: Zondervan

Chapter One
Your Garden

Do not conform any longer to the pattern of this world, but be transformed by the renewing of your mind. Then you will be able to test and approve what God's will is—his good, pleasing and perfect will.
— Romans 12:2 (NLT)

Imagine that you are living your life in a garden, much like the Garden of Eden. Imagine the serenity that surrounds you. Everything is healthy and flourishing. Growth and abundance are evident everywhere. The beauty takes your breath away. You see lilacs and poppies, irises and petunias. The fruit trees are heavy-laden with abundant, ripe, and colorful fruit. Evidence of the Creator's hand is everywhere. You can find little evidence of disease or pestilence. Storms and natural hardships probably exist but never last long or have any devastating effect. Depression and overwhelming anxiety are nonexistent. No one gets panic attacks or suffers from the crippling effects of resentment and bitterness. No pain lasts for long and when it occurs, it always makes the residents grow stronger and more Godlike through their suffering. Joy and love always win and grow to new heights of intensity. When hardship does befall, you handle it with resilience and grace. This is the world God wants for you and intended you to inhabit.

Imagine now that your mind is that garden—that, in its natural state, God created your mind to be as hopeful, joyfully radiant, and abundant as the garden. Imagine, as Paul describes it, that when "the Holy Spirit controls our lives, he will produce this kind of fruit in us: love, joy, peace, patience, kindness, goodness, faithfulness, gentleness, and self-control." Galatians 5:22-23 (NLT)

Continue to imagine that you have just returned to your garden from a long vacation only to find it in disarray. Someone has trampled the property lines and fences of the garden, blurring the natural demarcation between your property and that of someone else's garden. Large patches of weeds full of rotting fruit and dead cuttings stand where beautiful flowers and trees once grew. The boundary of your property and that of the outside world is confused and unclear. What is yours to control is no longer apparent. Pests and vermin have infested your fruit trees and flowers. A sickening pall of winter and death covers your garden and the hope of spring fades in the growing darkness.

Pests and Vermin in Your Garden

The Pests and Vermin in this story are metaphors for the destructive thoughts that exist within all of us. Our English language uses the word "worry" for this mental activity. Anxiety, depression, resentment, and irrational fears are some by-products of this irrational and destructive thinking. These malicious little pests trigger behaviors that rot away at the fabric of our lives. Addictions, eating disorders, avoidance behaviors, escapism, violence, rage, and abuse are just a few examples of the degradation caused by these thought maggots that invade our minds. Ridding your mind of these pests and vermin will allow God's abundance to regrow in your life. It will accelerate your development emotionally and spiritually. Character development and a more fulfilling sense of meaning and purpose will blossom in your life.

The first and most important step is taking personal responsibility for the recovery of your garden. Many people like to blame others for their problems. We could quite naturally shout in protest about the injustice served upon us by the trampling of our property lines. We might righteously demand that the government, the church, our neighbors or family assume the liability for mending our violated property lines and restore the health of our garden. Some people rail on for years about how helpless they are to overcome such a tragedy. We could wallow in our self-pity, mourning the insurmountable loss of the God-given beauty once bestowed upon our garden. From another perspective, someone might convince us that all this happened to us because we are just not good enough to deserve a great garden anyway. Now, some of you are going to get quite motivated reading this. You may have already decided that it is time for some serious gardening in your life. You may be willing to accept the discipline of daily weeding, fumigating, watering, mending fences and nurturing. Sadly, others will just read on, hoping for some magic "God thing" to do the work for them. Those of you who take up the gardening seriously will reap huge rewards and experience a dramatic rejuvenation in your lives. Those that merely read this book hoping for a magic fix will continue to get what they have always had, and for some that may be acceptable.

Fence Repair

Once you have spotted and fumigated the pests and vermin, you will need to repair the fences around the property line of your garden. After that, you will want to post sentries at the entrances that will filter out all destructive influences (thoughts) in your life. Simply doing the gardening is not enough. You need to insure that the infestation never occurs again. At that point, you can start the process of replanting the garden with new and healthy growth. Merely clearing your garden of all the infestation and restoring it to the original beauty and abundance God intended for you is insufficient. You need to learn how to *maintain* your garden in a style that is joyous, fruitful and God-honoring.

As Christians we believe in the existence of evil in this world. Just as the Garden of Eden is a metaphor for the state of grace that God wants for us, we can use another metaphor for the destructive thoughts that come into our minds and play havoc with our desire to be the people God wants us to be. As we mentioned in the Preface, we want you to think of the prompting to entertain negative thoughts as the accusing Voice. Charles Stanley, pastor of the First Baptist Church in Atlanta, Georgia, tells us that "spiritual warfare is fought every day on the battlefield of your mind. The Adversary knows that if he can direct your thinking, it's only a matter of time before you're vulnerable to the allure of sin."[1]

---

1 Stanley, C. F. (2004). *When the enemy strikes: The keys to winning your spiritual battles.* Nashville: Nelson Books.

But isn't blaming the Voice for our destructive thoughts just a way of avoiding personal responsibility? Not at all. It will actually help you to consider all your worry and negativity as coming from outside of you. We want you to do this because you are not ultimately responsible for having this mental negativity. You were not born with it, you never read a book on how to worry, and you have never prayed to become the world's best worry wart. By attributing this negativity to an outside source, you can gain some distance from these mental obstacles. You can then recognize yourself as the owner of your internal thoughts that are positive and constructive. The Voice is the owner of all that weighty mental baggage you thought belonged to you, and which the Voice prompts you to lug around throughout your life. But, of course, you don't have to do that. You aren't responsible for having the Voice, but you are responsible for minimizing its influence in your life.

Faith

If you are still seeking and not convinced yet of the benefits of faith, just look at the faith references in this book as metaphors. You can still obtain a significant impact from the tools we are going to present to you. If this book inspires you to consider faith as a new way of life, the skills you will learn will make the path that much easier to travel. In his book, *The Purpose Driven Life*, Rick Warren writes: "The Holy Spirit releases His power in us the moment you take a step in faith."[2]

The Bible can be a magnificent guide for telling us what to do. Unfortunately, it is not a psychology textbook any more than it is a medical textbook. As Isaiah writes: "The farmer knows just what to do, for God has given him understanding." The Lord Almighty is a wonderful teacher, and he gives the farmer great wisdom" (Isaiah 28:26, 29 (NLT). We assert that any knowledge which helps a farmer or gardener produce good, healthy mental "crops" is in line with God's will and can take us toward the abundant life that Christ promised for us in John 10:10.

---

2 Warren, R. (2002). *The Purpose Driven Life*. Grand Rapids, MI: Zondervan.

Truth

The Bible tells us that the enemy "couldn't stand the truth because there wasn't a shred of truth in him" (John 8:44, MSG). This is another one of the basic precepts in this book: all of your negative, destructive thinking is a lie. The lie may be buried deep within your thoughts. How does the Voice get away with lying to you? You will discover that it has many successful tactics. One of the best is to make you think it doesn't exist. It wants you to believe that it really is *you* who owns all of this self-destructive mental garbage and not be aware that it comes from outside you.

Two Favorite Weapons

The Voice uses its two favorite weapons to accomplish this: *speed* and *secrecy*. In less than a fraction of a second it can overwhelm you with destructive thoughts. Psychologists call this process "automatic thinking." It is a style of thinking that occurs so rapidly and can be so habitual that it occurs without you really noticing it anymore. It is barely perceptible on the edge of your awareness.

Your destructive thoughts are like an iceberg. Above the surface are your noticeable thoughts. Below the waterline exists the unseen automatic, silent assumptions. Even though they are "subconscious," you will learn to recognize those thoughts through training and practice. Much of your learning will involve writing because that will make it easier to slow your mind down enough to hear those quick and quiet thoughts that are ordinarily inaudible to you. This is where the Voice loves to hide and release its pests and vermin. By using the tools and exercises we are going to teach you in the following chapters you can easily defeat the Voice.

Importance of Writing

We are going to show you how to slow down and identify these distorted silent thought patterns and defeat them with the light of truth. In *Too Busy Not to Pray Journal*, one of the world's most inspiring Christian leaders, Bill Hybels writes: "So I developed my own disciplined approach to stillness before God. It is the only spiritual discipline I have ever really stuck with, and I am not tempted to abandon it because it has made my life so much richer. After I reflect on the previous day and write out my prayers, my spirit is quiet and reflective…. The moments that follow are the ones that really matter. This is where authentic Christianity comes from."[3] Writing will also be your key to unearthing the Voice's pests and vermin, fumigating them and letting God restore your orchard and garden to health.

You see, Christ had the ability to see the Voice, and was able to always spot its tricks so he never fell prey to them. In Mel Gibson's movie, *The Passion of The Christ*, Satan (the Voice personified) was always visible to the movie viewers and to Jesus. In one poignant scene in the Garden of Gethsemane, Satan peers right over the shoulder of Christ and tempts him with distorted truths about the nature of the task ahead of him. Christ was in a period of intense mental anguish knowing the reality of the cruelty and torture he was about to suffer. And Satan, true to his devilish nature, jumped in during a moment of weakness to tempt Christ out of the noblest act any human has ever performed. "No man need go through this. This is more than any man should bear." Being who he was, Christ had the ability to clearly see what the "Master of Lies" was up to and consequently was able to resist. Then, in a very poignant moment, in fulfillment of Genesis 3:15, the incarnate Son of God "crushed the serpent's head" under his heel before going off to meet his destiny on the cross.

This is how the Voice works on you too—lurking, ready to pounce. The main difference is that we often do not know the Voice is there. When we do notice what seems like inner negativity we must realize that is the Voice talking to us but trying to hide inside of our head. In this way, the Voice wants us to be the originator of all the mental garbage. Again, Rick Warren writes: "Temptation starts when Satan suggests (with a thought) that you give in to an evil desire, or that you fulfill a legitimate desire in a wrong way or at a wrong time."[4]

Often, we only feel the destructive feelings that come from the thoughts and feel powerless to do anything about them because we have not learned how to recognize the source. The Bible tells us what to do: "There must be a spiritual renewal of your thought and attitudes" (Ephesians 4:23, NLT). This book will show you how to do it.

---

3 Hybels, B. & Nystrom, C. (1998). *Too busy not to pray journal*. Downers Grove, IL: Intervarsity Press
4 Warren, op. cit.

Testimonies

Christine: Christine, a facilitator in one of our classes, realized she was creating her own upsets with her grown daughter by trying to control behavior that was none of her business. By writing about her upsets and using the tools in this book, she was able to let go of a situation over which she had no control. The results brought her relief and a new sense of peace with her daughter.

Kim: Another student, Kim, realized through her writing that she was not responsible for her grown son's anger. She does not feel guilty or responsible for his feelings anymore. Neither does she feel compelled to react to his outbursts. She is free.

Jenn: A life of continual conflict with men was brought to a halt through an intense writing effort. Our friend Jenn realized that she had silently assumed that "all men leave," and so to protect herself, she drove her new boyfriend away fulfilling this belief.

Melissa: Never would she have believed that the secret to weight loss was paper and pencil. Melissa lost 20 pounds using these tools. She also realized how she manipulated her husband, but now is content to let him be himself.

Abundant Life

Perhaps you have been a Christian all your life but have never really developed that sense of happiness that some seem to have. Perhaps you are a new Christian and wondering how you get that life of inner peace so many other Christians seem to have. Perhaps you are just a seeker trying to figure out life like the rest of us. You may have a nagging sense of something being wrong inside you but you can't quite get your finger on it. You do all the right things: you go to church, you read the Bible, you pray continually, you may even serve faithfully, and yet that deep down sense of abundant joy seems to elude you. We're going to show you why that is and how you can enhance your personal spiritual growth.

Writing, Writing, Writing

The purpose of this book is to teach you strategies that will make your life better. The best way you can learn these strategies is by writing, and by writing a lot!

The ones who gain the most from our course are those who take time each day to list all the negative thinking they can recall from the previous twenty-four hours. Seeing the truth objectively on a page has an amazing ability to clear muddled thinking. Your log should include the situation that you were in at the time, the negative thoughts, what you were feeling emotionally, what you did, and what happened as a result of it. The appendix entitled "Life Events Log" will help you walk through this process.

Try to make this a daily discipline so that it becomes a lifestyle. We suggest a half hour per day for such reflection. The goal is to make an extensive list of all the situations that have triggered you into negative thinking—especially those thoughts that you have not fully addressed but are nevertheless lurking around your brain as an amorphous blob of background worry. Such a journal provides the raw materials you'll need as you learn the tools in upcoming chapters. As the Voice attempts to keep you worried, you will learn to attack its pests and vermin but the process begins with a journal of your negative thoughts.

Trying to improve the health of your mental garden without writing is extremely difficult; it is like trying to learn math without writing down numbers and doing calculations. It can be done, but it's difficult. On the other hand, if you are like some in our classes that simply do not like to write, please don't be turned off by our emphasis on making lists and journaling. Some have told us that they have still benefitted without doing the writing. The insights gained from the new material were enough in themselves to give them a new start. As in Pat's case, remembering the material and picking up a pen later (perhaps at a time when the pain and desperation are intense enough) will still help you find a way out of the next pit you fall into. Overwhelmingly, though, the students who experienced the greatest and most immediate changes were the ones who did the most writing.

Keeping Your Writing Private

Your writing must be very confidential. Keep it in a safe place where you're sure no one will find it. Some of you might even need to keep it under lock and key. In extreme instances, you can even destroy it after you write it down. This is an exercise for *you* to clarify all the nonsense that rattles around in your brain every day. It is not intended for other eyes. Some people have objected that writing down their negative thinking may make such thinking more powerful and cause the negativity to become

8

more real. This is one of the Voice's lies. It wants you to believe the writing will not help you. In fact, just the opposite is true. Exposing distorted thoughts to the light of day is essential in analyzing and defeating such distortions.

Some have told us they are too busy to do the homework. This is another one of the Voice's tricks to keep you from growing. It knows if you take the time to start writing, it will be finished running your life. Others have told us they just don't have anything negative in their lives to write about. Our answer is that life will not be smooth sailing forever. Calamities await all of us, and the better you equip yourself to handle the storms of life now, the better off you will be when the gale winds blow.

Our Promise

We can make you three promises about what to expect from mastering this material: 1) You will experience less suffering and when you do undergo suffering, you will experience it in shorter durations; 2) You will experience an increase in happiness and will experience it more often; 3) You will have much greater control over your life. One student in the class challenged us by stating that she hoped we could deliver on our promises. Our answer to her and to everyone was that the results were entirely up to her. If you do the writing faithfully, one-half hour or more per day, and diligently learn these materials and incorporate them into your lives, your results will be beyond anything you can now imagine. Without the effort this may just become another interesting self-help book.

I'll Show You!

Years ago, Terry had an experience that illustrates this point. A client who had reached a plateau and was not writing, came to a therapy session with a striking breakthrough. She explained what had led to it. She had decided to prove Terry wrong in his emphasis on the importance of writing. She would do a marathon writing exercise, determined that it would demonstrate that nothing changed in her life. Consequently, she spent over ten hours that week writing and working on all the skills she had been taught. Although she had intended the exercise to undermine the value of writing, it was she who was surprised by what happened. The insights gained through the writing led to a major breakthrough in her therapy.

Changing Habits

This book is designed to help you change your habits (psychologists call these "adaptive mechanisms"). Habits are all learned, and many that you have learned took place a long time ago. Childhood is a time of intense learning and exploding brain development. When this learning window shuts, the things we learned tend to stay with us and are sometimes difficult to change. As a child, you may have learned to cope with a strange, sometimes confusing, and frightening world. You may have automatically developed ways of dealing with your environment because they were effective for you at that time. These newfound habits made you feel secure and worked as well as they could for your age. As we so often find in adulthood, many of our self-destructive habits are just the old coping habits of that early learning period. For example, when you felt threatened, maybe you threw a temper tantrum and the people who threatened you backed off and left you alone. Adults who fly into rages and lose their tempers are often just continuing what they learned about a scary world when they were younger.

You probably did not learn how to cope with life through deliberation and planning. Your early brain chemistry did this for you. Neural pathways were developed and reinforced every time you engaged in those early coping behaviors. We know that the brain is very malleable and is capable of tremendous change. Nevertheless, those old pathways are never entirely removed. As an adult, when you find yourself in situations similar to the experiences of childhood, you automatically continue and reinforce those old habits. The good news is that as you deal with life in new and different ways, you will actually be instrumental in changing how your brain functions.

Replacement Behaviors

Many people have told us that if they decided to rid themselves of those old patterns of behavior, they would be afraid of feeling like they were living in a vacuum—they would not know how to handle themselves in tough situations. This is why psychologists stress the importance of *replacement behaviors*. It is much easier to give up old habits (the "old baggage" we talked about in the Introduction) if there is something equal to or better to take its place. We will be showing you how to find replacement behaviors that the science of psychology has found to be effective with people.

You may have already guessed that we are talking about learning new skills. All your life, you have been learning new skills: reading, riding a bike, making friends. Some were easy, some were difficult. Either way, you found that the more you used your new skills, the better you became at using them. That is the "secret" to this book. Daily practice is vital. You will notice that we never use the word "perfect." We do not expect you to practice your new skills perfectly. You will make many wrong turns, slip into old habits, feel discouraged, and crave an easier way to improve your life. Since God gave you stewardship over your life, that is your most important job. Stewardship does not mean maintaining the status quo. At its very heart, stewardship is involved with change. It involves work, diligence, mistakes, accountability, setbacks and allowing yourself to be transformed by God's grace.

You are not reading this book because you are defective or morally incomplete. When you came into this life, no one gave you a manual. None of us got one. You are now holding a manual in your hands that we hope will provide you with some of the answers you are seeking . You are very similar to thousands of our clients and class members. We wrote this book because we not only believe in what we are doing, but because of the joy and fulfillment we personally experience when we see the lives of people change in front of our eyes. People who have felt dead for years suddenly become alive. People who went through life cowering in fear, now feel confident and unafraid. People who have been wracked with guilt have had the life-changing experience of self-forgiveness.

You, too, can become part of this growing number of people who are walking in grace and living their lives to the fullest. This is what God wants for your life, and you will honor God by taking this personal journey of improvement. This is the good news of the Gospel: that you might have life and have it more abundantly. Spiritual and personal growth means being able to tear down all the impediments that have kept you from experiencing such a rich, full life in the Spirit.

Assignment

Begin doing a daily writing log, as shown in Table 1-A. Focus each page on one specific event. Format it in three columns. The first being the "who, what, where, and when," the second labeled "emotions" and the third labeled "thoughts, beliefs and interpretations." Fill in column #1 first and try very hard not to put any interpretation, judgments or feeling here—just the facts. The interpretation comes later. Next, fill in column #2, emotions. Try to list as many different feelings as possible that were associated with the event. Then, fill in the #3 column; start with the first feeling at the top of #2 and identify any thoughts that were occurring while you were experiencing that feeling. Move down to the next emotion in the list and come up with a thought, belief, or interpretation that could be associated with that one and so on down the list.

That will be enough for now. The more pages of specific incidents you have, the quicker you will master the material. The exercise for now is just to get very good at discriminating an event from an interpretation and an emotion.

Table 1-A

WHO, WHAT, WHERE, WHEN	EMOTIONS	THOUGHTS, BELIEFS, INTERPRETATIONS
(Step 1)	(Step 2)	(Step 3)
My girlfriend dumped me.	Hurt, rejected, angry	This proves I'll never have a female in my life; I'm never going to date again; My life is miserable
I got chewed out by my boss for no reason.	Mad, scared, confused	He is the most evil person I've ever known; I'm gonna get drunk after work.

Writing Tip

Your first assignment, a three-column daily writing diary, will begin to help you develop and maintain a significant life-long habit of putting internal thoughts and emotions onto paper. The more information you can obtain, the better you will do in subsequent chapters. This is not necessarily about quality, but rather about quantity. Don't be concerned about doing it perfectly. Just do the best you can.

You will use your writings to help complete future lessons. Remember to keep this diary in a private place. The Voice will say the most awful and embarrassing things to you. You need this information but no one else does.

Chapter Two
The Big "H"

I've learned by now to be quite content whatever my circumstances. I'm just as happy with little as with much, with much as with little. I've found the recipe for being happy whether full or hungry, hands full or hands empty. Whatever I have, wherever I am, I can make it through anything in the One who makes me who I am.
— Philippians 4:11-12, MSG

Shipwrecked three times, flogged five times, three times beaten with rods, stoned once, imprisoned twice. Such was the experience of Paul, the author of the words that began this chapter. This devoted servant of God had the presence of mind to say he had found the secret to contentment in all things and in all circumstances. Paul had discovered the difference between Happiness (Big H) and happiness (little h). Since ancient times, people have understood that humans can experience two different kinds of happiness.[1]

As children we learned to understand happiness as events that made us feel good or excited. Tasty treats, thrilling rides at amusements parks, vigorous play activities with our friends. These

Figure 2-A

---

1   Waterman, A.S. (1993) Two conceptions of happiness: Contrasts of personal expressiveness (eudaimonia) and hedonic enjoyment. *Journal of Personality and Social Psychology* 63(4), 678-691.

are all examples of happiness with a small "h." You can identify little "h" because it includes such experiences as pleasure, excitement, and fun. "Little h" is easy to get. Short term gratification is all around us. Great food is in abundant supply. We have an unlimited variety of recreation available to us. Television, radio, DVDs, movies, the Internet and other media are always available. These sources of "little h" happiness are not bad things intrinsically. It's how we use or misuse them that is important.

As we mature, we begin to recognize a different kind of happiness. We will identify this as the Big "H," which also goes by other names such as tranquility, contentment, serenity, composure, and inner peace. Paul describes true Happiness when he writes about the fruit of the spirit—love, joy, peace, patience, kindness, goodness, faithfulness, gentleness, and self control (Gal. 5:22-23, NLT). Notice the last attribute on the list. It is only when we achieve "self-control," as St. Paul advocated, that we can experience this "Big H" kind of happiness throughout our lives. Research on control continues to find that it is often one of the key elements for experiencing Happiness. By self-control we do not mean that we are inflexible and "wound too tightly." Rather, it is the ability to make good choices in response to what happens around us. We also know it is a skill because the more we practice, the easier it becomes.

Big "H" does not just come to us because we are Christians or because we plead with God to give it to us. We need to (in the words of Scripture) "work out our salvation." We need to practice spiritual discipline, the self-control that helps us "keep at it," applying the principles we'll be discussing throughout this book. What sets the Big "H" and the little "h" apart from each other is how pain and discomfort are experienced. Happiness, in the Big "H" sense, is not the absence of pain or discomfort but the ability to cope with it. In contrast, little "h" withers and disappears in the presence of pain, discomfort or inconvenience, because it is dependent on events outside of us.

Won't Money Make Me Happier?

Researchers at the University of Michigan asked people what would make them happier and the unanimous response was "more money."[2] This finding

---

2 Campbell, A. (1981). *The sense of wellbeing in America*. New York: McGraw-Hill

illustrates the confusion most people make between the Big "H" and the little "h." It seems to most of us that outside resources will make us happier. And that is true—sort of. More money will make us feel better temporarily, but it will not improve the quality of our lives. When the *Chicago Tribune* asked people how much money would make them happier, the result was enlightening. People who were making $30,000 a year said that $50,000 would really improve the quality of their lives—they wanted another 67 percent more money. However, when they asked wealthier people—those who made $100,000 a year—the same question, they said they needed $250,000. In other words, they could only be happier with 150 percent more money.[3]

When we fail to make the distinction between Big "H" and little "h" we assume that if we can amass enough little "h," we can then convert it to the Big "H." That is why our drive for material wellbeing never translates into psychological wellbeing. As we spend more time on getting a "better" life (little "h"), we have less time to spend on those activities that can contribute to the Big "H."

In fact, as Swedish economist Stephen Linder pointed out, making more money takes time. That means that the time we spend making money becomes more valuable. Consequently, we begin thinking it does not make sense to spend our free time on anything but making money.[4] As a result, we get to spend less time on those activities that bring us the Big "H," such as listening to music, going for walks with friends, or spending time with our children.

Balancing Big H and Little h

We are not suggesting that little "h" is bad and Big "H" is the only good type of happiness. Our lives need a balance of the two. Big "H" gives us the stable platform on which we can live life during good times and bad. We all want to experience as much little "h" as we can, but as with many other things in life, too much little "h" can be counterproductive. Research

---

3 *Pay nags at workers' job views*. (1987, October 18) Chicago Tribune.
4 Linder, S. (1970). *The harried leisure class.* New York: Columbia University Press.

has shown that within the United States the very wealthy are only a trace happier than people with average incomes.

This tells us that Big "H" has very little relationship with the little "h." Except under extreme conditions, people with a minimum of little "h" can still enjoy a life filled with the Big "H." Additionally, little "h" is more real when it is within the context of Big "H" because we can experience little "h" for what it is worth and not as the defining experience of our lives.

Since Big "H" is a product of a mature spirit inside us and is not dependent upon outside circumstances, any of us can, like St. Paul, develop the ability "to get along happily" (experience the Big "H") in all things. The tools we're presenting in this book will help you gain control over your thoughts and emotions so that you can maintain the Big "H" for a lifetime. The accompanying table (Table 2-A) shows you the differences between Big "H" and little "h."

Happiness and Discomfort

As we mentioned earlier, little "h" and discomfort are opposites. They each drive the other one away. Just when you feel on top of the world, something from outside you can occur that takes away your little "h" and forces you to live with high levels of pain and discomfort. The only way to get rid of the pain is to find more little "h."

On the other hand, the Big "H" stays with you even during times of high stress and emotional trauma. It allows you to have a sense of peace in the midst of emotional suffering and mental anguish. Many people have heard of others who live in the worst possible circumstances and yet have a tranquility that seems incomprehensible given the environment. Likewise, we know that some people who have "everything" will put a gun to their head because of their internal distress and misery.

Happiness and Its Source

As Table 2-A shows, little "h" comes from the outside while the Big "H" resides within the recesses of your soul. We have learned from childhood that the good life depends on how well we succeed—either in our relationships or in reaching our goals. We bring this knowledge into adulthood and constantly strive for more and more little "h." We have been told that we can have as much little "h" as we want if we learn to master our environment. In Western society the three most popular methods for instant gratification are what Pat and Terry call the "mouth solutions:" food, booze, and drugs. Feeling better is just too easy, which robs us of our motivation to seek deeper and more profound pathways to the Big "H."

Table 2-A: Two Kinds of Happiness

LITTLE H	BIG H
The happiness that comes from the absence of pain and discomfort	The happiness that comes from coping with pain and discomfort
Cannot coexist with pain	Can coexist with pain
Comes from outside you —LIFE	Comes from within you —SELF
Is easy to find because there are so many places to get it	Is difficult to find because there are only four places to get it
Only lasts a short while	Can last forever

Most of us know intuitively that long-lasting peace of mind comes from within. Unfortunately, this is a rather vague notion. It sounds good, but few know how to achieve it. The major goal of this book is to show you how to get this elusive experience. Since living a life of peace and serenity is not easy to come by, we would like to serve as your guides as you walk along the path.

Happiness and Prospecting

A prospector wants to work at finding minerals that will have value. The easier it is to find a particular rock, the less value it has. Because little "h" comes from your environment, the sheer volume of resources to "feel good" is seemingly infinite. When we get discouraged, anxious or stressed, life offers many ways to feel better. If one source does not work, we can easily find another quick fix.

In contrast to the many little "h" sources, we will find that the Big "H" can only be found in four places, which we'll discuss below. Four is a minuscule number compared to the entire universe of places where we can get the little "h." The prospector can easily find gravel, but prospecting for gravel would not be cost effective, even though silicon (which can be made from gravel) is used for manufacturing computer chips. There is just too much gravel. It is not a scarce resource and so is less valuable. In contrast, prospecting for gold takes work and perseverance. When found, it is one of the world's greatest assets. So it is with happiness. Little "h" is "gravel" in contrast to the "gold" of the Big "H."

Happiness and Time

Another problem with living a life built exclusively on the little "h" is the short life span of the little "h." The Big "H" can last forever if you stay tapped into the resources you are going to develop. When the occurrence of the little "h" evaporates, it is our nature to want it back as quickly as possible. We begin to believe the illusion that we can have a lifetime supply of little "h" if we could just control the source. If we could just get that person to love us more, then we could be happy forever. If only we could just have a guaranteed money flow, then we could be happy forever. If we could sidestep health problems, then we could be happy forever. If we could be certain that our children would grow up to be good people, then we could be happy forever. The notion that we have ultimate control of these events moves us to buy into the fantasy that we can control the outside world. When we try this, we set ourselves up for continual frustration and disappointment.

We spend an inordinate amount of time trying to control people, places, and things that are beyond our control. We worry about our children's thoughts and feelings, we get stressed about the future, we feel guilty about the past and a whole universe of other circumstances we have absolutely no control over. We do this because of a worldly belief that if only we could make life fit our wants and needs then we could be happier. Yet even when the world allows this to happen, we only achieve the "little h" kind of happiness, which is short-lived even in the *most ideal* circumstances.

B-E-S-T

By now you are probably wondering about those four sources of the Big "H." There are only four—not three or five—because these four elements represent the four pieces of human nature: behavior, emotions, sensations, and thoughts. They are easily remembered by using their first letters to form the acronym B-E-S-T. We are people who engage in actions (*Behavior*) and we also experience certain kinds of feelings (*Emotions*). Physical

Sensations are part of our daily happenings. Finally, we are creatures with an active *Thought* life by which we interpret, judge, assess ourselves and our surroundings.

You experience the Big "H" by properly managing your behavior, emotions, sensations, and thoughts. When your life is "out of sync," it is because some or all of these four pieces are not working together in the way they should be.

People engage in destructive behaviors either by engaging in actions that are not in their best interest or by failing to act in ways that would be good for them. In a similar sense, few people understand the difference between healthy and unhealthy emotional pain. Consequently, they hang on to the unhealthy variety and try to get rid of the healthy pain. People in our society are also proficient at getting stressed (sensation), but few know how to rid themselves of stress in a healthy way. And finally, many people worry about life when they only need to be concerned. (See the Appendix 1 for the difference between worry and concern).

Try to imagine your life when each of these elements is being properly managed. Ask yourself the following four questions:

- What would my life be like if I could consistently choose to act in ways that were spiritually growth producing instead of ways that stunt my growth in God's grace?
- What would my life be like if I were able to accept healthy emotional pain and knew exactly what to do to rid myself of debilitating, destructive emotional pain?
- What would my life be like if I could maintain minimal levels of daily stress regardless of the circumstances?
- What would my life be like if I could spent most of my mental energy being responsibly concerned about life rather than wasting time and effort worrying about events that are beyond my control?

Jesus teaches us that "The thief comes only to steal and kill and destroy; I came that they may have life, and have it more abundantly" (John 10:10, MSG). The Voice (i.e., "the thief") wants you to stay focused on pursuing the little "h." By keeping you concentrating on what you cannot control in the world around you, the thief tries to rob you of abundant life, keeping you from growing and becoming a mature believer. That abundant life is attainable by learning to master the B-E-S-T life. The Bible tells us: "A river flowed from the land of Eden, watering the garden and then dividing into four branches" (Genesis 2:10). We are going to look at the four areas that water the gardens of our lives as the most important and only things we can really control. As we do so, the B-E-S-T life becomes the *best* life —the abundant life. So how do you get the B-E-S-T, abundant life? You get it by managing the four parts we just mentioned: your behavior, your emotions, your sensations and your thoughts —the four components that make up all human beings. God created us this way. One or more of these four parts relate to all other aspects of human nature. For example, spirituality, as an innate aspect of human nature, is the combination of our thoughts and behavior.

Property Lines

The property line that surrounds your garden contains your behavior, emotions, sensations and thoughts. These are the parts of life you are responsible for and the only things you have any control over. Everything else outside that property line is ultimately beyond your control. People are not puppets. As much as we would like to, we cannot control our kids, our spouses, our friends, neighbors, or associates. We can persuade, teach, influence, discipline, request, but the final

Figure 2-B: Your Garden

behavior of others is solely in their control. Any time you spend thinking about trying to control people or things outside your property line wastes your time—this kind of thinking is called worry. Spending your energy inside your own property lines is the most productive, character-building and growth-promoting thing you can do.

One morning before school Pat had a conflict with his young son, Kyle. He had gotten ready early and had earned the privilege of a few minutes of video games. When the time came for him to stop playing, he protested, claiming he needed more time. Pat gave him the choice of stopping then or losing his privileges for the day. Kyle protested loudly in a shrill and whiny voice as he turned off the T.V. His pain was clearly visible. In the past Pat had reacted to these displays by getting "plugged in" to his arguments. This time he recognized that his son's pain and the expression of it were outside his property line. Realizing his son's behavior and emotions were inside the boy's property line, not Pat's, gave Pat the tranquility to simply endure the outburst until it subsided. Pat and Kyle continued to school without any further trouble. This was a defining moment for their relationship. Pat learned that, when setting limits on his son's behavior, he did not have any right to change the way Kyle *felt* about his parenting and its consequences. Kyle's thoughts, feelings and behaviors were in his property line. Pat was not responsible for and could not control them. It is his duty as a parent to structure his child's life, not assume it is his prerogative to control the way his children feel about the structure.

Table 2-B shows those things that are inside and outside your property line. Studying this chart will give you a feel for the difference between the reality inside you and that of the world outside your property line.

Table 2-B: Property Line

THINGS WITHIN (POTENTIAL CONTROL)	THINGS OUTSIDE (NO CONTROL)
Behavior	What others do
Emotions	What others think of you
Sensations	How others react
Thoughts	Life events

The Annoyance List

Finding out what bothers you is the first step for recognizing whether you have any control over annoyances. Below is a list containing various daily occurrences that often annoy people. If the situation or person described is annoying to you, place a check next to the statement.

- ❏ A person telling me how to drive.
- ❏ Subscription cards loosely tucked into magazines.
- ❏ Getting a telephone busy signal or a phone without an answering machine.
- ❏ To see reckless driving.

- ❏ To hear someone talking loudly on their cell phone.
- ❏ To see an adult picking his or her nose.
- ❏ A person telling me to do something when I am just about to do it.
- ❏ A person continually criticizing something.
- ❏ A person being sarcastic.
- ❏ Junk mail whether the Internet variety or the paper kind.
- ❏ To have my cell phone go dead, my PDA lock up, my computer crash, or my GPS stop working.
- ❏ To have my thoughts interrupted.
- ❏ A person putting his or her hands on me unnecessarily.
- ❏ A person adjusting my TV set or car radio.
- ❏ A person giving me a weak handshake.
- ❏ A person picking his teeth.
- ❏ A person who does not know when to go home.
- ❏ A person continually trying to be funny.
- ❏ Being asked almost constantly to do something.
- ❏ To be evaluated critically by a relative stranger.
- ❏ Movies on TV that take as much time for commercials as for the movie itself.
- ❏ To have to walk on slippery sidewalks.
- ❏ Computerized telephone operators.
- ❏ To hear a person talking in the movies.
- ❏ To be unable to find a restaurant seat. To hear loud music I do not like.
- ❏ A person watching me work.
- ❏ A door that squeaks when I close it.
- ❏ To hear racial remarks about someone.
- ❏ Someone frequently telling me about the person who is his or her romantic interest.
- ❏ Too much discussion of sex in mixed company.
- ❏ To have to kiss an unattractive relative.
- ❏ To have strangers talk to me when I want to be left alone.

- ❏ A person talking a great deal and not saying anything very important.
- ❏ Having to listen to a sales pitch I do not want to hear.
- ❏ Listening to too many TV commercials.
- ❏ A person interrupting me when I am talking.
- ❏ To have drivers cut me off in traffic.
- ❏ To be at a boring party and not being able to leave.
- ❏ Not being able to find my car keys.
- ❏ Being stood up for a lunch or dinner appointment.
- ❏ A person who criticizes what I wear.
- ❏ A person who tries to convert me to something (political party, religion, etc).
- ❏ To find a hair in my food.
- ❏ To run out of gas.
- ❏ Rude or discourteous people.
- ❏ Not to be listened to.
- ❏ To be given impractical suggestions.

This list is merely to help you identify annoying situations that trigger each of the B-E-S-T components. When some of these situations happen to you, your ensuing behavior may be something you later regret. Your emotions may force you to do that dumb thing (you might clench your teeth or your fists). The sensations in your body may chew up your insides (your muscles might tense, your palms might sweat, maybe your breathing becomes rapid or shallow, your heart might start beating faster). Your thinking may go off on some destructive tangents (you may believe that someone is out to get you).

The more of these items you can identify each day, the more you will find the outside world running your life.

Sensations vs. Emotions

Behaviors and thoughts are easy to distinguish, but the difference between emotions and sensations is often confusing. People name both experiences by the same word, "feelings." Emotions and sensations are different though they may occur simultaneously. Examples of emotions include happiness, sadness, anxiety and fear. Sensations are *physical* feelings: urges, appetites, pains, muscular tensions, fatigue. These all come from our bodies and that is what identifies them as sensations. Recognizing the difference between the two is critically important. See Table 2-C

Table 2-C: Two Manifestations of Feelings: Sensations and Emotions

SENSATIONS ARE.....		EMOTIONS ARE.....	
"Feelings" associated with the stimulation of a sense organ or with a specific body condition.		"Feelings" that derive from our limbic system in the brain. They may be triggered from conscious thoughts or our "silent assumptions."	
Rapid, improper breathing	Sexual urges	Depression	Sadness
Muscle tension	Hunger	Guilt	Remorse
Racing mind	Thirst	Resentment	Anger
Muscle pain	Sleepiness	Helplessness	Weakness
Body fatigue	Cravings	Irrational Fear	Rational Fear

The Domino Metaphor

One difficulty in managing the B-E-S-T components is that they are interrelated. When you change one component, you affect the others. We use the metaphor of dominoes to understand these relationships. The memory device, the acronym B-E-S-T, helps us remember the inner *components* within the domino metaphor, but it does not tell us the order of the dominoes.

It's important to know the never-changing order of these dominoes: *Life, Thoughts, Feelings* (emotions and sensations), *Behavior,* and *Consequences.* Some people find this confusing at first. Eventually, it will become clearer. Then, you will find this idea to be a powerful foundation on which you can build as you apply the promises of the Bible, living out the life that God wants you to have.

The Behavior-Consequence Connection

It is often easier to understand how the dominoes work by looking at the last domino and working toward the front. The last domino (consequences) represents what happens because of your behavior—it is not about how you personally feel about your behavior. If you throw a chair through a window, the consequence is a broken window and maybe a broken chair. If you consistently treat your friend badly, the consequence is a broken friendship. Some consequences you are now living with have been the result of your behavior. If people are angry or disappointed with you, it is likely you have done something to make that happen. Your behavior can result in many life consequences—things you either did or failed to do. This relationship between behavior and consequences is easy to understand. It is important because it is the foundation for personal responsibility. We want our children to learn this at an early age so they can grow up to be good citizens.

The Emotions-Behavior Connection

The next connection—between behavior and emotions—is also easy to understand. Most of us are aware of how our emotions drive our behavior. We may mope when we are sad or discouraged; we may be noisy and boisterous because of our excitement when our team wins; we may act thoughtfully when we feel a sense of importance as we are engaged in a meaningful discussion. It is well accepted that emotions can be powerful drivers of behavior. If you ask someone "why" they did something, a common response is: "Because I felt like it."

The Thought-Emotions Connection

Unfortunately, the next link is the difficult one to grasp. When asked why we feel a certain way, our response is likely to point to something or someone in our outside world. One powerful example is the feeling of falling in love; another common source of overpowering feelings occurs when we lose a loved one. Most people point to the outside world out of habit. "If that hadn't happened, then I would not feel this way."

We want to show you that the truth is deeper than this. With one specific exception (a physiological response), it's what you think, not what happens to you, that is *always* the source of your emotions. Your emotional responses result from the way you interpret outside events. If you are late for an appointment with your boss and miss it because of car trouble, your feelings about the missed appointment will depend on how you interpret the missed appointment. If you thought the boss might have scheduled this meeting to criticize or fire you, you might find yourself feeling relief that the car trouble was causing you to miss the appointment. On the other hand, if you thought your boss was going to promote you to vice president, but would likely choose someone else because you didn't show up, you would be worried sick or angry about the car trouble. We want you to get used to accepting the fact that all your emotions (both painful and non-painful) are caused by your thoughts, whether you are aware of them or not.

Although the insights of cognitive psychology have been available for several decades, Christian authors are beginning to integrate these ideas into our understanding of the successful Christian life. One of the cleverest titles in the Christian book market is Joyce Meyer's *Battlefield of the Mind: Winning the Battle in Your Mind*.[5] She writes from personal experience that personal freedom and peace of mind are experienced by overcoming negative thinking.

Some people find it difficult to accept the equality of thoughts and emotions. They think one is more important than the other. Psychology has shown us they are of equal importance even though one proceeds from the other. Ken Blanchard and Phil Hodges are convinced that Christian leadership is at its best when the two are in equal proportion to one other.[6] Whether the heart or mind is more important is not a question of theology but psychology. God gave both to us to use for the glory of God. Mark Noll, a professor at the University of Notre Dame, has shown us how some Christians have hindered God's work in the world. He writes that Christians often neglect paying attention to matters of the mind.[7] This neglect of our mental life is contrary to Paul's teaching. He states it plainly when he says, "There must be a spiritual renewal of your thoughts and attitudes." Ephesians 4:23 (NLT)

---

5   Meyer, J. (2002). *Battlefield of the mind: Winning the battle in your mind*. Joyce Meyer Trade.
6   Blanchard, K. (2006). *Lead like Jesus: Lessons from the greatest leadership role model of all time*. Nashville: W Publishing Group.
7   Noll, M. (1994). *The scandal of the Evangelical Mind*. Grand Rapids, MI: William B. Eerdmans.

Dominoes and the Big "H"

This idea is important for learning how to live the abundant life with the Big "H." When all your dominoes are standing, you will be experiencing the Big "H." The problem is that when you look closely at the Dominoes chart (Figure 2-C), you will see that the first domino—life, the outside world—has a round bottom. It does not stand up easily and when it does, it is not for long. This indicates life itself. The outside world is constantly crashing into our personal space. Sometimes it does so in an annoying way that we can shrug off. Other times, life hits us so hard we wonder if we will ever recover. Almost reflexively, we reach down and try to put the first domino upright. Even when we succeed, it will eventually fall again, knocking all the other dominoes down. When the dominoes stand up for a while, we get to experience the little "h." When they fall, the chain reaction starts again.

The Domino Effect

We are going to teach you how to begin using a different strategy. Look again at the graphic (Figure 2-C) with which we open this section on The Domino Metaphor. Instead of trying to keep the first domino (life events) from knocking over the other dominoes, you will learn to change how you use the second domino (thoughts). You will learn how to lift the thought domino off the table, slather the bottom of it with super glue and firmly place it back on the table. When the glue dries, the second domino will be immovable, no matter how hard the first one hits it. The writer of Proverbs reminds us, "be careful how you think, your life is shaped by your thoughts" (Proverbs 4:23, TEV). Our personal experiences in life are often the effect of an unseen chain reaction. This chain reaction can lead us to believe that our lives are not our own. We become convinced that we are victims of a cruel and unfeeling world. We might even come to

Figure 2-C: The Domino Effect

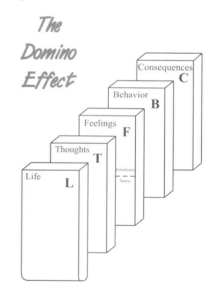

the conclusion that a God who is uncaring and even vindictive rules the universe. We call this chain reaction the *"Domino Effect."*

Thoughts and Personal Control

The first lesson you need to learn is that God wants you to acquire the skills to control this chain reaction by taking control of the thought domino. God designed humans to have to react to an unpleasant (or maybe even a pleasant) life event with an automatic thought response. Your brain wants to understand what is happening. It becomes a cluster of perceptions, interpretations, judgments and other mental activity. The most powerful thing you can do to transform your life and live more in God's will is to change the way you think about certain life events or triggers. We will use the words *life* and *trigger* interchangeably to describe the Life domino. The Bible tells us throughout that controlling the second domino, our thoughts, is an imperative step in obtaining the abundance of blessings God wants to bestow upon us when we conform to God's will.

Adam and Eve's Dominoes

Look at " Adam and Eve's Dominoes (Figure 2-D)." We have taken some liberty with the Scripture here because Genesis 3 does not tell us what they were thinking or even feeling. Genesis goes directly from the temptation (Life Domino) to their eating the forbidden fruit (Behavior Domino). Nevertheless, it is very easy to speculate that in the second domino the Voice was tempting them with thoughts like: "How wonderful it would be to know all that God knows" or "You can't stand knowing that wonderful fruit is right there in front of you and you can't have even a single bite!" or "maybe you misunderstood what God

Figure 2-D: Adam and Eve's Dominoes

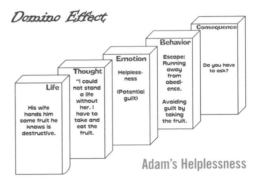

Adam's Helplessness

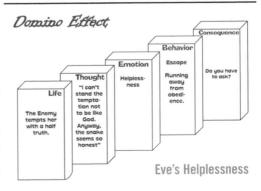

Eve's Helplessness

was saying," or perhaps "just one little bite won't hurt anything; besides, you've been good, you *deserve* it and, after all, I (the serpent) am only trying to help." This style of negative thinking results in helplessness—a feeling that the pressure is too great to resist. This emotion often leads people to destructive, rebellious, escapist behaviors. No one needs to guess what the consequences of Eve's and Adam's actions were. Their close relationship with God was broken and they were expelled from the garden, with the result that humanity has suffered ever since.

Silent Assumptions

The discovery by modern psychology that thinking produces emotions only reinforces what the saints and prophets have been telling us for ages. Until recently, what was not clear was how unnoticeable some of that thinking really is. The scientists call it "automatic thinking" or "silent assumptions." Some of our thoughts occur so rapidly that we cannot even perceive we had any thought at all. They seem hidden. Normally, we only perceive the audible thoughts in our daily lives. Destructive, paralyzing emotions such as guilt, anxiety and depression signal us that more devious thoughts are occurring quietly and rapidly enough to be just beyond our ability to perceive them.

Research has shown that the emotional effects of uncovering and replacing negative thinking with positive thoughts can produce the same pleasant brain chemistry as antidepressants. As a testimony to this, Pat was able to quit taking the prescribed antidepressant Serazone after mastering the materials we are presenting here. One of the key facilitators in one of our classes also was able to kick the habit of depending upon antidepressants as the only way to find relief from emotional pain. But please don't misunderstand what we are saying here, and heed this cautionary note: *In some cases, depression and panic disorders can be very serious and even lethal. We are not implying that all readers will be able to stop taking their medications. There are brain chemistry issues and other factors that must be taken into account on a case by case basis.*

We also want to make another important clarification here. We are not talking about the "unconscious mind" in the strict Freudian sense when we speak about silent assumptions. Currently, psychologists refer to the unconscious, not as some independent mechanism that determines our fate, but as the place in memory which may take more work to access.

As we begin show in chapter 4, you can all learn the skills of uncovering your self-talk that may be residing in the unconscious. All your thoughts are potentially accessible to you. Some of them are so quick and silent, perceiving them is impossible unless you slow your mind by writing out your thoughts.

Recently in one of our classes, while doing an exercise that helps us uncover those silent assumptions, one person discovered that he had about five separate negative thoughts occurring in less then one second. The Voice uses the speed of our minds against us. As we have mentioned, its favorite two weapons against you are speed and secrecy. The Voice "knows" that it can use this facility to introduce destructive, distorted thoughts through these channels. They will be processed so rapidly that we normally are not even aware of their presence.

The "Life" Domino and Choice

There's one important consideration to note about the "life" domino (the trigger or activator for thoughts, emotions, behaviors and consequences)—the matter of choice. Often, we can *choose* our environment, the context in which we live out our lives. In many cases, we can control what neighborhoods we live in, where we go to school, the friends we have, the churches we attend, or even whether or not we go to church or hang out at the local bar instead. The context in which we place our life as a result of our own choices affects us because of the domino effect. Other times, life circumstances force us to live in a specific context that we have *not* chosen. Those situations, too, need to be seen in terms of the domino effect.

Figure 2-E: The Voice Cycle

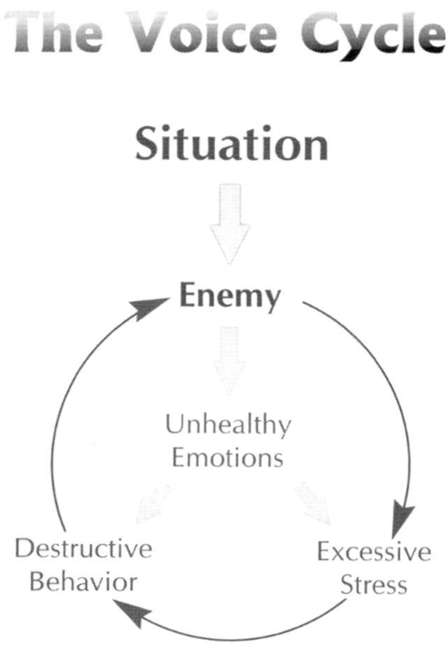

The Voice Cycle

Situation

Enemy

Unhealthy Emotions

Destructive Behavior

Excessive Stress

The Worry Cycle

Our dominoes do not always fall in a straight line. After the chain reaction from the life domino to the consequence domino has taken place, it may seem as if the consequence domino runs around to the front of the line and becomes a new life domino. Many people describe to us that they feel as if they are always running in circles. When the dominoes turn into a circle, it looks like Figure 2-E. We have changed some of the language to more accurately fit the real world.

Not all of life sets off a vicious cycle. Only certain situations in life activate the Voice. There is a big arrow between the situation and the Voice. This represents the speed at which certain situations set of the Voice. The often appears swiftly and silently. Psychologists call this a "conditioned response."

As you follow the arrows you notice the Voice then sets in motion toxic emotions (described in more detail in the next chapter) and excessive stress. These events are highly uncomfortable for us so we are motivated to do something to relieve us of our discomfort. Being creatures of habit, we will usually try something that has worked for us in the past. For most people this would include behaviors that drive away emotional pain and discomfort. Unfortunately, this action brings us the little "h" but not long term resolution. Then the Voice starts hammering us about what we just did to feel better. The cycle continues—much like an imaginary perpetual motion machine. Many of the people we have worked with tell us that this Worry Cycle is exactly the circle they keep running in.

The Voice keeps us running in circles by lying to us. These lies include incorrect perceptions, wrong interpretations, false predictions and irrational beliefs. These warped messages can be about you, the world around you or the relationship between the two. When we capture one of these distorted messages, we take the first step toward spiritual and emotional growth. In chapter 7 we will show you the five steps you will use to defeat these Voice lies and to replace them with the truth. Internationally acclaimed author and pastor of one of the largest churches in Southern California, Rick Warren, writes in his *Purpose Driven Life*: "Spiritual growth is the process of replacing lies with truth."[8]

---

8   Warren, R. (2002). ***The Purpose Driven Life***. Grand Rapids, MI: Zondervan

Embarrassing Example

The following is an example of how destructive the Worry Cycle can be. Although, only slightly exaggerated, it is based on a true story about Pat. The names have not been changed to protect the hero of this story. The story began as Pat was driving home from work (We will use abbreviations at the beginning of each sentence to denote which domino it would fall into: L=life, T=thought, E=emotion, B=behavior, C=consequence).

L: Pat had received a performance review at work that day and it had not gone well. His boss had made some "suggestions" for areas of improvement and had even made a wisecrack about Pat's weight.

T: While driving home he was thinking, "That jerk, he has no right to talk to me that way." Just then he saw a 7-Eleven and thought, "I'll show him; I'll have a brownie."

E: Pat is feeling a strong degree of resentment about now.

B: He stops at the 7-Eleven and buys a brownie, completely blowing his diet restrictions for the day. [Yes, we know this sounds stupid and irrational—how does buying a brownie get even with his boss? This is the way the Voice works].

C: He returns to the car defeated by his own behavior.

Now, the consequence domino becomes the next life domino:

L: Pat has exceeded his own desire and goal to limit his daily calorie intake. He has made a mistake.

T: He thinks: "What an idiot! Why did I do that? I shouldn't have done that. I should know better!" He now believes he is a loser for making such a dumb mistake.

E: Pat is beginning to feel very guilty about his misguided attempt to retaliate against his boss. His guilt makes it necessary to punish himself for making such a dumb mistake (buying a brownie).

B: His guilt guides him to another 7-Eleven and he has another brownie!

C: His body gets more calories

Again the consequence domino becomes the life domino for the next sequence:

L: Pat returns to the car feeling even more defeated.

T: He thinks, "What a worthless loser I am! Maybe the boss was right? I really am worthless. I can't even control my diet."

E: Now he's beginning to get depressed as a tide of worthlessness begins to engulf him.

B: Since Pat is worthless anyway, he might as well do what any good loser would do—Yep, have another brownie!

C: Back into the store he goes—and on and on and on goes the Worry Cycle.

You can see how drugs, alcohol, shopping, sex, or any other common human activity could easily replace the brownies in this example.

Concern vs. Worry

Believing that things cannot go wrong is foolish. Life will never be completely easy or pain-free. The first domino will always fall. When we anticipate and plan for problems that are likely to occur, we are showing concern about how life treats us. And such concern is good. Concern leads us to do things that improve us rather than wasting time worrying about things that we can't do anything about. When we are concerned, we are problem-solving. We are looking for constructive solutions to problems. When we *worry*, we are not solving problems but are spinning wheels and using our imaginations in unconstructive ways.

The main difference between concern and worry boils down to control. Worry focuses on things outside ourselves, which we cannot control, and often leads us to take the wrong kind of action. Concern, on the other hand, comes from recognizing our limitations and doing what we can to make ourselves and the world better.

By making a habit of setting aside some quiet time each day and writing about those things that are on our minds, we can distinguish between what we can control (concern) and what we cannot control (worry). We can then learn to accept the things we cannot change and take constructive steps to change what we can.

Writing

Learning strategies on how to switch from worry to concern helps you to better live in God's grace. The only way you can learn those strategies is by writing—a lot! Why do we keep insisting you must write and write and write? The answer is simple: You are learning mental skills.

If you are seriously committed to change and to experiencing more of the grace of God, you will need to list all the negativity you can recall each day. As one of the authors (Pat) puts it, "I begin each item in my writings with the prayer, 'Lord I'm worried that …' Soon I have a list of all the things that have been bugging me lately; especially those things that I had not yet fully addressed but were sort of background worry. From this list I can rapidly address the things that I cannot change or influence at all, and I write, 'Accept' across it."

You can only make changes to those things you can perceive and understand. Some people try to skip this important and vital first step. They want to get the next lesson and find the easy, magical formula they think is waiting for them. We have bad news for you. No easy formula exists. We have found that the more you write, the more you grow and change.

Summary

1. Although everyone wants to be happy and is constantly striving for it, the little "h" happiness is not sufficient for the abundant life. The Bible affirms the importance of the Big "H" as a necessary ingredient for living in God's plan.

2. You can only experience the Big "H" when you manage your God-given property well. This is more difficult than it sounds. In one of Jesus' parables (Mat 13:24-25), he tells the story of someone who planted good wheat seed in his field. When he was sleeping, an enemy came and spread weeds among the wheat, and snuck away.

3. The Voice wants you to be a poor tender of your garden where the Big "H" is located. It does this by convincing you that you can only get the little "h" which is outside your garden.

4. Within your property line you need to learn how to manage your thoughts, emotions, sensations and behavior. Of these four, the most

critical is your thought life because this directly affects the other three.

5. Each of the four Big "H" ingredients is related to each other like a line of dominoes. When they are all standing, they represent a life of the Big "H." Events continually push the first domino (Life) over. The Voice makes certain that the second one (Thoughts) will topple easily and knock over the rest.

6. Since you have no control over the stability of the Life Domino, your only recourse is to make the Thought Domino immovable. This is the goal of *The Worry Free Life*.

7. To gain control over your dominoes, you must first learn to distinguish between them. Managing each domino requires a separate skill set. If you do not know which domino you are dealing with, then you will not know which skill to use to manage it.

Assignment #1

To help you get a better understanding of your property lines, you can take the Property Line Quiz. We have given our opinions on the answers at the end of the quiz.

Table 2-D

PROPERTY LINE QUIZ		
Define which of the following situations are within your property line which one's are not. Remember, only those things that are within your control are within your property line.		
	IN	**OUT**
1. Your mother is mad at you because you ruined her Thanksgiving by not coming for dinner. Instead you had dinner with your friends.		
2. You are angry because the car in front of you just cut you off.		
3. Your wife/husband calls you stupid because you forgot to pick up one of the things on the shopping list when you went to the store.		
4. You know people at work who you insist do not deserve a promotion. This situation gets you to hate your job and only perform at 50% when you are there.		
5. For years you have been mad at your parents because you think they favor your sibling more than you.		
6. Your teenage son is hurt and upset at you because you decided you could not afford to buy him the new motorcycle you promised him.		
7. You overhear your coworkers talking about how selfish they think you are because you accepted the promotion for a job that they themselves wanted. You clearly knew they wanted the job, and they have been with the company longer than you.		
8. Your husband/wife/child makes you feel so angry when they forget to do things you asked them to do.		
9. "Life Sucks!!!!!!! Nothing good ever happens to me. I'll never feel like I did in the good old days."		

	IN	OUT
10. You are a husband and your wife says, "We've got to talk." You instantly panic.		
11. You are a wife and when you try to tell your husband you feel hurt about something he said, he replies, "I don't want to discuss it" and walks out the room. He refuses to talk to you for four days.		

This is how we see property line issues in the situations above:

1. You cannot control your mother's anger—only your response to it.
2. You cannot control the behavior of the other driver, but you can decide whether you want to feel angry.
3. You cannot make your spouse stop calling you names; you can speak up about how you feel about it.
4. Of course good things happen to people who do not deserve them. However, it really has nothing to do with whether you like or dislike your job. It is still the same job.
5. It is unfortunate that your parents may have favored your sibling. You can't change it, so find a way to adapt.
6. Your teenage son has a right to be upset even if it is for the wrong reasons. You can choose how you want to deal with it.
7. No one has the power to stop the wagging of tongues. How you handle it is within your property line.
8. You need to decide whether anger is something you want to feel or if it is a motivator for getting them to change. You do not have to be angry. Or you can choose to do so. It is up to you.
9. Life goes on for good or bad. Your only choice is what you are going to do about it.
10. Get used to it, men. Women need to talk. Learning to listen and be a part of their verbal world is much better for you than avoidance and panic.
11. You cannot control your husband's behavior. If it is important you tell someone about how you feel, you will need to find alternatives: a close friend, a relative, a professional counselor.

Assignment #2

Dominoes Questionnaire

As with Pat's story, your next step is to figure out the dominoes for some of the annoyances in the Annoyance List on page 21. The questionnaire below can help you to do this. This writing assignment will help you get a better sense of what is inside and what is outside your property line. When you experience difficult times, it may seem as if you have a big pile of mixed up dominoes. The following *Dominoes Questionnaire* will help you learn the difference among all your dominoes

You may use the *Annoyance List* or think of an incident in your life that was difficult for you to handle. When it was happening, you may have experienced it as something devastating and overpowering. In actuality, that overwhelming event was composed of several smaller pieces. Those pieces are the five dominoes. This questionnaire has six parts because we have broken the third domino—feelings—into its component parts: emotions and sensations/stress.

Each domino has a few common suggestions from other people's experiences. Although these will help you get started, you will probably check the "other" box and add more items. The only domino that will not require an answer will be number six, the consequence domino. Domino six, like number one, refers to something outside your property line. It always pertains to something that happened in the environment as the result of your action

Table 2-E: Dominoes Questionnaire

Name of Annoyance_____

Life Domino
- ❑ Were you at work or home?
- ❑ Were there other people present?
- ❑ Were you doing anything unusual?
- ❑ Was anyone making the situation difficult for you?
- ❑ Others?

Thought Domino
- ❑ Were you putting yourself down?

- ❑ Were you using labels about yourself?
- ❑ Was your thinking muddled?
- ❑ Was your mind racing?
- ❑ Others?

Feelings Domino [Emotions]
- ❑ Were you feeling depressed?
- ❑ Were you feeling guilty?
- ❑ Were you feeling helpless?
- ❑ Were you feeling resentful?
- ❑ Were you feeling anxious?
- ❑ Were you feeling fearful?
- ❑ Others?

Feelings Domino [Sensations]
- ❑ Were you feeling nauseous?
- ❑ Did you have butterflies?
- ❑ Did you have a headache?
- ❑ Were you tired or fatigued?
- ❑ Did you have a panic attack?
- ❑ Did you hyperventilate?
- ❑ Were your muscles tense?
- ❑ Others?

Behavior Domino
- ❑ Did you shut down and do nothing?
- ❑ Did you punish yourself?
- ❑ Did you run away?
- ❑ Did you retaliate?
- ❑ Did you avoid something?
- ❑ Did you insulate yourself from others?
- ❑ Others?

Consequences Domino
- ❑ Did you end up in the hospital?
- ❑ Were you abandoned?
- ❑ Did anyone try to hurt you?
- ❑ Did you lose anything; e.g., your job?
- ❑ Others?

Writing Tip

Learning to sort out the dominoes will establish a solid foundation for learning the skills in the rest of this book. You want to complete at least one Dominoes Questionnaire each day until you have internalized the ability to quickly sort out the dominoes in most of your life situations.

Continue to complete your 3-column diary that you began in Chapter One of this book. The more pages you fill, the better the foundation you will have for learning new skills

Chapter Three
Emotions

Why do you let your emotions take over, lashing out and spitting fire?
— Job 15:12 (MSG)

What if you never had to feel depressed or guilty again? What if you could say goodbye to corrosive feelings like bitterness, helplessness, severe anxiety, or irrational fear forever? It's possible for those "what ifs" to become reality. We can't guarantee you a perfect life, of course, for none of us will ever be perfect; but we can promise an increased quality of life. It has happened to thousands of others through the principles presented in this book.

Let's think about the dominoes again and this time concentrate on the middle domino—the "feelings" domino. The middle domino represents sensations and emotions. This chapter will teach you how to correctly identify your emotional experiences.

**Figure 3-A:
The Feeling Domino**

If you have been conscientious in your writing exercises, you are probably able to recall roughly how you felt when particular events have bothered you. *Naming* your specific emotions is sometimes harder, as is identifying your thoughts associated with the emotion. Being able to identify your emotions and then working back to the thinking that caused them are essential parts of improving the quality of your life and ridding yourself of old baggage.

Understanding Emotions

People experience confusion about the exact meaning of different emotions. Even in the mental health field, practitioners often lump different emotions together. We have devised a system for recognizing distinct emotions that we hope you'll find helpful. Such knowledge will give you insight into which skills you will need to manage these varied emotions.

Gender Differences

Because of differences in brain structure, most women generally find talking about emotions easier than most men. A woman's brain causes her to center her life around the inner world of emotions. Consequently, women have a more inclusive vocabulary for talking about emotions than men do. This chapter will be easier for women because they are accustomed to describing in detail how they feel. Their language of emotions begins at an early age and is continually refined throughout life.

For most men, talking about emotions is a much harder task because their brains are hard-wired to focus on the external world. Men have a rich vocabulary for describing the world around them, but less so for their inner worlds. The problem occurs when women want to know how men are "feeling." When the question, "what are you feeling (or thinking) right now?" is asked, the abbreviated male response doesn't satisfy many women. The list of words and phrases men use to express their feelings is short. Men are either "doing great" or "kind of bummed" or, using the universal phrase for being displeased, they declare, "I'm mad!" (or a similar expression). Being aware of these gender differences in expressing feelings can be helpful as we learn to understand our emotions.

Your Garden

Gardens need tending and keeping. To do this, you need specific skills and tools. If you were to return from vacation and find your garden in bad shape, you would want to bring it back to health. You would try to find out exactly what had infected your garden. Was its poor health caused by a plant disease? Insects? Animals? Weeds? With some detective work and a diagnostic understanding, you could pick the right tools to restore your garden to health.

You use the same process to manage emotions that are bothering you. You will find it very helpful to be able to precisely identify the sources of the problem in your "emotions garden." By so doing, you can find the correct strategy for cleaning out these weeds or other destructive forces and keeping them away. It would do your garden no good to use tools to eliminate a fungus if instead the destruction was being caused by gophers.

Emotions and Sensations Revisited

Before we begin discussing emotions, we need to review the distinction between sensations and emotions. Most people commonly call both sensations and emotions "feelings." And it's true; they *are* feelings, however, they are two significantly different kinds of feelings.

Sensations. Sensations are "feelings" that come from your body. Hunger, thirst, sexual desire, muscle tension, and fatigue are all examples of sensations. Addictive cravings are also sensations, though they are compounded, complicated, and empowered by unhealthy emotions. When we understand that we have a choice about responding to our sensations, they begin to lose some power over us. Pat recently lost twenty pounds by realizing that the hunger he felt was a bodily sensation and that, with the power of Christ, he was stronger than that sensation. He used to say "I am hungry." Now he says: "I have the sensation of hunger," knowing that God empowers him to be strong and able to control himself in any situation. By identifying hunger as a controllable sensation, Pat can seek God's help in reducing hunger's power over him. This is true for us with any sensation.

Emotions. Emotions, on the other hand, are feelings that are largely triggered by *thinking*. These thoughts may be either consciously recognizable or the "silent assumptions" we discussed in chapter 2. Emotions come in two varieties: pleasant and unpleasant. Most of you are not reading this book to figure out how to deal with *pleasant* emotions. The next skill you need to master is learning to identify your unpleasant, painful emotions. This is more difficult than it sounds because painful emotions also come in two varieties: constructive and destructive, and they need to be sorted out. You will eventually learn to cope with unpleasant emotions by knowing which kind you are experiencing. Both kinds can be intense and painful! To the surprise of many people, uncomfortable, hurtful emotions arising from life's calamities can still be constructive and healthy. God did not design us to live lives without pain. Sometimes God allows us to be in difficult circumstances to promote our emotional and spiritual growth.

Never Trust Your Emotions

You cannot always trust your emotions. An immediate, non-reflective response to your emotions is often called an intuition or a hunch. Intuition can be a dangerous tool to rely on for making decisions because it can be a reflection of misperceptions and misinterpretations. One would be better off assessing them cognitively, especially in important situations that have significant consequences. The exception to this is the instinctual decisions experts make. Their expertise has become so habitual that responses based on expert instincts can sometimes be more accurate than highly reasoned responses made by non-experts. For more information on the subject see the excellent book by Dr. David Myers called *Intuition: Its Powers and Perils*.[1]

Emotions that are more accessible can also be dangerous. This is often seen in gambling. People will make decisions that defy odds because they "feel" the decision is the correct one. Since emotions seem so personal and authentic, individuals tend to rely on them in situations where it would be best to be more cognitively reflective.

The uncomfortable emotions the Voice generates by its lies are destructive and unhealthy, and trusting such emotions is detrimental. Since we humans tend to believe that our emotions are an accurate reflection of life, the Voice can use that misconception as a strategy for seducing us to act upon these feelings.

Lynn was an intelligent and well educated person who generally made excellent decisions in life. One day a close friend of hers told her about a speaker in church who talked about a Christian investment opportunity that was a surefire way of guaranteeing a secure financial future. Her friend was excited about this opportunity and Lynn had recently been pondering how she and her husband were going to help their three children through

---

1   Myers, D. G. (2004). *Intuition: Its Powers and Perils*. New Haven, CT: Yale University Press.

college. As she and her friend talked, she became more convinced in her gut that this was the way for her. Many people in church had become enthusiastic about this opportunity, which was being wholeheartedly endorsed by the church staff. Based on her strong feelings, she invested her recent heritance of one hundred thousand dollars. After putting up the money, her feelings about doing the right thing became even stronger. She could hardly wait for the investment to double so that she could share the good news with her husband (who was not a churchgoer). Unfortunately, her world suddenly shattered when news spread among the investors that they had been scammed. In her bitterness and disappointment, she realized that she had put aside her intelligence to make this important decision.

Learn to be skeptical about the way you feel, and don't allow your feelings to decide how you must act. Feelings are like fire. Fire can be helpful or destructive. Fire is dangerous when raging out of control. When you contain it, fire can be very useful and productive. So it is with your feelings.

Emotional Skepticism

Some people believe that you must be either an emotional person (intuitive, caring, sensitive, and the like) or else you are logical (rational, cold, and calculating). This is too simple. It is not one or the other. Healthy people have a good balance between emotions and reason. Nevertheless, reason must contain and direct your emotions. Relying on emotions without reason is like hiking without a compass. Living solely on the basis of your reason with no emotion is like watching the compass but never noticing the beauty around you.

Constructive and destructive emotions are similar in some ways. One characteristic they share is the ability to be painful and intense. Painful emotions are not necessarily bad. Henry David Thoreau wrote: "Truth and roses have thorns about them." But neither are pleasant emotions always good for us. The relief of avoiding a confrontation with a difficult customer may at first seem like a pleasant, healthy emotion because it feels good to avoid the confrontation. But if the customer complains to your boss, you may have some explaining to do. Feeling good is not what this book is about, because the notion of "feeling good" relies on the little "h." We want you to experience your life at a deeper and more profound level—that Big "H."

Emotional Pleasure

God constructed our brains to seek pleasure and avoid pain. When we are in situations that make us feel good, we wish we could make time stop. As a child, I (Terry) remember times while playing with my friends that were so exquisite that I wanted the moment to last forever. Life always intruded, however, and sometimes I would try to recapture that time at a later date. It never happened.

Most people want to make cherished experiences last forever. Pleasure seeks to maintain the status quo. Although this seems desirable at first, further thought shows us the danger in such a desire. It would be a terrible experience even if it were possible. If I could have stayed in those magical moments as a child, I would still be a child. Growth and maturity can only come about through change.

Your spiritual journey is defined by change. This is often a scary idea, especially if life is going well and you would like it to stay that way. You are probably reading this, however, because life is *not* going well at this time. In searching for answers, you may also harbor the expectation that once you reach your goal of maturity, you won't have to face so much change. What you are likely to find instead is that when change takes you to the place you expected to be your destination, you will discover that this "destination" is merely a way station. A decade from now, your life will be far removed from anything you can now imagine.

Alan Watts[2] explained that pain and pleasure are both dimensions of being alive. When we work at eliminating emotional pain in our lives we wind up losing the chance to be fully alive. The more we chase after the little "h" as a counterweight to emotional pain, the more we lose the capacity to live fully as God intended.

Emotional Pain

To fully understand emotional pain, you need to discern the differences between healthy pain and unhealthy pain. There is no upside to unhealthy pain, but there is a major upside to healthy pain. Don't ever forget that unhealthy, destructive emotional pain comes from the Voice and is a quicksand to pull you down and stop your forward movement.

---

2   Watts, A. (1951). *The wisdom of insecurity*. New York: Random House.

Healthy emotional pain, on the other hand, is part of God's creation. Since none of us is likely to move forward willingly when life is going well (we want to pitch our tents right where we are in the comfort zone), the healthy pain serves as a wake-up call. It is the poke in the ribs that reminds us that we have more work to do. It is a reminder that God is not done with us yet. The healthy emotional pain is a call to arms—a reminder that we need to shut down the status quo, fold up our tents, and march forward. Healthy emotional pain can serve as God's "megaphone to rouse a deaf world."[3] Complacency in our incompleteness is easy for us. It is hard work to grow and become all that God wants us to be. "My friends, be glad, even if you have a lot of trouble," the scriptures tell us. "You know that you learn to endure by having your faith tested. But you must learn to endure everything, so that you will be completely mature and not lacking in anything" (James 1:2-4, CEV)

Distinguishing Healthy Emotional Pain from Unhealthy

In learning the difference between healthy and unhealthy pain, we need first to see how they are similar. They both can be *excruciating*. Suffering is suffering in either case. And they both can be *intense*. The feelings are strong. Healthy emotional pain, such as bereavement and grief, can certainly be as powerful as unhealthy emotions. In other words, you won't be able to tell them apart simply by how bad you feel as you experience them.

Healthy and unhealthy emotional pain can be distinguished, however, with their distinguishing characteristics showing up in four ways—ways that have to do with their source, their duration, and their effects (in terms of both growth and behavior).

Source of Pain

Constructive emotions are God-given, for "every good gift and every perfect gift is from above" (James 1:17, KJV). Constructive emotions are the sound of God's alarm bell. In them, we can know that "God is doing what is best for us, training us to live God's holy best" (Hebrews 12:11, MSG). In contrast, destructive emotions come from the Voice that tries to keep us from the rich, full, abundant life we can experience as participants in God's Kingdom.

---

3   Lewis, C. S. (1943). *The problem of pain*. New York: Macmillan.

Duration of Pain

Healthy painful emotions are of short duration and are time-limited. By their very nature they evaporate on their own without any help from you. They allow your life to be linear and to continue on your journey. "That is why we never give up. Though our bodies are dying, our spirits are being renewed every day. For our present troubles are quite small and won't last very long. Yet they produce for us an immeasurably great glory that that will last forever! So we don't look at the troubles we can see right now; rather, we look forward to what we have not yet seen. For the troubles we see will soon be over; but the joys to come will last forever" (2 Corinthians 4:16-18, NLT).

On the other hand, unhealthy emotions can last a lifetime. They hardly ever go away on their own. When they do, it is usually a temporary respite, and then they return with gusto. They cause your life to be circular, running around and around; expending time and energy going over and over again the same old hurts and disappointments, keeping you from your spiritual goals. The Bible warns us about this. As *The Message* paraphrases Hebrews 12:15. "Keep a sharp eye out for weeds of bitter discontent. A thistle or two gone to seed can ruin a whole garden in no time."

Maturity and Pain

Healthy emotions promote growth and leave you a stronger person with greater wisdom. They enhance Christian maturity by allowing your life to deepen to unexpected levels of experience. We know that people will often testify that they are better people because of the suffering in their lives. When this happens they are speaking of healthy pain and suffering. In contrast, unhealthy pain inhibits all emotional growth. This is why we often see people who are still the same people they were twenty years ago—still voicing the same complaints, still fighting the same battles, still holding the same grudges. The longer the Voice can keep you tied up with these emotional knots, the less likely you will be able to experience God's grace.

The Behavior of Pain

Finally, healthy emotions energize you to take constructive *action*—the fourth or "behavior" domino we discussed in chapter 2. These constructive actions build you up, develop patience, establish endurance, and build character. That is not to say that they always feel good. Accepting the notion that God gives us emotional pain for good reason is hard for us. The Voice would rather call us to continue in its damaging cycle where we continually seek relief from pain and discomfort through means that may not be in our best interest. The resulting temporary relief —the little "h" —feels so good that it blinds us to what we are missing. It's the "Esau syndrome" that the Scriptures talk about, "trading away God's lifelong gift in order to satisfy a short-term appetite" (Hebrews 12:16, MSG).

Emotional Recognition

As you learn to distinguish between healthy emotional pain and unhealthy emotional pain, you will find it is both easy and difficult. In one sense, it is easy because we can experience only six unhealthy emotions. In contrast, life offers us hundreds of healthy ones. The recognition task is easy because all you need to do is recognize the *unhealthy* emotions. Then anything else you experience is, by default, healthy.

But in another sense, the task is difficult because each of the unhealthy emotions looks like one of the healthy ones. This apparent similarity is a source of much confusion for people trying to sort out their emotions. As we mentioned earlier, even mental health professionals often group together these various emotions by describing one of the emotions in terms of the others.

The six unhealthy, destructive, toxic emotions are *guilt, resentment, depression, helplessness, unhealthy anxiety,* and *irrational fear*. Since all emotions are packages wrapped in *thoughts* (Domino 2—coming before the emotion) and behaviors (domino 4—coming after the emotion), let's look more closely at this packaging. The packaging allows us to more clearly define each emotion. Each emotion is defined by the thought that precedes it and the behavior that follows. Psychologists call this an "operational definition." Here's how each one of the unhealthy emotions works and the resultant behavior in each case:

Guilt

Thought: "I made a terrible mistake." The belief that you have violated an externally imposed rule causes guilt. People often couch this belief inside "should" language —"I should never have done that (or said that)."

Behavior: Self-punishment. Guilt is the emotion that gets you to punish yourself.

Resentment

Thought: "That person has disrespected me." Believing that someone has violated your rights causes resentment because you are convinced they are bad and worthless, rotten to the core.

Behavior: Retaliation. Resentment is the emotion a person feels when he or she is acting revengeful toward another person.

Irrational Fear

Thought: "I'm experiencing strong feelings, and I'm frightened about what I'm feeling." A belief that something inside you (emotion, sensation) is dangerous and unsafe causes Irrational Fear. "What I'm feeling could really hurt me." "Trusting myself is really scary and harmful."

Behavior: Insulation. Irrational Fear is the emotion you feel when you are spending time insulating yourself from the real world.

Helplessness

Thought: "I can't stand it." "There's nothing I can do about this." Helplessness is caused by the belief that something is happening to you that is literally inescapable and intolerable. "I can't take this anymore and will do anything to get away."

Behavior: Running away. Helplessness is the emotion you feel when you are desperately trying to escape from a painful situation.

Depression

Thought: "I am rotten because . . . " When you believe that you have no redeeming value as a human being, you will feel depressed. "If I were a better person, this wouldn't be happening to me."

Behavior: Lifelessness. Depression is the emotion you feel when you are being lifeless. Lifelessness is not restricted to inactivity. Some people who feel depressed overcompensate by doing too much for others. Often this proves to themselves they are good after all. They make the mistake of confusing extrinsic worth with intrinsic worth. If you feel depressed, you may put effort into helping other people focus on themselves so that they will not pay attention to the no-good you. On the other hand, you may try to relieve your feelings of depression by partying all night, or gambling away a weekend, or running up a credit card on a shopping binge. These behaviors are all considered lifeless because they have no purpose other than proving how worthless one is.

Unhealthy Anxiety

Thought: "Something bad is going to happen and I can do nothing about it." A two-pronged belief supports this unhealthy emotion: (1) the belief that a low probability event has a high probability of happening to you in the near future and (2) when it does, you will experience a personal catastrophe.

Behavior: Avoidance. Unhealthy anxiety is the emotion you feel when you expend effort to avoid something that you perceive as terrible but is probably blown out of proportion.

GRIHDU: A Way to Remember the Unhealthy Emotions

You can remember these six toxic emotions by learning the phrase: "**G**od **R**eigns **I**n **H**is **W**onderful **U**niverse." This mnemonic device (an antidote to the toxicity) will help you remember the six destructive emotions because the first initial in each word is also the first letter of one of the six deadly emotions: **G**uilt, **R**esentment, **I**rrational fear, **H**elplessness, **D**epression, **U**nhealthy anxiety.

Be aware that anxiety and fear are often confused with each another. People tend to use them in the same sentence as interchangeable experiences. They are vastly different from each other because anxiety is always related to the future while fear is always related to the present. According to this scheme, it is technically incorrect to say that you are afraid of that big interview tomorrow. Since it is not happening yet, the correct emotion is anxiety. To confuse this even further, you might be anxious about the interview but afraid of the anxiety. Experiencing irrational fear because of the unhealthy anxiety is a hallmark of panic attacks.

More often than not, these six emotions will not be found in isolation but in groups of two, three, or more. The definition of a bad day is when you get hit with all six. Psychologist Carol Tavris likens emotions to grapes because they often come in clusters.[4] As you track your emotions you will probably find that several of them regularly occur together.

Destructive emotions are corrosive and come from the Voice with its lies and partial truths that often hide the thoughts that generate these destructive emotions. Because these emotions are circular in nature, they can last indefinitely. They rob us of our ability to take constructive action. Like a cancer, they eat away at us and prevent our spiritual growth, and can keep us in bondage for a lifetime. The good news is you have the power to rid your garden of these destructive emotions, and banish them from your life. Nevertheless, it will take commitment on your part—a commitment to learn this material and to do the daily writing and exercises.

Because of our upbringing, many people think they have no control over their emotions, especially negative ones. Many of us lead lives resigned to the darkness of bitterness, depression, and anxiety, believing "that's just the way life is." We think we are victims of bad temperament and that our families are just "cursed" that way and nothing can be done about it. So we medicate ourselves in all kinds of destructive ways to find temporary solace from the pain (seeking little "h"), even though we know that the darkness will inevitably return. We have many unhealthy ways to escape from the pain of destructive emotions. People can use almost anything to relieve their discomfort: Booze, drugs, shopping ("retail therapy"), work, sports. All these things work for a short period, but eventually the pain returns and continues to rot away the quality of our lives.

The Other Side of the Emotional Coin

So far, recognizing unhealthy emotions should be an easy skill to learn. Most people can memorize and eventually recognize six items. What makes this task more daunting is the similarity between these six toxic emotions and six other *healthy* emotions. The next step is to tease these six pairs apart so that you can stop being confused as to which emotion is healthy and which one is unhealthy. This is a critical step. You will use different skills for handling unhealthy emotions than you will for handling healthy ones.

---

4   Tavris, C. (1989). *Anger: The misunderstood emotion*. Carmichael, CA: Touchstone Books.

52

First, we will look at the healthy emotions that are the polar opposites of the unhealthy ones. The accompanying chart shows this relationship.

Table 3-A: Unhealthy vs. Healthy Emotional Pain

UNHEALTHY EMOTION	HEALTHY EMOTION
Guilt	Remorse, Regret, and Shame
Resentment	Anger
Irrational Fear	Rational Fear
Helplessness	Weakness
Depression	Sadness
Unhealthy Anxiety	Healthy Anxiety

Guilt vs. Remorse, Regret, and Shame

The opposite of guilt is not about never feeling bad for messing up. When you have made a mistake, your concern about the mistake will allow you to feel the healthy alternatives to guilt, namely remorse, regret, and shame. Remorse and regret are healthy emotions that we need to identify and accept as emotional pain that helps us to grow. Accepting remorse as part of a healthy life allows us to learn from our mistakes. It is true that making mistakes can open up new learning opportunities for us. In addition, we need to forgive ourselves when mistakes are made. The self forgiveness moves us from the emotional pain of remorse and regret to a place of clarity and forward movement.

Shame also is another misunderstood emotion. It is an emotion that follows the breaking of community ties through inappropriate behavior. Being ashamed when we violate community standards is healthy for us. As a Christian, I would be ashamed if I committed adultery. It would prod me to ask for forgiveness and work at the difficult task of reconciliation to restore the broken relationships with my family and church community. However, if I let the toxic emotion of *guilt* creep into my mind, I would spend more time punishing myself, thanks to the Voice's lies. The more time I spend punishing myself, the less time I would have for the process of reconciliation and atonement.

Shame, then, is community based, whereas remorse and regret are more personal. Shame is experienced when I disconnect from my community.

Remorse results from a disconnect from my core values. By forgiving myself (in the case or remorse and regret)—or asking forgiveness from my community (in the case of shame)—I will be able to learn from my mistakes. Learning from our mistakes propels us forward in our spiritual journey.

Guilt, on the other hand, runs us in circles. Even though it is unnecessary and destructive, people commonly believe that guilt is necessary as a motivator for getting people to do what is right. The Voice gets us to internalize society's rules so every time we make a mistake our instant emotion is guilt. The Voice makes us guilty by telling us we should or should not do something.

Drs. Henry Cloud and John Townsend in their best-selling book, *Boundaries*,[5] state, "We have been so trained by others on what we 'should' do that we think we are being loving when we do things out of compulsion." This compulsion (another way to describe behavior driven by silent rules) to always do the "right thing" (hoping to please others by following their assumed expectations) can make our lives miserable.

Words like "should," "have to" and "ought to" represent a tipping over of the thought domino that triggers the emotion of guilt. The Voice is lying to us by insisting that we live our lives by rules and external expectations. St. Paul expresses this beautifully when he describes the end of the "Law" with the coming of Christ:

> "The law no longer holds you in its power, because you died to
> its power when you died with Christ on the cross. Now you are
> united with the one who was raised from the dead. As a result,
> you can
> produce good fruit, that is, good deeds for God . . . the law
> aroused those evil desires that produced sinful deeds. Now we can
> really serve God, not in the old ways by obeying the letter of the
> law, but in the new way, by the spirit" (Romans 7:4-6, (NLT).

---

5   Cloud, H. & Townsend, J. (2002). *Boundaries: When to say YES; When to say NO to take control of your life*. Grand Rapids, MI: Zondervan.

Christ gave us permission to make mistakes. Making them is a vital part of God's plan for our learning process. Some of our most important learning occurs from the mistakes we make.

Resentment vs. Anger

When we feel resentment towards someone because they have violated our sense of right and wrong or violated our personal integrity, the Voice wants us to retaliate. The problem is that the person at the other end of your retaliation may also have a strong Voice that tells that person to retaliate towards you. Now you are locked into a double circle called a feud. By thinking for yourself when you have been violated, you can experience the healthy emotion of anger.

Anger can be a very constructive emotion—that is, when it's used properly. An abundance of research has dispelled some commonly held beliefs about anger. Pop psychology has led us to believe that ventilating our anger is always healthy, that we need to get it all out. Just the opposite is true: in most instances venting our anger only fuels more anger. It produces a state of physiological arousal that usually prolongs the emotion.

The second myth is that withholding our anger can make us sick, can cause the anger to grow inside us and eventually transform itself into illness, depression, or even violent acts. A preponderance of research shows that holding back an angry outburst will usually lead to a more diplomatic and productive outcome. It also will allow time for the physiological responses to calm down and give you a clearer head.

This is not to say that you should just always try to forget it when someone violates you. Dr. Tavris shows that anger will keep resurfacing until you confront the cause of the violation and reach a resolution.[6] Emotions, and especially anger, are like fire: controlled and used thoughtfully and strategically, anger can be very useful, but allowed to rage out of control it can be devastating in its consequences.

A few years ago, a car mechanic delayed in completing needed repairs on my car. I (Pat) was leaving for vacation and needed my car back. As the day for leaving approached, I prepared myself for yet another delay. Without

---

6   Tavris, op. cit.

my personal car, I would be forced to spend hundreds of dollars renting a car. Sure enough, the repair shop told me again my car was not ready. Having anticipated this response from them ahead of time, I controlled my temper and confronted them with the facts about their broken promises and their responsibility to make amends for their mistake. They agreed, and I persuaded them to pay for my rental car. My car was done the following week. Perhaps Mark Twain said it best: "If you're mad, count to ten, if you're really mad, count to one hundred."

Resentment is not the same as anger. Resentment is a cancerous emotion that is like turning a loaded gun on yourself. It smolders inside us like landfill fires and tire fires that sometimes burn underground, polluting the environment. The Voice urges us to degrade each other's value as human beings. It delights in our thoughts of revenge, retaliation, and demeaning language that drive wedges between us and others, poison relationships, and tear families and friends apart. Even the most commonly used and seemingly innocent characterizations can be a mild form of retaliation. Phrases like, "that turkey" or "what a jerk" usually only serve to subtract a little more love from the world. Revenge is never a substitute for appropriate confrontation. And retaliatory action ("I'll show that so-and-so! He can't cut *me* off") has caused many an accident and death, as the phenomenon of road rage on crowded highways shows.

Irrational vs. Rational fear

Fear is quite reasonable when a visible and imminent threat presents itself. A man pointing a loaded gun at you would be a very real cause for a fear reaction. This would be rational fear. However, when the fear is not imminent nor external but focuses on your internal pain, irrational fear is probably at work.

Irrational fear is unreasonable because it is a fear of something inside you. It points to emotions or sensations that you have mistaken for something outside you. Any one of the other five toxic emotions can also lead you to think that danger is present when it is not. Some men have this irrational fear whenever their wives or girlfriends make the request, "we gotta talk." They do not know why they are afraid; they just get flooded with an overwhelming feeling that they need to insulate themselves immediately. Maybe run down to the corner store and pick up something, anything!

In its extreme form, irrational fear leads to phobias and panic attacks. The tsunami of feelings on the inside gets mistaken for something on the outside. People with phobias, such as the fear of high places, are not really afraid of high places. They are afraid of the terrifying panic that overwhelms them when they are in high places. Irrational fear is triggered by something uncomfortable inside oneself that is not usually dangerous. Rational fear is highly focused on the outside toward something that is objectively lethal to one's wellbeing.

Helplessness vs. Weakness

As Clint Eastwood once said: "A man's gotta know his limitations." When life has pushed us up against our personal limitations, feeling weakness is normal and healthy. It an uncomfortable but healthy alternative to helplessness. When we feel weak, it leads us to seek self-improvement. The Apostle Paul said, "When I am weak, then I am strong" (2 Corinthians 12:10, NLT). Helplessness, on the other hand, is the feeling of being trapped and boxed in with no place to go. When this feeling escalates high enough, you will try to escape any situation.

The unhealthy emotion called helplessness can also be the force that powers human addictions. It comes from a belief that you cannot *stand* your current situation. The Voice convinces you that you are boxed in or trapped. It tells you that you have no choices left. It then delivers the final blow and assures you that the only course of action is to escape. All addictions are an attempt to self-medicate (run away from) the internal pain of feeling helpless. Being helpless means being powerless to avoid excessive drinking, eating, or dangerous sexual behavior. Some addicts live with the belief that they are powerless to conquer the addictive behavior, because they have not yet learned to conquer the destructive emotion of helplessness. The addictive, destructive *behavior* follows the destructive *emotion*, it does not precede it.

When you are convinced that you are helpless, you cannot stop yourself from doing something to ease the emotional pain, even if the something is to run. Knowing there are two other dominoes between a life event (for example, an argument with your spouse or friend) and your destructive behavior (getting drunk or high) frees you from the lies and distortions that lead to helplessness. Recognizing that your kids are not really driving you crazy allows you to slow down and rethink your alternatives to the stressful situation. Understanding the sequence (triggering event–thought–emotion–behavior) is the antidote to helplessness.

When conflicts and struggles arise, it's important to know when to stop or when to choose differently. Without that self-awareness you can hurt yourself. Recognizing a weakness is different from feeling helpless. Knowing when you are overwhelmed, knowing that you have a weakness for booze or drugs, perhaps certain types of food, or even inappropriate sexual behavior, can save you from unwanted consequences. Knowing that you lack patience or tolerance in some settings can prepare you to endure those situations more gracefully. Whatever it is, if you know you have a weakness for something, you can prepare yourself and make better choices for handling it in a mature, responsible way. You can step back mentally and rethink the situation, choosing more appropriate and healthier attitudes to address a conflict. Being aware of your weaknesses frees you up to spend more of your time doing the things that you enjoy.

Depression vs. Sadness

Have you ever felt better after a good cry? Studies have shown that crying releases an endorphin-like chemical in the brain that produces pleasant feelings. Crying is a natural part of emotional healing whenever we encounter loss. Healthy sadness recognizes that a loss does not devalue us personally. We are not our money or our things; we are not our performance or what other people think about us. Our worth as believers comes from being alive. God's loving us wholly and unconditionally establishes our value for all time. It is faith that keeps us connected to God, His unlimited redeeming grace, love and infinite worth, forever. As the Scripture says, "We who have run for our very lives to God have every reason to grab the promised hope with both hands and never let go" (Heb.6:17-18, MSG).

In contrast to healthy sadness, feelings of depression strike deeply at the core of our value as human beings and the worth of our lives. When we experience any degree of loss, the Voice may urge us to react in a way different from sadness. The Voice may tell us that the loss diminishes us as a person and that our life has become a whole lot less valuable. By valuing ourselves by our performance, net worth, friends or family, salary, reputations or others' assessment of us, we can never feel completely worthwhile. When anything goes wrong in any of those areas, our assessment of our self-worth will shatter if we do not have a solid faith in our infinite worth to prop us up.

Self-esteem is a different issue from self-worth. Many people mistakenly think self-esteem is a necessary step before a person can be healthy enough to have a good life. Recent research has shown that self-esteem follows the mastery of challenges in life. Don't you feel better about yourself when you have done a good job mowing the lawn, cooking a great meal from a new recipe, solving a puzzle, or assembling a child's toy or piece of furniture? We often feel good about ourselves after successfully spending an evening being a good parent, helping a friend who needed comforting, or finishing a satisfying day of hard work. These are all moments of high self-esteem. It occurs when you complete a task at a satisfying level of performance.

A large movement in this country spearheaded by the school system and bolstered by pop psychology attempts to enhance a person's self-esteem by structuring the environment to minimize mistakes and failure. Some schools avoid awarding failing grades for fear that they might tarnish a student's self-esteem. This is the opposite of teaching children to master life's challenges. Children are smart enough, the studies show, to know when someone is pandering to them. After all, "if everyone wins, then no one is a winner." This kind of false self-esteem simply promotes mediocrity.[7] Your worth is your intrinsic, infinite, God-given value simply because you are alive; self-esteem is something you earn by striving and failing and finally mastering a task.

Unhealthy Anxiety vs. Healthy (Performance) Anxiety

Have you ever stood up to speak in front of a crowd? Ever competed seriously in any kind of contest? Ever asked someone out on a date knowing that their rejection could be very painful? If so, you have experienced healthy anxiety. This emotion is associated with the "butterflies" or "stage fright" and is often called performance anxiety. It is another God-given emotion that prepares you for a challenging task. The brain signals the

---

7   Seligman, M. (1996). *The optimistic child: Proven program to safeguard children from depression & build lifelong resilience.* New York: Harper Paperbacks.

body to begin producing adrenaline. This increases the heart rate, helps you think faster, and provides the energy needed to perform at your best. Athletes could not reach peak performance without this performance anxiety. Before Pat gives a talk, he looks forward to and expects that anxiety to appear to help him do his best.

Figure 3-B: Peak Performance

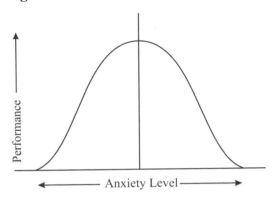

The bell curve to the right will help explain this. When the anxiety level is too low, sufficient arousal is not available to produce maximum performance. If the anxiety level gets too high (unhealthy anxiety) performance also diminishes. It is in the mid-levels of healthy anxiety that performance reaches its peak. Like the other healthy painful emotions, healthy anxiety is both painful and helpful. The anxiety you feel when paying the bills or during the excruciating work of putting together a budget is an emotion you need to embrace for emotional and spiritual growth. Such anxiety is good for you. It produces healthy planning and a positive outcome in your life.

Unhealthy anxiety and healthy anxiety may feel the same but are radically different because they originate in different places (the Voice, in the one case, and you, in the other). They also drive people to engage in behaviors that are strikingly different (*avoidance*, in the one case, and *planning*, in the other). The belief that something tragic will happen to you in the near future drives unhealthy anxiety. The Voice convinces you that what will happen will be so bad you'll be disabled and unable to make any more personal choices. At its extreme, psychologists call it a panic attack. Normal anxiety becomes destructive or counterproductive when the Voice introduces thoughts of the possibility of impending disaster.

What the Self-destructive Emotions Have in Common

The one thing all six of the self-destructive emotions have in common is their robbing you of your ability to choose. Later, when we get to chapter 5, we will talk about the destructive thoughts that trigger each of these toxic emotions. These are the "vermin" that cause all the trouble in your life. Recognizing the toxic thoughts that precede each poisonous emotion will be your first step for introducing real change and freedom into your life. Identifying and then changing those thoughts into positive and constructive statements is the key to life-long happiness with a capital H and true spiritual transformation.

Other Healthy Emotional Pain

Throughout the Psalms, David wails and bemoans his predicaments, which were at times life-threatening due to no fault of his own, and at other times were self-created. In both cases, he learned what he was feeling and expressed it with all the intensity and detail that he could muster. David is one of the great heroes of the Bible, not because he was a powerful ruler but because he gives us so much insight into his humanity. He was very emotional, but he usually kept his emotions reigned in enough to let God's wisdom prevail in his life. He *almost* never let emotions be the final arbiter of his course of action. We say almost never because we know he let his passions get the better of him when he bedded Bathsheba, another man's wife, and then had the husband killed in battle. Eventually, he rose out of his self-created pit and endured the intensely painful, but healthy grief he had to go through as he suffered the consequences of his sin. In the end, David emerged heroically as he redeemed himself with God. His patient endurance of intense grief built the character of one of the most beloved figures in the Scriptures.

Like us, David experienced many different kinds of emotional pain. Anger, performance anxiety, sadness, weakness, rational fear, and remorse are not the only painful healthy emotions. Loneliness, envy, boredom, even jealousy, are examples of other emotions that can be healthy and constructive, depending upon the action they prompt.

Jealousy

Jealousy is not commonly considered a constructive emotion. The Bible tells us that even God, who is perfect, gets jealous: "Don't worship any other god. GOD—his name is The-Jealous-One—is a jealous God" (Exodus 34:14, MSG). We experience jealousy when someone attempts to take from us something or someone we highly value. Without the emotional junk the Voice puts into our heads, the natural behavior of jealousy would instead be to put effort into keeping what we value. If it is a person, we would resolve to spend more time with them and work on strengthening the connection. Unfortunately, when the destructive emotions of resentment and bitterness team up with jealousy, the results are corrosive. The Voice uses any of the six unhealthy emotions as pollution devices by inserting them into normal, natural painful emotions.

Loneliness

Loneliness is designed to motivate us to reestablish our relationships and social connections. It occurs because we realize that we are all by ourselves and that we would like to be with other people. Loneliness can be positive and healthy if it impels us to take action and show initiative in reaching out to others. If this emotion gets polluted with depression or unhealthy anxiety (such as in a social phobia), the normal act of reaching out gets crushed by these unhealthy, devastating emotions stirred up by the Voice with its lies. ("You'll never have friends." "You're not worthy of being in a relationship." "Nobody likes you." "No one wants to be with you." "Your phone will never ring.")

Boredom

Boredom is also a healthy emotion because it, too, motivates us to take constructive action. Our brain is wired to make us feel discomfort when we are bored. It is a signal that we are no longer receiving any stimulation that is necessary for being alive (this is different than meditation, because boredom is passive and meditation is self-directed). Boredom is the result of being in a setting where nothing is happening that grabs our attention. This is most common in younger people because the brain is still maturing and needs the stimulation for growth. As adults, the Voice wants us to use boredom as an incentive to engage in destructive behavior when it is really designed to move us toward a different kind of behavior, namely, finding something to do that keeps us alive and interactive with our environment. Such action can occur in the presence of others or as a solitary but nonetheless rewarding endeavor.

Envy

By itself, envy is another natural, harmless healthy painful emotion. It is only when the corrupting influence of the six nasty emotions pollutes envy that it becomes harmful. Envy is the flip side of jealousy. The thought that you would like to have what someone else has produces envy. When the toxic emotions are not present, you will work to obtain something like that which you envy. If the Voice can pollute this natural emotion with such devices as resentment and helplessness, you may do something illegal or unethical to get what you want. These unhealthy emotions would divert your energy into violating another person's dignity in your drive to obtain the goal. If the Voice adds helplessness to the mix you would be convinced that you "could not stand" being without the desired target. The requisite escape behavior could drive you into some form of self-medicating behaviors.

As you think of other healthy painful emotions, try to understand them within the package of thoughts and behaviors. Since all emotions are part of a larger package, their definitions depend on the other parts of the package. But always remember that all emotions are prompted by a thought and followed by a behavior. Consequently, to clearly understand what an emotion is, we need to "operationally define" it by these two components. For most people, actions are much more obvious than thoughts and beliefs. Therefore, defining the emotion in terms of its behavior is easier but often counterintuitive.

Mindfulness

Unfortunately, healthy painful emotions can be excruciating at times. Merely recognizing them and naming them may not help much. In the 1960s, the University of Massachusetts hospital developed a strategy for managing emotional and physical pain in patients who had severe chronic pain. They call their program the Mindfulness-Based Stress Reduction program and it has successfully helped thousands of people learn to tolerate extreme discomfort. Psychology has adapted the strategies so that they can be successfully used with emotional pain.

It is beyond the scope of this book to teach you the difficult-to-learn skill of mindfulness. However, many resources on this topic are available to you. The originator of the program, Dr. Jon Kabat-Zinn, has a number of books available if you want to explore this powerful skill further. We recommend *Full Catastrophe Living*[8] as an introduction. Although the program is relatively new, the concept is not. Jesus lived and demonstrated a life filled with mindfulness.

You may want to try our abbreviated version of mindfulness, as presented below. If that is not sufficient, you may want to see a psychologist who has been trained in the skill, attend a workshop, or obtain books and videos for your benefit. We teach people to use a simple four-step procedure for managing their healthy painful emotions. The simple version is as follows.

Step #1: Observe

Notice the painful emotion, but do not judge it. Making a value judgment about emotional pain is almost reflexive for humans; for example "Oh, this is awful" or "I can't stand this." Mentally and emotionally you want to stand apart from yourself and just notice what is happening. As you do, tell yourself what you are observing: "I'm feeling an intense sadness right now" or "I'm feeling anxiety and stress about my meeting with the boss tomorrow." When you find yourself being drawn back into the pain by evaluating it, interpreting it, or reacting to it, back away and start to observe it again nonjudgmentally.

This is a crucial and difficult step. You need to train yourself to be *neutral* with respect to the pain. Trying to make sense of what is happening is normal for your brain, but that's not what you will be doing in this step. Instead, you will be training your brain to do something that seems contrary to the way it should be done.

---

8   Kabat-Zinn, J. (1990). *Full catastrophe living: Using the wisdom of your body*. New York: Dell Publishing.

During this observation phase, you can use any self-soothing techniques that work for you. When you become comfortable with this first step, you can add the next one.

Step #2: Define

Try to decide whether this emotional pain is healthy or unhealthy (remember GRIHDU). If the emotional pain is unhealthy, stop using mindfulness and immediately switch to your coping strategies for handling this type of emotion (you will learn this in chapter 7). When you have dispatched the unhealthy emotion, begin step one again.

If the emotional pain is not one of the six unhealthy emotions then, by default, it will be healthy. If it is healthy, then try to correctly name it: sadness, anger, boredom, remorse, loneliness, anxiety, rational fear, and so on. Naming it will help you recognize it as a necessary part of your faith journey. Even as you name it, continue to be a neutral observer. If judgments or interpretations come back, gently move back to step one. This movement between steps is meant to be done gracefully as if you were riding waves that move you up and down. This allows you to go with the natural momentum of your brain rather than resisting it.

Step #3: Accept

This important step keeps you from equating yourself with your feelings. Emotions are something you experience, not who you are. *Feelings are not facts.* Just because you are angry does not mean you are an angry person. You are always more than your emotions. By *not* making your emotions a standard to decide who you are, you are free to be more than your emotions. You can view yourself as the person God intends you to be. Separating your being from the pain frees you from a personal investment in fleeing it or fighting against it;. The emotion is not you, but merely something happening to you.

Accepting your healthy pain will reduce the sensation of pain. As you may know, the more we fight pain, the more it hurts. You have probably had the experience of being momentarily distracted from emotional or physical pain only to wonder why you felt nothing while you were distracted. Pain research has established that when you stop fighting it, you can reduce the sensation of pain. The problem is that fighting the pain seems the right thing to do.

Step #4: Embrace

As we have already pointed out, healthy, painful emotions exist to motivate you to better yourself. Your anger will lead you to confront the situations that violate your dignity so that you can value what God has created. By crying when you are sad, you heal wounds that can keep you from reaching your divine potential. When you forgive yourself for making mistakes, you grow that much closer to the goals that God wants for you. Planning for dealing with difficult situations in the future helps you become more competent and adept at dealing with those problems that life throws your way.

Summary

1. Emotions are louder than thoughts. We are often aware of them before we become aware of the thoughts that generate them.
2. All painful emotions are either healthy and constructive or unhealthy and destructive. The former come from God, the latter from the Voice.
3. Of all the hundreds of emotions available to humans, only six are unhealthy; the rest are important for your spiritual growth.
4. Learn to accept the healthy pain through techniques such as mindfulness.
5. Later, in chapter 7, you will learn techniques for dispatching all six of the unhealthy emotions from your life.

Assignment

Begin a three-column emotions log for identifying destructive, unhealthy emotions. Determine the time of day you experience the emotion, then the setting. The setting might include who, what, where, how often. In the last column name the unhealthy emotion. Remember, we mentioned that emotions can cluster like grapes, so don't be surprised to see more than one emotion occur at the same time. By faithfully keeping this emotions log, you will begin to see patterns and relationships between the three columns. The example below will help you get started.

Table 3-B: Unhealthy Emotions Log

TIME	SETTING	DESTRUCTIVE EMOTION
9:30a	Home alone	Depressed
1:00p	Didn't call my mother	Guilty
3:30p	Sitting in car at busy stop light	Helplessness
5:15p	Boyfriend [or girlfriend] didn't call	Resentful
7:40p	Worried about talking to my boss tomorrow	Unhealthy Anxiety
10:25p	Feeling tired, upset, nauseous	Irrational Fear

Writing Tip

Keep this log for at least a week. The more writing you do, the more you will learn and the easier the following chapters will be. The ideal method for logging this information is in real time. However, because it is a new skill and you may have limited time you can fill out the log whenever you have time. One of the best tricks our clients and students use is to break up the day into two-hour blocks of time. At the end of each two-hour block, take a few minutes to recall the existence of any of these six unhealthy emotions. Make a quick note and then at the end of the day pull all your notes together and put them in your emotions log.

Chapter Four
Pests Get in the Garden

And then [Jesus] added, "It is the thought-life that defiles you."
— Mark 7:20 (NLT).

This chapter is a good place to pause briefly and see how well you have learned the approach thus far. We began by using a metaphor of a garden, reminding us of the story in the second chapter of Genesis. It tells us that when God created the Garden of Eden, it was perfect. The trees and plants were free from disease and pestilence. No bugs were present. No vermin hindered and destroyed the beauty of the garden. But in Genesis 3, we see that evil ruined it all. Evil came at the expense of innocence. Humans came to know pain, suffering, and even death.

This ancient explanation of how evil entered the world runs contrary to what God wants for you in your personal world today. God wants you to be able to transcend your flawed life and live in the fullness of his glory. For many of you, this may be a difficult task, but not for lack of desire or motivation. The apostle Paul admitted that he, too, often did things that he did not want to do and did not do things he wanted to do.

Remember the dominoes? They illustrate how your thought life powers your behavior through your emotions. Because of human imperfection, the Voice still negatively affects our thought lives. For example, you may want to stand up for someone who is being ridiculed and mistreated, but the Voice whispers a hundred reasons to stay out of it. You may want to do something constructive to get rid of your emotional pain, but the Voice convinces you to do something that is not good for you instead, such as abusing alcohol or food. The Voice tells you that these things will make you feel better. As with all lies from the Voice, this is a half-truth. These things will make you feel better—but only temporarily. The Voice likes to sidetrack you from the Big "H" to the little "h" whenever possible. When you do some things to feel better, you believe the illusion that this behavior is the right thing to do.

Active Participation

Your battle against the Voice is as old as the human race: "For we wrestle not against flesh and blood, but against principalities, against powers, against the rulers of the darkness of this world, against spiritual wickedness in high places" (Eph:6:12, KJV).

You want to make sure that you do not make the mistake of being a spectator in your own garden. You are *not* watching a struggle between good and evil. If this were so, then you would be the prize that goes to the winner of the struggle. The cartoons that show a devil on one shoulder and an angel on the other shoulder are funny but incorrect. If you perceive your struggle this way, you will lose the ability to take your life back from the Voice.

Though you may feel as if two people are inside you, you want to change this perception. Just one person lives within you—you! *Only* you. The Voice wants to live inside and be part of you, but it must continually be forced out. One of our successful students commented that no matter how well his life is going, the Voice with all its lies and accusations continually tries to sneak back. The Voice even tried to convince him that his life would be better if he would just let it back willingly. Another person told us that the Voice apologized for being so mean. If the person would just let it back, then they could work on life together. If you have ever felt like someone else was running your life, that you are not in control, then you have identified the Voice. Not only do the lies of the Voice affect your behavior, but the lies also force the six nasty and devastating emotions into your life. As you'll recall from the preceding chapter, these painful emotions are of a different variety than the healthy painful emotions that all humans experience. Painful emotions that are healthy help us to grow into grace, while the painful emotions that are unhealthy make us run in circles, forever enslaved by the Voice.

You must never forget that the Voice would have you believe that your struggles are really against yourself. The greatest deception it can ever perpetrate on you is to make you believe it does not exist. If your worry is really just a part of your nature, then the Voice has a resting place within your soul. When we err, the Voice will tell us, "I'm not telling you to cheat on your spouse. This is really *your* idea, and it's a good one!"

Remember, Christ was able to clearly discern the voice of temptation and false belief, and with Christ's help, you can also grow continually more perceptive to the presence of that Voice. Without training, people hear the deceptive lies of the Voice as their own inner thoughts. Even worse, since your silent assumptions are not audible, you may only feel that a nagging emotional war is going on inside you.

The Bugs

The Voice has many ways to harm the garden of your mind. It can unleash a horde of pests to destroy it and keep you from producing the "fruit of the spirit." When you learn the Five Steps to Grace in chapter 7, you can fumigate your mind against the negative-thinking vermin that are so destructive. To begin moving in that direction, we want you to begin examining some simpler "mind pests" that the Voice may use against you. These bugs are a catalog of distorted thoughts and misperceptions—mistakes about life, other people, and yourself. They may be small and apparently insignificant, but they can bore into your thought life, making it more difficult for you to have clear and realistic thoughts.

The Either-Or Bug

Life must be lived in the extremes, says the Voice. You must always see your day-to-day experiences as either-or. You are either happy or miserable, either a wonderful person or a rotten person. When this bug invades your mental garden, you cannot live in the middle ground where life's rainbow of color exists. The Voice says you only have two choices. Everything is either black or white. As you fumigate this bug, life becomes richer and more colorful. For most human beings, the necessity of choosing one or the other extremes in a given situation is rare. Usually, you'll have a number of options. The either-or bug is particularly devastating for relationships because humans are so complex. Viewing your relationships and the people involved as either "all this" or "all that" narrowly defines them as one-dimensional shadows, thereby demeaning them.

Blind Alley Bug

The Voice likes to send this bug when you have really important decisions to make. It wants you to believe you have only one good way to make a decision. When you are in a tough situation, the Voice wants you to believe that drinking or taking pills, for example, are the only possible methods for satisfactorily dealing with what is happening. The Blind Alley bug has the potential to blind you and limit your capacity for creativity and spontaneity. By following this path the Voice has set for you, you will often find yourself at the end of a blind alley. It will appear that all of your good choices have evaporated.

Busy-Busy Bug

If the Voice can keep you running as fast as possible, it can keep your mind too occupied to listen to what it is saying. This is a common bug that infests the lives of successful people. Meeting goals, making more money, getting more promotions, running a business as if you lived in a world of thirty-six-hour days, spending all of your time helping other people—these worthwhile activities can make it very difficult to hear the Voice. If you can't hear the Voice, then you can't defeat it. Remember to slow down internally and keep your mind open to hearing the Voice. As Anne Lamott said, "If the devil can't get you to sin, he'll keep you busy."[1]

Comparison Bug

Many of our class members tell us this bug is more common and pervasive than cockroaches. If the Voice can erode your ability to maintain a strong sense of self, it can control you much easier. This common mental pest is always comparing you with other people, but only in a way that shows you as inferior to others. What is not always apparent is that this is a cheap shot. When you think about it, finding someone who can do something "better" than you is an easy task for the Voice. You must not let the Voice compare you with anyone else. To do so is a losing game.

---

1   Lamott, A. (2005). *Plan B: Further thoughts on faith*. New York: Penguin Books

Comparison bugs always keep you in a one-down position and you must vigorously oppose them.

Control Bug

This pest wants to drive you crazy by convincing you that you should be able to control the way other people behave. This bug tends to show up in families. The perfect family does not exist. Consequently, your children or spouse can easily behave in ways that annoy and irritate you. This will drive out any little "h" you may be experiencing. This bug wants you to believe that if you just plead, nag, or request something hard enough and long enough that other people will finally go your way. The Voice secretly knows that if you accept the fact that you cannot change anybody but yourself, you'll be much happier. And it cannot allow that. Learn to fumigate the Control Bug and keep it out of your garden. You can't control other people, no matter how hard you try; you are only in charge of yourself.

Demands Bug

The Voice likes to tell you what to do by bringing this bug into your garden. That's because the Voice's main goal is to run your life. The Demands Bug will make you feel like a slave, unable to make your own decisions and manage your own life. Your antidote to this trick is to insist that you make all of your own decisions. You do this even if it means doing the same thing the Voice just told you to do! The difference is between a choice *you* make and the obedience you give to the Voice.

Emotional Reasoning Bug

The Voice will try to get you to assume that what you feel is the absolute truth. For example, it may try to get you to believe that if you feel stupid, then you must be stupid. This pest is one of the more common bugs in people's mental gardens. Because feelings are so much a part of our daily existence, convincing us that we *are* our feelings is easy for the Voice. The truth is that you are a person who *has* feelings. It makes no sense to think that the feelings you have can define who you are as a person. What if the Voice tried to get you to believe you were a bicycle simply because you *had* a bicycle? Would that make you a bicycle?

Exaggeration Bug

The more the Voice can exaggerate what happens in your life, the better chance it has of increasing your confusion. You can bet that most of what the Voice says to you is some type of exaggeration. You can spot this bug by listening for words such as "always," "never," "most," "forever." "I can never say the right thing." "I mess it up every time." "Everybody always blames me for everything anyway, so why even try?" The Voice will try to make you believe a situation is either worse than it is or not as bad as it is. This bug may be found attached to other people, specific situations, or even yourself. By continuing to pollute your garden with this bug, the Voice can cloud your thinking about reality.

Interpretation Bug

This is also a very common bug because our brain is continuously seeking to make sense of life. Most people find it very difficult to live in ambiguous environments. When something does not make sense to us, we automatically try to find reasons for what is happening. However, the Voice takes advantage of this naturally occurring process. The Interpretation Bug allows the Voice to interpret your life for you. Unfortunately, this bug puts you in the position of being a child, not knowing what is best for your life. You will do much better if you insist on sticking with facts rather than interpretations. God's gift to you—a rational mind—will let you exterminate this bug.

Jump Ahead Bug

The Voice may initiate this bug by telling you that you are not learning the material in this book fast enough. It wants you to go on to the next chapter quickly before you have mastered the skills in the present one. This does not mean you cannot browse ahead, but you must remember that the skills in this book are interlocking. Learning the more advanced skills depends on how well you have mastered the previous skills. If the Voice can infest your garden with enough of these bugs, your chances of failure increases—exactly what the Voice wants. You don't need to let this happen. Be patient.

Label Bug

By using this bug on things—especially people—the Voice forces you to deal with the world in a limited way. Labels, such as "stupid," "lazy," "incompetent," are self-limiting because they allow for no flexibility or change. This is a pesky bug that sneaks into our lives easily because labels seem like a shortcut to understanding people. "That person is a_____(fill in the blank), so there's nothing else I need to know about her or him." But labels usually demean people and violate the principle of Christian love. This bug violates human integrity because it takes the wholeness of a person and reduces it to a single word or phrase, a caricature of humanity. The Label Bug also pretends to protect us from people whom we find threatening. The most common variety of this bug is rampant in racism, gender and sexual discrimination, and tribal religious perceptions.

Magical Thinking Bug

One can easily spot this bug by the phrase, "If . . . then . . . " Example: "If you would just be a better person, then you could get everybody to like you." Or, "If you would just read the Bible more, you wouldn't have all these problems." This bug and the Control Bug are related. The magic in this thinking is believing that you can control other people's behavior if you just change the way you treat them. It is also magic because this bug keeps you from understanding the natural laws of nature. The most dangerous toxin this bug can infect you with is the illusion that God is a Divine Santa Claus who will grant your every wish if you just "try hard enough to be a good Christian."

Mind-Reading Bug

This bug will pollute you with the silly notion that you can read another person's mind. It wants you to believe that you really know that another person is angry with you even if they say they are not. In truth, you can make guesses, even lucky ones. However, nobody can be certain that they know what someone is thinking or feeling. No person in the history of humanity has ever read someone's mind accurately. Magicians can appear to do it, but it is always a trick.

Myth of the Good Friend Bug

This bug's toxin has the opposite effect of the previous bug. That bug had you thinking you could read someone else' mind; this bug wants you to believe that the other person can read *your* mind. The effect of its poisonous myth is to persuade you that if someone cares about you, they should know what you are thinking and feeling—without your telling them. When you allow this bug to stay in your garden, you set yourself up for feeling disappointed and rejected when another person does not respond to your suffering in silence. Since women tend to be more aware of their feelings than men, they often have more trouble with this bug. If you want someone to know how you are feeling or what you are thinking, you must tell that person.

Predictions Bug

Like the Mind-Reading Bug, this one fouls your brain by making you convinced that you can predict the future. Since most people are sincerely curious about the future, this bug is very easy for the Voice to sneak into your garden. Mark tells us (13:32) that even Jesus admitted that the future is unknowable by anyone except God. A mutation of this bug is for the Voice to agree that you cannot see into the future. Then it tries to convince you to agree that it can read the future for you.

Silence Bug

As you get better at engaging the Voice, it will try to put the Silence Bug into your garden. Defeating the Voice is easier when you know what it is saying to you. It will try to fool you by remaining silent when you try to listen to its lies. You can counter this several different ways. The simplest method is to do absolutely nothing. The Voice is then tricked into thinking you are not paying attention so will start trying to hammer you all the more. Secondly, if you want to irritate the Voice and get a response, make something up. Write down what it *might* say to you. The more outrageous, the better. If the Voice says, "I didn't say that," you write down, "I didn't say that." Finally, you can use material from your past. You have plenty of that. It is also a good start to begin the process of cleaning up your past, especially those parts that continue to linger.

Stereo Bug

One of the most amusing bugs for the Voice is the Stereo Bug. This is similar to listening to music through a set of headphones—you get different information in each ear. When you listen to music going to each ear, the different outputs complement each other. This is the opposite of what the Voice does. It will put different bugs in each ear. It might tell you, "You need to do your homework for this book now" in one ear. The other ear will hear, "You really don't have time for that now. You can do it later." Either instruction you follow, the Voice wins because it is now running your life by telling you what to do.

Success Bug

This bug is fairly rare, but you need to be able to spot it should it appear. It is also late appearing in that it seldom appears in the early stages of your faith journey. However, as you become stronger and more successful in defeating the Voice, this bug may suddenly appear. The Voice will use this to discount your successes. When you become strong enough to succeed on a regular basis, the only tactic the Voice has left is to keep you from internalizing your achievements against it. This way your successes never become a part of your nature and remain detached and distant. You can spot this bug when you hear the Voice telling you that your personal growth was just luck, or that it won't last, or that the risks you took to be successful are just too scary. More lies.

Surprise Bug

This bug is one of the most persistent pests. It will probably be with you for the rest of your life. No matter how often you swat it, it will come back. This is not really important because the stronger you get, the more you'll develop immunity to its bite. The Voice will always try to catch you off your guard. It will try to send this bug in when you least expect it: when you are happy and enjoying life, when you are confident about a certain area of your life, or in an area of life where the Voice has never appeared before. As you get more experienced, the Voice will be less and less able to surprise you. Remember this motto: Never Be Surprised by Surprises.

Why, Why, Why Bug

Normal human curiosity makes all of us susceptible to the bite of this bug. Our brain is constructed to always ask why. The Voice enjoys confusing you with "why" questions. Our society spends a lot of time asking "why." Even mental health professionals used to spend inordinate amounts of time trying to find out why their clients were feeling or acting a certain way. Often this is a path that leads nowhere productive. You will find life more prosperous when you begin to change each "why" question into a "what" and a "how" question. For example, instead of asking yourself why your best friend treated you badly, you can destroy this bug by asking yourself, "*What* did she do?" followed by, "*How* am I going to deal with it?"

Wishful Thinking Bug

The last bug on the list can be just as damaging as the previous ones. There is nothing wrong with wishing that things were different. This bug, however, confuses wishing with *expecting*. Wishes are future events that have low probability; expectations are future events that have high probability. When this bug gets into your mental garden, you will confuse wishes with expectations and begin expecting things that are not very likely. The Voice wants you to waste your time wishing for things rather than taking action to get your needs met. You want to learn the difference between wishing and expecting. When you learn and practice this distinction, this bug will be effectively fumigated.

Summary

1. Now that you can hear the Voice more clearly and more often, you can begin to look more closely at how it is trying to undermine your success at having a beautiful garden.
2. The Voice has many pests that can invade your garden—usually more than one at a time.
3. You recall from earlier chapters that the Voice always lies. These pests are metaphors for the lies. This is the next skill you will begin to develop. These pests represent all the minor lies the Voice tries to get past your mental gates.
4. In the next chapter, you will learn how to identify the six big, powerful lies (the vermin) that provide the foundation for the Voice's running and ruining your life.

Assignment

Every good gardener is proficient in recognizing garden pests that will destroy the plants and fruit. Your next assignment is to familiarize yourself with these self-defeating bugs in your mental garden. For at least a week, you need to spend time each night reviewing the following list of bugs and identify which ones invaded your garden during the day. You can use the following form to do so. When you are adept in recognizing these bugs, you will have accomplished two objectives.

You will be able to recognize more clearly that these buggy thoughts are not from you. They have been placed there by the Voice. They do not belong to you; they have no place in your mental life. You are also not responsible for having the pests in your garden but you are responsible for getting them out of your garden.

Secondly, you are not a bad person for having these thoughts. You have been victimized by the Voice into believing you are defective because these worrisome thoughts invaded your property line. You are no longer responsible for having these thoughts; you are only responsible for correcting them in order to live the grace-filled life that God intended for you.

The Bug and Pest Worksheet

BUGS	MON	TUE	WED	THUR	FRI	SAT	SUN
Black & White [or Either -Or Bug]							
Blind Alley							
Busy-Busy							
Comparison							
Control							
Demands							
Emotional Reasoning							
Exaggeration							
Interpretation							
Jump Ahead							
Label							
Magical Thinking							
Mind-Reading							
Myth of the Good Friend							
Predictions							
Silence							
Stereo							
Success							
Surprise							
Why, why, why							
Wishful Thinking							

Chapter Five
Routing Out the Vermin

Search me, O God, and know my heart; test me and know my thoughts.
— Psalm 139:23 (NLT)

In chapter 4, we identified the "mind pests" or little bugs—erroneous ways of thinking that cause us trouble. But as bad as all these annoying little pests are for your garden, it's the *vermin* that cause the major devastation. These vermin infiltrate your thought life with profound lies and distortions that guarantee a life of pain and misery. If we were to change the metaphor to a military image, we could say that the vermin are the Voice's super weapons. These vermin are sneaky. Just when you think you have mastered them, the Voice reinvigorates them. Yielding to these vermin can drag you down into those old familiar, painful worry cycles. And you can find yourself stuck there indefinitely.

As we've been seeing throughout this book, the Voice operates on the basis of lies. All of the lies are bad for us, but some are especially bad. If the bugs are the minor lies that the Voice lets loose in our garden, the vermin are the major lies and can cause great destruction. But we need to recognize them and learn how to deal with them and get rid of them. This chapter and the next two chapters will provide you with strategies for doing both.

Guarding Your Garden

When the psalmist wrote the words we've chosen for the epigraph under this chapter's title, he knew that life would always bring us challenges. In those challenges our thoughts, emotions and behaviors reveal our inner character. God searches out our heart and helps us explore our inner character, developing and refining it so that when adversity strikes we perform as spiritually mature Christians.

Because we're not aware of most of our thoughts, the Voice can take advantage of us. About 95% of what we think is non-conscious.[1] Thoughts, beliefs, and interpretations occur so quickly that they are barely perceptible and can fade quickly from memory. Yet these automatic thoughts and silent assumptions make us feel lousy without our knowing why. It's in this nether region where the Voice dwells. It is here that it twists and distorts our thinking, while lingering in the shadows where its dirty work goes largely unnoticed.

A property line surrounds our garden, keeping the bad outside and the good inside. It needs to be marked by a sturdy well-built fence that protects us from the destructive forces bombarding our minds daily. The entrance to your garden is where you stand guard as the sentry. This is where you decide exactly what thoughts get in and which ones you are going to throw back into the abyss. You are going to train yourself to examine the credentials of every thought that arrives at your gate. You want to assume that every thought that appears in your mind is suspect. All thoughts are considered to be from the Voice until you have evidence otherwise. Very few of your thoughts are all bad or all good. Probably ninety percent of them are in a grey area between healthy and unhealthy. Most of your thoughts have a degree of truth and distortion within them. It is your job to check them out. You are not your thoughts; *You are the sentry that decides which thoughts are acceptable and which are not!*

Watch Your Pronouns

By now you will have an extensive compilation of Voice messages that you have been recording since the beginning of this book. Your writing is the raw material for uncovering the "silent assumptions" and the "automatic thinking" that the Voice uses to manipulate you. It tries to influence your feelings and behavior in ways that make you feel as though you are not in control of your own life.

---

1   This number is a best guess by those who have been doing the research in this field. Although the figure is not exact, we know that when we compare the conscious material with unconscious material the amount of conscious information is far less than the unconscious information.

The first step in fighting the Voice is to *think of it as external to you* rather than coming from the essence of who you are. The best way to do this is to change the pronouns in your writings from "I" statements to "you" statements. Instead of "I'm worried about making my house payment this month," you will change it to "You are worried about making your house payment this month." This puts the negativity in the mouth of the Voice and back outside where it belongs. By doing this, you take the first step to separating yourself from the Voice and becoming less likely to believe its lies.

As we mentioned in the preface, some clients and people who attend our workshops tell us they find it useful to think in terms of spiritual warfare and therefore equate the Voice with the devil, whom Jesus called the "father of lies." By envisioning the contest as a spiritual battle, they are fighting Satan, the author of destructive thoughts designed to keep us from what God wants for our lives. Some Christians have asked if it is biblical to engage in such dialogue with Satan as the personification of evil. But we need only remember that Jesus did so, each time answering with Scripture, culminating with his strong words, "Get thee behind me, Satan." Or as *The Message* translates Matthew 4:10: "[Jesus'] answer was curt: 'Beat it, Satan!' He backed his rebuke with a third quotation from Deuteronomy: "Worship the Lord your God and only him. Serve him with absolute whole-heartedness." We're told in 1 Peter 5:8, "Be alert, be on watch! Your enemy, the Devil, roams around like a roaring lion, looking for someone to devour. Be firm in your faith and resist him" (GNT).

Since the Voice, regardless of how you wish to conceptualize it, wants to survive and grow, it will do anything to keep you from exposing it, including using some "pests" from the previous chapter to convince you that this way of thinking about thoughts and emotions is just too much work or not worth doing. One common pitfall at this stage is a fear of opening the Pandora's box of negativity. The Voice might tell you that doing this assignment will only make you feel worse. "You would be much better off if you just stopped thinking about this stuff and just try to be positive."

The truth is that no matter how much negative self-talk you uncover, it need not be overwhelming because it does not belong to you! You need to uncover all of it so that you know and recognize the Voice. Knowledge is power. The more worry you can uncover, the more ammunition you will have to take back your life. If you believe that the worry belongs to you, you will find yourself running in circles. "How can the negativity in my mind get rid of the negativity in my mind?" Instead of fighting yourself in circles, you need to fight the Voice head-on to make headway against a real and deadly antagonist.

Ultimately, all of the worry and negativity will no longer overpower you. You will begin to believe the truth that you are not the author of this painful chatter. All this venom comes from and belongs to your spiritual enemy—the Voice. It will try to convince you that these new skills are all nonsense and that you really are just a negative, pessimistic person by nature and can never stop worrying. Just remember these thoughts are not yours. The accusing Voice is feeding them to you. You became exposed to these distortions when you were very young and were unable to see their inconsistencies. As life continued, you internalized these thoughts and beliefs. Eventually they took up residence within your mind and became habitual and automatic until they assumed a life of their own.

Facts about the Voice

Now you need to find out some important information about the Voice and how it works. Only with such awareness will you be able to counter it. Here are some facts about the Voice's tactics.

Fact #1

The destructive taunts of the Voice plague everyone. Since none of us are perfect, all humans must struggle against their own destructive self-talk, the Voice. Even the happiest people have a Voice trying to gain a foothold in their lives. They are merely fortunate to have either good genes, a nurturing childhood, or both. Remember that you are not alone in your struggle with the Voice. Even Saint Paul wondered: "I don't understand myself at all, for I really want to do what is right, but I don't do it. Instead I do the very thing I hate." (Romans 7:15, NLT).

Fact #2

Some people envision this struggle as literally taking place between God and the devil, and that you're just caught in the middle as they battle for your soul. But God settled this struggle long ago. Christ has triumphed over sin and death. You are now left to deal with the remnants of that struggle—the "mopping up" operation, as it were. God breathed his spirit into you when you were created in the image of God. That spark of divinity is God's energy, an energy deep within you. The outdated and twisted theology that Satan and God wrestle for your soul is the stuff of B grade movies and C grade theology. There are only two participants in the battle we are talking about: you and the Voice—not a trio of God, the devil, and you as a spectator. But you have the edge because God's power—the power that has triumphed over evil and death—is available for you. "God's Spirit is in you and is more powerful than the one that is in the world." (1 John 4:4, CEV).

Fact # 3

The only goal of the Voice is to run and ruin your life! Up to this point, it may have been doing a very good job of it. You are not responsible for the silent assumptions it has planted in your garden. However, you are responsible for unearthing the weeds, destroying them, and making it difficult for them to grow back. Learning to identify, attack and overthrow the Voice is the most powerful tool you will ever learn to promote your personal growth.

Fact #4

Eventually you must win the battle against this Voice. The Voice cannot stand up against the light of truth. "You will know the truth and the truth will set you free" (John 8:32, NLT). The truth will defeat the lies. When you find specific lies, you will use specific truths to counteract them.

Fact #5

The Voice always lies. Sometimes this may be obvious, sometimes not. Our adversary is quite skilled at twisting the truth into partially distorted rationalizations. The Voice wants you to believe that it is the sweet call of reason. The Voice wants you to believe it is your closest confidant and only trusted friend. This is how, for example, it gets addicts to repeat their destructive behavior until they die of their addiction.

Fact #6

Society has a common perception that hearing voices is a sign that someone is certifiably crazy. Recent research shows that this is not always true. A small percentage of "normal" people have auditory hallucinations but these hallucinations are helpful rather than harmful. People whose hallucinatory voice tells them to harm themselves or others will eventually find themselves in a psychiatric hospital and given strong medications. Another distinction is that healthy hallucinations are taken for what they are—brain experiences similar to a waking dream. Psychiatric hallucinations, in contrast, are very difficult to separate from reality.

For some people, their automatic thinking is so quiet and quick that it is inaudible. For others, they clearly hear the thoughts. Both circumstances are "normal;" they are just different experiences for different individuals.

Fact #7

To defeat the Voice, you need to interrogate it, just as a military officer interrogates captured enemy soldiers to learn what the other side is up to. This will be the next skill you will learn. Knowledge is power. By interrogating the Voice, you will begin to uncover subtle nuances and whispered lies you have never heard before. As your mortal antagonist, the Voice will try to keep you from doing this by unleashing a variety of its "pests." The following are some samples of what it may tell you to try to throw you off-track:

> . . . "This may work for others but it won't work for you."
> . . . "Go ahead and do the assignments, but not now—you have too many other important things to do first."
> . . . "If you learn all about me you will only get worse. I'm too powerful for you and will gain more control over you if you try to find how I operate."
> . . . "You aren't really getting better; it's just luck."
> . . . "The more you succeed now, the worse your fall will be when you eventually stumble."
> . . . "You won't be able to change your life enough to make any real difference."

The following is a "dossier" on the Voice to help you be aware of the type of lies/vermin the Voice sends your way.

The Voice's Dossier[2]

You might be surprised to know the Voice has a "dossier," a list of characteristics and strategies that you need to know in resisting its attempts to run your life. Check over this dossier for more understanding of the way your adversary operates.

1. The Voice always lies.
2. The Voice completely distorts reality.
3. The Voice hates change.
4. The Voice likes everything in black and white.
5. The Voice wants me to think I am worthless and powerless to change my life.
6. The Voice wants me to obey an unreasonable set of rules.
7. The Voice is repetitious, habitual and dull!
8. The Voice wants me to judge other people based on their behavior.
9. The Voice will use subtle messages to enslave me.
10. The Voice loves to make me feel obligated by using the "should" word.
11. The Voice knows exactly what buttons to push with me.
12. The Voice is malicious, nasty and sneaky.
13. Everything the Voice says is logically flawed and, at best, a half truth.
14. Beware of the Voice's observation/assumption trick.
    For example: *Observation*: Your friend did not want to come over tonight. *Assumption*: That means you must have done something to hurt her feelings.
15. To agree with the Voice, no matter how reasonable it sounds, is to always be defeated.
16. The Voice wants me to get caught in an undertow of emotions, seemingly fighting myself around and around in circles.
17. The Voice's best weapons are speed and secrecy; I must expose it and slow it down.
18. The Voice is like the wizard in the Wizard of Oz; a tiny, frightened

---

2 Adapted from Sandbek, T. J. (1993). *The deadly diet: Recovering from anorexia and bulimia.* Oakland, CA: New Harbinger.

thing trying to get me to believe it is larger than life and quite terrifying.

19. The Voice uses illusion to put fear in the hearts of those who are stronger than it is.

20. The Voice wants to convince me that its cheap tricks are part of the real world.

21. The Voice is a coward! It loves hitting me when I am down.

22. The Voice's only purpose in life is to survive.

23. If I am not actively fighting the Voice, I am automatically agreeing with its messages.

24. I need to anticipate times of stress because this is when the Voice will try to regain a foothold in my life.

25. Guilt is one of the Voice's tricks to keep me dependent upon the unrealistic expectations of other people.

26. The Voice wants me to be resentful so that I will eventually cut off all human support and caring.

27. The Voice is my worst enemy and wants me to be miserable.

28. The Voice likes to play it safe—the Voice is gutless!

29. The Voice tries to trick me by insisting that a low probability event has a good chance of happening.

30. When I take risks, I challenge the Voice—the Voice wants to immobilize me with fear.

Interrogating the Voice to Find the Vermin

When you first try to expose the Voice by writing down your thoughts, it might scurry and hide. It will leave you thinking nothing further is left to check out. The major purpose for interrogating the Voice is to find its most basic and powerful lies—the vermin. Fortunately, only six lies exist. This should not be a surprise since there are only six destructive emotions—one nasty emotion for each nasty lie.

Keywords

We will go into more detail about these lies in chapter 6. To make it easier for you to recognize these vermin, we have represented each Big Lie with a *keyword*. We call these words "keywords" because they are the keys to discovering what words the Voice uses to trigger your devastatingly unhealthy emotions. All you need to do in this chapter is to try to force the Voice to give you that keyword. The keywords are:

- **Should** (as in the Voice's statement, "You should or should not . . . ")
- **Worthless (them)** (as in "That person who caused you pain is a worthless so and so.")
- **Danger** (as in "Those are dangerous feelings you are having.")
- **Stand** (as in, "This is too much for you; you can't *stand* it.")
- **Worthless (me)** (as in "You are a worthless human being.")
- **Tragedy** (as in "Some dreaded thing is going to happen to you, and that will be a tragedy.")

After you write down your thoughts and look at the Voice's words on your paper, see if you can find a keyword. If you cannot find one, then you will begin to interrogate the Voice. Interrogation has three forms based on the method the Voice uses to lie to you. If you find no keyword, the Voice can only cover up the Big Lie to you in *statements, demands,* or *questions.* Distinguishing these three styles can be a challenging process at first. Interrogating the Voice is a discipline that is not natural and is not taught anywhere. As you persist in your interrogation of the Voice, you will begin to find you are more in control of your thoughts. Additionally, you will have more control over your emotions. The following are the responses you will learn to use for each of the three lying styles: If it's a *statement* from the Voice, you'll provide a "So what if you think that" response. If it's a *demand,* you'll be ready with a "Why should I" response. And if it's *a question,* you'll tell the Voice to mind its own business.

> Statement: "So what if you think…"
> Demand: "Why should I.."
> Question: "It's none of your business!"

Statements

A class attendee, Melissa, felt uneasy about accepting compliments from others. When someone said to her "You are so creative," the Voice rushed in with its own statement to counter the compliment. The Voice would say something like, "No, that's not really true. They are just saying that to be nice." At this point we taught Melissa to interrogate the Voice by saying, "So what if you think I'm not creative?"

When you use the "So what if you think.." response, you are telling the Voice, "Tell me more. Keep talking to me. I want you to tell me *all* your lies." Your intent is to expose more of the Voice's silent and secretive beliefs about you. For many people this goes against their instincts. They would rather *not* hear all the negativity, thinking that if they do not attend to it, then everything will be okay. Nothing could be further from the truth.

To conquer the Voice you need to know as much about it as you possibly can. We cannot emphasize it enough: *knowledge is power*. The more you can get the Voice to talk to you, the more you become aware of its lies and distortions. By demanding that the Voice tell you more, you are not agreeing with anything this little deceiver is telling you. You are simply trying to make the private lies public. If you are forceful enough with your interrogation, the Voice will always talk back to you. It might angrily try to overpower you with more lies. No matter what it says in response to your interrogation, *you keep interrogating it*. In Melissa's case it went like this:

Voice: "Well, you know you just get lucky sometimes; you don't really have any talent"
Melissa: "So what if you think I just get lucky sometimes?" "So what if you think I don't really have any talent?"

Voice "You screw up more than you get it right."
M: "So what if you think I screw up more than I get it right?"

Voice "Your friends won't want to be with you anymore."
M: "So what if you think my friends won't want to be with me anymore?"

Voice "You won't be able to make new friends."
M: "So what if you think I won't be able to make new friends?"

Voice "You'll be lonely."M: "So what if you think I will be lonely?"

Voice "That would be a tragedy."
M: "Ah-ha!! I got you that time. You just used the 'tragedy' keyword."

You will notice that Melissa interrogated the Voice by including its own words after the "So what if you think . . ." phrase. This is very important because it anchors your interrogation to the specific message from the Voice.

When the Voice shifts to another message, you follow it and anchor it again. No matter what it says, you anchor its message to your interrogation.

Notice that eventually Melissa found the keyword. This is a bit confusing at first because you are working in parallel: you are interrogating the Voice and watching for a keyword at the same time. Sometimes the Voice starts repeating itself before you find the keyword. When that happens, quit and take a break until you want to begin again. The important thing to remember is that *you* decide when to take a break, not the Voice. This helps you begin to take control of your interactions with the Voice. You are developing an attitude, and you are saying, "Hey, Voice, I'm not going to let you run my life anymore!"

Demands

Demands are another way of hiding the Big Lies. A demand is nothing more than a statement that has a sense of urgency built into it. Often, the Voice wants you to take some kind of immediate action. It could have told Melissa, "Pick up the phone and call your friend right now." Upon spotting this demand, she would have responded with a different question, "Why should I pick up the phone and call my friend right now?" Usually the Voice will come back with another statement—"Because you need to know if she is still really your friend." Melissa would respond with, "So what if you think I need to know if she is still really my friend?"

The Voice hit one class attendee, Rick, with, "Work harder if you want to do better." We taught him to respond with, "Why should I work harder if I want to do better?" That opened a whole floodgate of responses from the Voice,, such as, "You're going to die broke and alone; You're heading for utter ruin; No one will love you; You're a failure; You were born to lose." On and on it went. The interrogation of that single demand about doing better exposed a whole series of distorted beliefs that had been quietly plaguing Rick for many years.

He was overjoyed when he found these lies because that knowledge gave him some real nuggets with which to work. When he examined each of these statements individually and carefully in the light of truth, the falsehoods became apparent. Rick's faith assured him that real wealth is not in the material world but in the riches of God's abundant love. No matter what his financial situation brought, he had already won; and the Voice of doom could not take it away. Rick discerned that the Voice was lying by predicting a bleak, dark, and hopeless future for him. No one can predict the future, not even the Voice. Rick's life was rich with love. He had a huge church family, the infinite, overflowing, and abundant love of Christ, and legions of friends. Because of his deep compassion for others, life gave him never-ending opportunities to meet new friends. His investment of time and energy in them was not an indication of failure but quite the opposite.

Questions

The third type of the Voice's cover-ups is the question. Questions are like ringing telephones—they are hard not to answer. Having a conversation with the Voice by answering its questions is the worst thing you can do. Doing so will allow it to pull you into its circle of influence. To avoid this you must respond to all questions, regardless of content, with the rejoinder, "It's none of your business!" If the Voice had said to Melissa, "Don't you care if you are lonely?" she would have replied, "It's none of your business!" If the Voice had asked Rick, "Don't you care if your peers are doing better than you?" he would have given the same response. We have discovered that some of our class members added harsh language between the words "your" and "business." We will leave it to your imagination what that might be.

Practicing Interrogation

Role-Play with Statements

One of the most powerful and effective ways of learning to deal the Voice is by practicing your interrogation skill with a friend, your Grace Partner, or someone else who is learning these skills. This is because of the emotions you generate when doing it with another human being. When we role-play with our class members and clients, we start by having them be the Voice. Someone picks a situation for us to play. We have them begin by just using statements (we play one of the class members). They are told to speak mercilessly. We tell them to be so mean and vicious toward us that we will get on our knees and beg them to stop. The results are always eye-opening. No matter what they say to us, we just calmly use the "So what if you think . . ." response. If they get stuck, we tell them to get meaner. At some point, we stop and ask them, "Who has the upper hand here? Who is winning?" Upon reflection they say with surprise in their voice, "You are."

Reverse Role-Play

We discuss what this process was like for them pretending to be the Voice and trying to beat us up and intimidate us. Then we reverse the roles and we play the Voice. We use the same situation and try to stick with the same issues that are personal to them. To give them practice, we eventually escalate our statements by making them cruel and vicious. At some point, the person agrees with us. At that point, we stop and remind them to continue interrogating the Voice. We do this enough times until they begin to experience this new and powerful response to the Voice. We then talk about how different this strategy is. They learn that their automatic agreement with the Voice is no longer the only option. Most people are excited and hopeful that we have now given them a skill that will propel them forward on their faith journey. This is why we recommend simulating your interrogation with a caring human being.

Introduce Demands and Questions

Next, we introduce demands, questions, and keywords into the simulation to make sure that these responses eventually feel comfortable. As in the children's game, Hide and Go Seek, we get a volunteer in our classes to be "it." The rest of the class is the Voice and begins firing statements, demands, questions, and keywords at this target person. We act as coach to this "victim" and often whisper the proper response when needed. Every class we have conducted reports that this is one of the most rewarding classroom experiences.

As helpful as role play is, it is not the real thing. Now you must do these interrogations with the Voice as much as you can. The ideal is to interrogate the Voice *every time* it talks to you. Obviously this is impossible. You can start by dividing your days into two-hour segments—either even hours or odd hours. At the end of each time segment, write down what the Voice has been saying to you in the last two hours. A two-column format is helpful (see example below).

Do the same thing two hours later. At the end of the day, review your writing and add anything that you might have missed. As we keep stressing, your success will depend on how much you write. In more than two decades of clinical practice, Terry discovered a direct connection between the amount of writing a person does and the amount of progress he or she makes. The research also supports this observation.[3] Although you can write too little, you can never write too much.

Interrogation Log

Your Interrogation Log might look like this:

THE VOICE'S WORDS	MY RESPONSE TO THE VOICE
You really blew it today.	So what if you think I blew it today?
If you keep this up you will lose your job.	So what if you think I will lose my job?
How will you pay your bills?	It's none of your business!
Your family will suffer.	So what if you think my family will suffer?
Don't you care?	It's none of your business!
You sure have a bad attitude about this.	So what if you think I have a bad attitude about this?
If you lose your job you will never get another one.	So what if you think I will never get another job?
What will your friends and family say?	It's none of your business!
You should work harder.	Gotcha. That's the "should" keyword.
This is stupid and won't work.	So what if you think it is stupid and won't work ?
Go to work this weekend.	Why should I go to work this weekend?
If you don't, you'll lose your job.	So what if you think I will lose my job?
Ad nauseam......	Ad infinitum.........

Sometimes people report that the Voice is silent after an interrogation response. If this happens to you, just remember this is one of the Voice's tricks to throw you off base. What you can do is just make stuff up and see if that provokes a response. If that does not work, do nothing. With enough silence, the Voice will begin its inane chatter by telling you to get busy. Another alternative is to use material from your immediate or distant past.

---

3 Parr, G., Haberstroh, S. & Kottler, J. (2000). Interactive journal writing as an adjunct in group work. *Journal for Specialists in Group Work* 25(3), 229-242.

Most of the people we work with have a warehouse full of past messages from the Voice.

One morning at a time when Sharon, one of our small group members, really needed some extra sleep, she was awakened by her young daughter. Sharon recalled being irritated at her daughter and then feeling guilty for having those feelings. This made her distress even worse. Upon reviewing the incident with the group, she began interrogating the Voice. She heard the message, "Doesn't she realize how tired you are? Why can't you get any sleep?" After bringing these thoughts out into the open, she began to realize that the Master Home Wrecker was trying to make her feel resentful toward her innocent little daughter. Her daughter was only bored and just wanted the comfort of her mother in the natural way kids do. She learned that the next time thoughts with unanswerable questions arose, she was going to shut the Voice down by emphatically retorting, "It's none of your business!"

Take time to pick out an example from your own Events Log and interrogate the Voice. Keep writing so that you can find the keyword. When you have found it, listen to what the Voice says to you. See what kind of insight you develop regarding the effectiveness of your interrogation techniques.

Substitute key words

One further note. Some people have told us that they do not find a specific keyword but can find other words that mean the same thing. For example, maybe the Voice never tells you that you *should* do something. However, you might hear the words "have to" or "must" instead. Using substitute keywords is perfectly okay, just so they have the same power to rob you of your dignity as the standard keywords. For example, the Voice's telling you that you did not *like* something is not a good keyword substitute for *stand* because it is not strong enough. But if the Voice tries to convince you that a catastrophe is awaiting you, you know you're dealing with an alternate key word (catastrophe).

The Voice uses endless variations to the six keywords to trap you into destructive thinking. From the writing you are doing, you can discover for yourself your own variations to these keywords. Once you recognize your own variations, synonyms and phrases, you can spot the Voice and defeat it much easier.

Below are just some suggestions for possible substitute keywords you might discover in your own writing:

Figure 5-A: Examples of Substitue Keywords

EXAMPLES OF SUBSTITUTE KEYWORDS	
Stand	"Heck with it," "Forget this!" "Too hard," "You hate this," "You're trapped," "You have no choice," "You're boxed in"
Should (not)	"Have to," "Need to," "Must," "Ought to," "Shouldn't have," "Got to"
Worthless (me)	"You're terrible, deficient, unacceptable, unlovable, a fool, no good, pond scum, lower than the stuff you scrape off the bottom of your shoe."
Worthless (them)	Any negative judgment about another person's innate value. Swear words or magnified generalizations are a good tip-off that this vermin is at work: "Bad person," "no good," "rotten." Even seemingly innocent rebukes like "turkey," "jerk," "butthead," can be a tip-off that the Voice is at work. There are no bad people—just bad behaviors!
Tragedy	"Catastrophe," "disaster," "awful," "terrible." You can often spot this keyword with the phrase, "If... then.."
Danger	"Danger," "Hazardousness," "Terrifying," "Frightening."

Summary

1. Your goal in this chapter is to find out as much as you can about the Voice—even if it takes several weeks.

2. You can dissociate yourself from the Voice by writing all its thoughts as though it is speaking to you using the pronoun "you." Whenever you give yourself a pep talk, use the pronoun, "I." (*Voice message*: "You are worthless and unlovable." *Pep talk message*: "I am a beloved child of God."

3. The more you know about the Voice, the more advantage you have to defeat its lies. To help you increase your awareness, we suggest you read the Voice Dossier aloud to yourself every morning just after you wake up.

4. The Voice treats everyone differently. Some people get many questions.

Others hear nothing but statements or demands. Still, others get a combination of all three. Some people also tell us that they hardly every hear keywords. Other people say they get nothing but keywords. Let the Voice lead you. You follow along by writing down everything it says.

5. In the next two chapters we will go into more detail regarding the keywords, why they are so devastating, and how to combat them, routing the vermin from your garden.

Assignment

Switch your record keeping from the three-column layout to a two-column layout. In the left column write what the Voice is saying to you. Look for a keyword. If you find one, name it in the right-hand column. If there is no keyword, use the right-hand column to interrogate the Voice is see if you can find the Big Lie keyword (vermin).

Use the example above entitled, Examples of Substitute Keywords as a guide for identifying the keywords. Your writing is getting more important by the day. The next chapter will use the keywords you find to go after the Voice more aggressively. But stay with this chapter until you are confident that you know how to interrogate the Voice and find its keywords.

Writing Tip

Don't guess at the keyword. If the Voice says, "You are ugly," you might think this "sounds like" *worthless me*. If you guess at a keyword, you have an 83% chance of getting it wrong (five out of six). The Voice wants you to guess because you are then easier to fool. The "ugly" comment might have been heading toward the "should" keyword ("You *should* take better care of yourself") or the "stand" keyword ("You can't *stand* being ugly") or any of the other keywords.

You need to use your interrogation response: "So what if you think I'm ugly?" Then the Voice might say: "You will never be able to change." You would counter that with "So what if you think I will never be able to change." The Voice might then try to zing you with a Big Lie: "That would be a *tragedy*!" Now you have found the keyword but it is different than what you originally thought.

We have noticed that it is better to do more interrogation in order to find the keyword than to hurriedly guess the keyword. If the Voice can get you to rush through this chapter, it can sit back and enjoy you building a shaky foundation for the next chapters.

You are just beginning to learn and master this skill of identifying keywords, so allow yourself time to become proficient at it. We would rather you take more time than less time practicing your interrogation skills. If you move on before you are ready, you will find that the next skills you will be learning will not work well because they directly depend on your ability to quickly and accurately identify keywords.

We will repeat ourselves again: Only by writing can you expose the Voice enough to make significant changes in your life. You are trying to capture those "automatic thoughts" that we all have just on the edge of awareness. They are fleeting, barely perceptible statements that the Voice says to you throughout the day. Although they are fast and thus hard to detect, they directly generate feelings that are quite often self-defeating in nature. Your success in the upcoming chapters will depend on well you master the skills in this chapter.

Chapter Six
Putting It All Together

Carefully guard your thoughts because they are the source of true life.
— Proverbs 4:23 (CEV)

By now we hope that you have become proficient at spotting the Voice's "keywords" that we called the "vermin" in our metaphor of the garden. These keywords are important to recognize because they provide the key to defeating the Voice.

This chapter will tie together what you know about emotions, the Voice, and the keywords. We will analyze the lies behind the keywords and show you how to turn them into Christian truths. When you have learned these skills, you'll be ready for the battle with the Voice that we'll discuss in chapter 7.

Watch Out!

The Voice will keep trying to sneak those "silent assumption" vermin through your garden doorway. It can happen so quickly and quietly that you might not even recognize your thoughts as vermin. Writing your thoughts on paper will help bring clarity and transparency. Clarity is the great nemesis of the Voice—it will do anything to keep you from writing. The Voice will continually tell you that writing is too much of a hassle, or that you can do well without it. It might try to tell you that writing is not your "thing," or that this writing stuff will not work anyway. If it succeeds in keeping you from writing about it, the Voice can guarantee that this material will not work and can be disregarded as just another useless self-help book. The great American author Henry David Thoreau once said:

"Things do not change; we change." It cannot be emphasized too strongly: continuing to write is the best way to make a significant change that will have a positive effect on your life and those around you. Write daily, write often. You are merely transcribing the lies from the Voice.

Linking the Lists of "Sixes"

By now you have probably noticed that the number six has come up in two different contexts. We've looked together at six destructive emotions and six keywords. Next, we want to show you how these two lists of "sixes" are related. Each of the destructive emotions has one basic distortion (vermin) lurking behind it. You can unlock the door to understanding those distortions by using not keys but *keywords*. We introduced them in the preceding chapter. Now, we'll be examining each one in greater detail.

We especially want to help you understand how the Voice uses these six "vermin" lies in an attempt to run your life. Here's an example. Sally told us that she had done something really stupid several days before one of our classes. Afterwards, she felt rotten, awful, and most of all, guilty. The Voice machine-gunned her with lies like, "You really screwed up! That was terrible. You shouldn't have done that!"

The Voice can easily bombard a person untrained in spotting and analyzing its lies and the related destructive emotions. It is difficult even to recognize, much less fight, the Voice in this situation. Using the information from this chapter, Sally was able to tune into the Voice's message within seconds. She said to herself, "Since I'm feeling guilty, the Voice must be using the keyword *should*. I am going to look for this keyword. When I find it, I will know that the Voice wants me to punish myself. It is telling me I have to play by the rules and that any serious infraction is a major failure for me." This analysis of what the Voice was doing allowed her to fight back and dump those nasty emotions of feeling rotten and guilty.

Keywords of the Voice

In Table 6-A, you'll see the six keywords in the Voice's message and the accompanying emotions. We want to help you understand what they mean and how they are really distortions of reality. If you temporarily leave the garden metaphor and go back to the domino metaphor, you'll see that for each keyword you will learn to identify five things: first, the environmental trigger or life event (Domino 1), second, the message of the Voice through thoughts (Domino 2), third, the emotion the thought generates (Domino 3), fourth, the behavior that accompanies the emotion (Domino 4), and, fifth, most importantly, the Truth. You are familiar with Jesus telling you that "the truth shall make you free" (John 8:32, NATB), and you will find that this is exactly what happens when you know, believe, and act on the truth—a whole new experience of freedom will open up to you.

Learning the Truth about each of these lies from the six vermin is the core strength of this chapter. We will go through each keyword separately and explain why the lie is a Lie and why the truth is the Truth. The Voice will fight you as you read this information. Its most potent lie is to tell you that you don't believe this material. Our response is to agree on the surface with that assessment, but with one important difference. We do not expect you to believe it *yet*. Your goal right now is to *understand* it. Belief will come later. If you already believed the six Truths, you would have no need to read this book. Table 6-A illustrates the relationship between triggers, lies, emotions, behavior and truth. Following this table is a thorough explanation of what the table means. You may wish to refer back to this table as you go through the explanations.

Table 6-A

SOURCE (TRIGGER)	MESSAGE (LIE) (KEYWORDS ARE IN BOLD)	EMOTIONS TOXIC	BEHAVIOR	REPLACEMENT TRUTH
Mistake	You should (not) do that	Guilt	Self punishment	"I can make my own decisions because I am a responsible adult."
Violation (something that someone does or says against you)	The people who hurt you are worthless because.	Resentment	Revenge	"No matter what they do, they still have infinite worth."

Feelings	Those feelings you are having are hazardous; they pose great danger to you.	Irrational Fear	Insulation	Even though these feelings are
Conflict	You can't stand it	Helplessness	Escape	"I have been standing it all my life."
Loss	You are worthless because . . .	Depression	Lifelessness	"No matter what I do, I still have infinite worth."
Threat	Something bad will happen and that will be a tragedy	Unhealthy Anxiety	Avoidance	"Nothing can happen to me that will keep me from making choices."

Dissecting the Attacks by the Vermin

It's important to understand how the vermin work in undermining your happiness. You learned in chapter 3 how the six unhealthy, destructive, toxic emotions (remember GRIHDU?) result from heeding the lies of the Voice activated by particular triggers. Here we'll look at how that works. We'll examine the keywords embedded in each of the false messages generated by the Voice.

Keyword # 1: Should

The Trigger: Making a mistake
The Emotion: *Guilt*

Message from the Voice: The Voice can spend your entire day reciting all the rules you broke: "You *shouldn't* have had that cigarette (or that candy bar)." "You *have to* do more volunteer work." "You *haven't* been doing all you *should*." "You didn't call your mother like you were *supposed* to last night."

For believers, God has absolved us of all guilt. That means we are innocent, free to make mistakes. Since God does not condemn us, we do not have to condemn ourselves for our behavior.

The Voice may try to trick you by including worthwhile goals in its "should" message. For example, it might tell you that "you should work harder on conquering your problem." This is definitely a worthwhile goal. Nevertheless, the insertion of "should" by the Voice undermines the validity of the goal by making it a mandatory obligation (and thus a source of guilt) instead of a reasonable and controllable choice that you can make on your own.

The Behavior: If the Voice can get you to feel guilty, you will spend most of your time punishing yourself instead of fixing whatever it was you did. Often the Voice will get you to beat up on yourself by getting you to repeat the mistake again and again. "Since you already binged, you can punish yourself by really doing it up right and finishing off that container of ice cream and the rest of the cookies." When you eventually learn to get rid of the Voice, you will forgive yourself for your mistakes instead of punishing yourself.

The Replacement Truth: Stated as simply as possible, the Truth for this keyword is that for adults there are no "shoulds." This may seem to run directly counter to all of your moral and ethical upbringing. Yet when you look at this truth more closely, you will see that it enhances your own set of moral values.

Society uses the word "should" to make rules. Rules are necessary for irresponsible adults and for children. Rules help and encourage them to make wise choices about life. These same rules are devastating for responsible individuals. When you were a child, adults gave you rules to help make you a better person and avoid danger. The rules also helped you to become more socialized. Unfortunately, by the time you became an adult, you had developed a very strong habit of making decisions on auto pilot, based upon hundreds of rules.

As an adult you need to use a better method for making decisions and choices for your life. As we pointed out earlier, your decisions now are best for you when they are based upon an awareness of the consequences of your choices.

The problem with moving from rule-based decision making to consequence-awareness living is that "should" rules are very convenient and comfortable and it's hard to discard them. If you are a person who lives a legalistic life, based on the "shoulds" and expectations of others, your life is highly predictable. This drive for safety, and security keeps you locked into a life of rules and is costly. You pay the high price of *guilt* when you fail to follow them.

The other alternative, a life based on awareness of consequences, is a life of freedom, spontaneity, growth, and surprises. Of course, choice exacts a cost, too—vulnerability, unpredictability, and risk taking. Such a life buffets and tosses you about by many unforeseen events. In other words, you pay a cost whether you live a sheltered life of rules and regulations or whether you live a life of growth and freedom. In weighing the respective costs, you will find that the Voice tries to convince you that the cost of freedom is far too high. It would have you believe that following rules is the way to avoid risk and uncertainty. This notion is totally contrary to the Christian path.

Scriptural support for combatting keyword "should" with truth

And you will know the truth, and the truth will make you free. (John 8:32, NATB)

Being made free from sin, you became servants of righteousness. (Romans 6:18, WEB)

So Christ has really set us free. Now make sure that you stay free, and don't get tied up again in slavery to the law. (Galatians 5:1, NLT)

Why don't you choose to be led by the Spirit and so escape the erratic compulsions of a law-dominated existence?" (Gal. 5: 18, MSG)

When I was a child, my speech, feelings, and thinking were all those of a child; now that I am an adult, I have no more use for childish ways. (1 Corinthians 13:11, GNT)

Keyword # 2: Worthless (Other Person)

The Trigger: Violation
The Emotion: *Resentment*

Message from the Voice: When the Voice convinces us that another person is awful—just a plain no-good louse, we automatically feel resentment towards that person. The flip side of depression is resentment—not anger, as we used to believe. If you apply the "worth is determined by behavior" belief to another human being, rather than to yourself, you will find yourself feeling resentment toward that person. The Voice would have you believe that the other person's behavior, which has affected you in some way, means he or she is worthless as a person. So when you listen to the Voice's assessment of another person as a rotten, shiftless, unspeakable, son-of-a-gun, you're thereby setting yourself up for hatred and bitterness. One clue that you are feeling resentment instead of anger is the use of name-calling and derogatory labels.

Our students and clients have given us the following examples of messages from the Voice in reference to someone they felt feel had violated them in some way. "You bonehead, what were you thinking? Don't you ever listen to what I say?" "That jerk just cut me off. That dirty &%$#%$#%^!!! I ought to give him what he's got coming." "That moron just ruined my new shoes." "My ex just lied in court and cost me thousands of dollars. I hate that wench! I'd like to wring her neck!" "That stupid brother of mine! He just told the rest of the family what he swore he would keep a secret." "I work my tail off for this company and I don't get squat! Those SOBs can go to hell!"

It is ironic that we treat total strangers better than we sometimes treat our own families. We have all heard it said that we always hurt the ones we love. Why do we treat complete strangers with more respect and civility that we do our own kin? Because the Voice can maintain more control over us the more we mistreat those to whom we are closest. Pat tells his class that once he realized this, he began no longer allowing his two young boys to use even the slightest degree of slander against each other without apologies and fence-mending. He reports that this raised the level in his family's emotional fuel tank tremendously.

The Behavior: The Voice wants you to retaliate and get revenge on those who have wronged you. By wasting your time and energy in planning how you'd like to "get even with that so and so," and make that person suffer the way that person caused you to suffer, you'll have no time and energy to get angry and confront the individual. Yet, confrontation and anger are much more healthy and productive for you. Another problem with revenge is that it might trigger the Voice's maneuvering in the other person and the person will then retaliate back. If this happens, you are in the middle of a feud with the Voice on both sides. You might want to avoid this!

The Replacement Truth: The replacement truth is identical to what it is when the Voice is trying to persuade you to think of yourself as worthless. Despite what someone else does to you, they still have infinite worth. When John tells us that God so loved the entire world, there is no footnote name those who are excluded. The Voice wants you to believe that since you aren't God, you don't have to love everybody. It wants you to believe that hatred is justified if directed towards "evil" people.

This does not mean that infinitely worthwhile people do not engage in incomprehensibly awful behavior. Nor do you have to ignore what they have done to you. Nor does it mean that you cannot get angry at those who violate your integrity. You have the right to get mad when someone has violated your basic rights. You do not, however, have the right to retaliate in kind. You have the right to get them to stop harassing you.

You can see another distinction, now, between resentment and anger. Resentment means you are judging and evaluating another person's value *as a person*—based on what they have done to you. Anger shows that you are confronting that other person's *behavior*. Resentment concentrates on the worth side of the equation; anger concentrates on the behavior side.

Scriptural support for combatting key word "worthless (other person)"

But I tell you, love your enemies, bless those who curse you, do good to those who hate you, and pray for those who spitefully use you and persecute you.—Matthew 5: 44, WEB

A stone is heavy and sand is weighty, but the resentment caused by a fool is heavier than both. —Proverbs 27:3, NLT

Let all you do be done in love. — 1 Corinthians 13:1, BEB

Love does not keep a record of wrongs. — 1 Corinthians 13:5, GNT

Keyword # 3: Danger

The Trigger: Feelings and sensations
The Emotion: *Irrational fear*

Message of the Voice: The Voice first tries to get you to tune into something uncomfortable happening inside your body—whether physical sensations or emotions. When you become aware of what is happening, the Voice then tries to convince you that what is going on inside you is dangerous. "These feelings you're experiencing are scary and could really hurt you!" You will notice this is the only message that has an internal trigger. All other triggers are found outside you. Jennifer told us about the Voice's message to her when she was anxious about a presentation at work the next day. It said, "This feeling is really abnormal. Something is really wrong with you. You are in serious trouble. This feeling could even possibly kill you. There is no escape from it!" We have also heard other messages such as, "You don't know why you can't sleep or relax. There is too much going on. You can't figure it out. You can't stop thinking about it. Your chest gets tight and you feel panicked. You're going nuts!" Someone else reported they heard the Voice say, "These feelings can never be changed. You were just born this way. The world is just too scary a place. You can't handle this. Don't leave the house, don't call anyone, don't let anyone know what is happening. If you do, they will think you've gone crazy." You're not crazy, this Voice message is crazy.

The Voice loves to introduce this vermin immediately after using some different vermin. For instance, when you are feeling depressed, the Voice will point to this feeling and try to convince you that you need to be afraid of it. So now, besides depression, you have a bonus emotion—irrational fear. The Voice enjoys getting you so absorbed in and terrified of destructive emotions that you become absolutely certain they can destroy you.

Other common triggers are fatigue and sickness. Karen told us that the Voice got her to feel irrationally afraid when she was feeling tired after a hard day's work. As she was relaxing on her couch, she heard the Voice say, "Uh-oh, watch out, do you feel that? It's dangerous." Now besides feeling tired, she felt fearful.

Feeling sick or having a fever can also trigger this message. When you feel bad from the illness, it is often difficult to mentally switch gears and become aware of the presence of the Voice. Finding the keyword is not easy when you are sick.

You may have noticed by now that this message points up a significant difference between rational and irrational fear. Rational fear always points to something outside you; irrational fear always points to a feeling within you. For years, the mental health community was not aware of this and was puzzled by people's irrational fears. When clients brought up the subject, the well-meaning therapist would discuss all of the things in the person's life that they could possibly perceive as dangerous. Therapists were looking for the feared object in the wrong place. Irrational fear is always concerned with what is happening inside, not outside, of you.

The Behavior: When you feel irrationally afraid you will begin to insulate yourself from the outside world. One natural instinct of fear is a withdrawal from the environment. Someone not trained in combat, automatically flinches or withdraws if someone tries to hit them. By getting you to feel afraid of your emotions, the Voice will tell you to withdraw and let your fear keep you from reaching out to those around you who can help you.

The Replacement Truth: The truth is quite simple—dangerous feelings do not exist. Feelings may be painful or uncomfortable, but they are not dangerous. Remember that irrational fear generally focuses itself on something inside you. The Voice tries to convince you of something that is simply not true: namely, that those feelings and sensations inside you can hurt and destroy you. They may be unpleasant, but they cannot destroy you.

Scriptural support for combatting the keyword "danger"

> The LORD is my light and my salvation—so why should I be afraid? The LORD protects me from danger—so why should I tremble? —Psalm 27:1, NLT

> You will keep in perfect peace him whose mind is steadfast, because he trusts in you. —Isaiah 26:3, NLT

> For I am the LORD, your God, who takes hold of your right hand and says to you, Do not fear; I will help you. —Isaiah 41:13, NIV

Do not be anxious about anything, but in every situation, by prayer and petition, with thanksgiving, present your requests to God. And the peace of God, which transcends all understanding, will guard your hearts and your minds in Christ Jesus. —Phil. 4:6-7, TNIV

Keyword # 4: Stand

The Trigger: Conflict. Conflict can be internal or external. External conflicts can be with people or objects. Internal conflicts can be realistic conflicts with yourself or unrealistic conflicts with the Voice.
The Emotion: *Helplessness*

Message from the Voice: "This thing that is happening to you right now is uncontrollable, awful, unstoppable," the Voice says. "You can't stand it! You are trapped, hopeless, out of control forever." The Voice wears you down, trying to convince you that something is driving you up the wall and that you're going to go crazy if you stay in this situation any longer. You simply can't bear it. Various people have given us some examples of how the Voice uses this keyword. "You know that eating like this is unhealthy, but you just can't resist these cravings. Put a plate of donuts in front of you and you're utterly helpless." "Everyone tells you that you drink too much but you just can't stand to go home without a couple of drinks first." "Your kids are driving you nuts! You can't take it anymore. Have a smoke!"

The Behavior: When the Voice uses this keyword with you, it will often try to confuse the difference between "leaving" and "running away." You want to leave any situation because it is your *choice to do so*—you can decide whether leaving is the better part of valor. Leaving a situation can sometimes be quite constructive and helpful.

Running away, however, is never helpful, because it's not your choice. It's giving in to the insistence of the Voice, which has many ways to get you to "run away" from something. The most obvious is to remove yourself physically from an uncomfortable situation. Less obvious, but just as common, is to run away emotionally. Using food or drink to feel better when life stresses you are also ways to run away from the stress. Unfortunately, it generally works. Because you experience happiness with the lower-case "h," it feels like running away was the right thing to do. Most people who use these methods feel better for a short period. Unfortunately, they play right into the tactics of the Voice. As you get better at combating lies with truth you'll be equipped to remain in conflict situations. And you'll improve yourself by learning to cope successfully with what is happening around you.

The Replacement Truth: The truth for this vermin-generated lie is quite simple. In fact, it is so obvious that most people tend to miss it. It goes something like this: while the Voice is saying that you cannot stand something, you are in fact standing it. Right at that very moment. It is quite likely that you have been standing it most of your life. You may not like it, but you have been standing it. The message, "You can't stand this," is clearly a bold-faced lie.

In clinical medicine, it has been observed that people who decide they can stand a physical illness (though they do not like it) are the ones who are more likely to get well. Those who convince themselves that they cannot stand it are generally the ones who worsen. The same holds true for mental health. By resisting this lie with the Replacement Truth, you can tolerate seemingly unbearable situations.

The Replacement Truth is that you can stand anything, but you *do not have to like it*. In fact, you can hate it. You can dread being in a situation. You can even wish that you had made a different choice. Nevertheless, while you are in any given moment, you are in actuality standing it. You may have to stay in the situation a little longer—but you can stand and survive what you greatly dislike. The Voice will try to confuse you about this important distinction between disliking something and the inability to stand it.

Scriptural support for combating keyword "stand" with truth

> Our ancestors trusted in you, and you rescued them. You heard their cries for help and saved them. They put their trust in you and were never disappointed . . . Yet you brought me safely from my mother's womb and led me to trust you when I was a nursing infant. I was thrust upon you at my birth. You have been my God from the moment I was born.
> —Psalm 22:4-10. NLT

> Bless the LORD, who is my rock. —Psalm 144:1, NLT

We can rejoice, too, when we run into problems and trials, for we know that they are good for us—they help us learn to endure. And endurance develops strength of character in us . —Romans 5:3-4, NLT

They attacked me at a moment when I was weakest, but the LORD upheld me. —Psalm 18:18, NLT

He gives power to those who are tired and worn out; he offers strength to the weak. —Isaiah 40:29-30, NLT

For I can do everything with the help of Christ who gives me the strength I need. —Philippians 4, NLT

Each time he said, "My gracious favor is all you need. My power works best in your weakness." So now I am glad to boast about my weaknesses, so that the power of Christ may work through me. (2 Corinthians 12:9, NLT)

So if you are suffering according to God's will, keep on doing what is right, and trust yourself to the God who made you, for He will never fail you. —1 Peter 4:19, NLT

Every test that you have experienced is the kind that normally comes to people. But God keeps his promise, and he will not allow you to be tested beyond your power to remain firm: at the time you are put to the test, he will give you the strength to endure it, and so provide you with a way out. —1 Cor. 10:13, GNT

Keyword # 5: Worthless (Me)

The Trigger: Loss (personal, tangible, or abstract)

The Emotion: *Depression*

Message from the Voice: The Voice taunts, "You are a worthless good-for-nothing. What you just did (or said or didn't do or say) proves it." Yes, "worthless" is the same keyword we examined in reference to what the Voice tells us about other people when we feel resentful, but now we're going to see how the Voice instructs us to apply it to ourselves. To get you depressed, the Voice will try to convince you that you are utterly worthless. It will not just declare what a terrible person you are but will try to *prove* it. The voice will tie your alleged depravity to a specific action or inaction. In so doing, the Voice tries to convince you that your worth as a human being depends on your behavior. We describe this Voice concept by using the phrase: worth is determined by behavior.

Since nobody is perfect, this equation makes your worth go up and down like a yo-yo. When you do well, you can feel good about yourself. When you make a mistake, your worth plummets. When you really blow it, your worth drops low enough for you to get depressed. By accepting the concept that your worth equals your behavior, you are forced to be a perfectionist to avoid depression. "If only I wouldn't screw up anymore, then I wouldn't have to get depressed." Of course, since you cannot be perfect, you will continue to get depressed as long as you allow the Voice to use this vermin in your life.

Maybe some of these examples might be familiar to you. "Everyone tells you that God loves you and that you are forgiven, but you really can't believe that. It may be true for others but not for you. Deep down you just know you aren't worthy." "That was really stupid what you just said. You really suck!" "Just give up because you never were cut out to succeed at this kind of thing anyway." "You are lower than the stuff you scrape off the bottom of your shoe."

The Behavior: When the Voice has finally convinced you that you are rotten and corrupt, you will begin to shut down and stop doing all the things in life that you normally do. Doing nothing is what depressed people do. Becoming lifeless and lethargic for an extended period is a sure sign of depression.

Learning to recognize this vermin and battling against it will allow you to stop being depressed and shutting down. After you have rid yourself of the depression, you can, if appropriate, express your emotions over the loss you have experienced. Some people who have been effective at this have found themselves crying for the first time in many years. Should this happen to you, this is a good thing. Crying is God's natural way to help you heal from a loss.

The Replacement Truth: Your worth does not depend on what you achieve, and it certainly does not depend on your behavior. Rather than accepting the equation "worth = behavior" as a description of reality, you need to know that your worth is not equal to your behavior. The Bible tells us that because we are alive, we all have infinite worth! Since God makes all humans in His image, there is no way to measure our worth. Because God is infinite, your worth is infinite.

No matter how badly you mess things up, you are infinitely worthwhile. You cannot change the infinite worth you were born with. This Truth is difficult for many people to accept, even some Christians. The stumbling block is their hanging onto a worth = behavior equation as a reality. It is an illusion. Once you begin separating your worth from your behavior, you can make headway against the vermin that produces depression.

Scriptural support for combatting keyword "worthless (me)"

He lifted me out of the ditch, pulled me from deep mud. He stood me up on a solid rock to make sure I wouldn't slip. He taught me how to sing the latest God-song, a praise song to our God. More and more people are seeing this: they enter the mystery, abandoning themselves to God.
—Psalm 40:2-3 MSG

God created people in his own image; God patterned them after himself; male and female he created them
—Genesis 1:27 NLT

Are you not conscious that your body is a house for the Holy Spirit which is in you, and which has been given to you by God? —1 Cor. 3:17, BEB

What is the price of five sparrows—two copper coins. Yet God does not forget a single one of them. And the very hairs on your head are all numbered. So don't be afraid; you are more valuable to God than a whole flock of sparrows. —Luke 12:6-7, NLT

And I am convinced that nothing can ever separate us from God's love. Neither death nor life, neither angels nor demons, neither our fears for today nor our worries about tomorrow—not even the powers of hell can separate us from God's love. No power in the sky above or in the earth below—indeed, nothing in all creation will ever be able to separate us from the love of God that is revealed in Christ Jesus our Lord.
—Romans 8:38-39, NLT

Keyword # 6: Tragedy

The Trigger: Threat (to your well being)

The Emotion: *Unhealthy anxiety*

Message from the Voice: The format for this keyword message is generally, "What if such and such happened, that would be a tragedy!" Notice that this sentence has two parts: a "what if" and a "tragedy." The "what if" part is usually a prediction. The Voice wants you to believe that it can tell the future and it is warning you of something dire in your future.

Tragedy, the second part of this message, is the most dangerous portion of this message. It is the word that generates the emotion of unhealthy anxiety. The "what ifs" do not contribute much to the unhealthy anxiety. It is the addition of the tragedy part that makes this vermin so harmful.

The Voice wants you to believe that something will occur in your life that will make it impossible for you to make choices any longer. By losing the ability to make choices, you will give up your humanity and the control of your destiny. You'll be acutely aware of that loss and doomed forever. This is the stuff of Greek tragedy.

See if you are familiar with this vermin we found running around in one of our classes. It's the common "money-tragedy" vermin. "If you don't make a sale soon you'll lose your job. What then? You will probably lose your house and have to declare bankruptcy, and then your kids will live in terrible, destitute poverty. They will grow up to be criminals. It's going to be horrible! You need to start worrying about your house payment. What if you are late making your payment? Do you wonder what it will feel like if they come to foreclose on you? You should prepare yourself for the worst, just in case it happens. If you plan the whole thing out now, then when you lose the house you will be ready for it."

The Behavior: If the Voice can get you sucked into this lie about inevitable tragedies befalling you, you will no longer be running your own life. This lie causes you to avoid everything that you perceive as a threat— whether it is or not. By continually avoiding things that you are anxious about—changing jobs (what if I fail, and then what if no one else wants to hire me), deciding to return to college (what if I can't pass the entrance test? And what if the younger students make fun of me?)—your life will become more restricted. As the joy of life begins to drain away, you become more miserable. Fighting back will allow you to encounter these threats on your terms and by that allow yourself to live a full and rich life. You will feel stronger and more courageous as you tackle more threatening situations. Strategic and careful planning will eventually become easier and more natural.

The Replacement Truth: You need to know that two lies are associated with this vermin and thus there are two replacement truths. You must first be able to tell distinguish between the two lies. By doing this, you can know what the Voice is telling you and therefore how to respond. Since the "what if" part is usually more visible than the tragedy part, this is where you will want to begin. When you hear the "what ifs," you need to remember this is a distortion of probability. The tragedy closely follows this distortion of logic. Let us look at the first lie, the "what ifs." When the Voice tells you this, it is trying to make a prediction. As you have already learned, no one, not even the Voice, can accurately predict the future.

The tragedy vermin is a mutant because the likelihood of an awful, terrible thing happening to you is extremely low. Ask yourself how many of the Voice's predictions have come true in your lifetime. The answer is very few—if any! The odds are in your favor that something awful will *not* happen. The odds are always working for you. Responding to this distortion reduces the mountain back down to its original molehill. You need to understand the Voice cannot read the future!

Be watchful when you have conquered this first part and are convinced that a particular "what if" has one in a million chances of occurring. The Voice will counter this response with "Yeah! But this could be that one time." Embedded in this statement is a further notion: "if this were that one time, it would be a tragedy."

It is at this point you need to concentrate on the second part of the message. To do this, you need to understand what the word "tragedy" really means to the Voice. Most of us use the word "tragedy" differently than the Voice does. We think it is a tragedy if our clean car gets rained on. Yet the Voice uses tragedy in its more classical meaning. A tragedy to the Voice means that two events occur simultaneously: (a) your loss of the ability to make choices and (b) your conscious knowledge of this loss. This idea has been well developed in the stories and plays of the ancient Greeks.

Looking at this idea in the light of the real world, you can quickly recognize that there is no such thing as a personal tragedy. No matter what happens, you still have choices. Only a few events can keep you from doing even this—a coma or death. However, even these two things would not be personally tragic, because you would not be aware of them.

Challenging this Truth, Peter asked us, "What if I were flying in an airplane at thirty thousand feet and the wings fell off. As I am plummeting to earth, what are my choices?" After we thought about this we replied, "Your choices are definitely limited. Nonetheless, you can die with dignity or you can die like a fool. That is your choice." At times, interpreting an event realistically may be your only option.

Once you have recognized that a personal tragedy is not a possibility for you, you knock out the supports from under this message. Remember that tragedy always has another part. The lie in the first is in the over-blown probabilities of the "what if" statement. This "what if" statement is really referring to a very low probability event, but the Voice wants you to believe that it is a high probability event.

Nevertheless, no matter how low the chances of such an event happening, it still could! If it did, it would merely be unfortunate, inconvenient or uncomfortable—not tragic. It would not be tragic, because no matter how bad it was, you would still be capable of making decisions and doing something! Even dying does not take away our choices. As Christians we have faith in eternal life. Therefore, nothing can happen to us that is ultimately more than an inconvenience.

Scriptural support for combatting the keyword "tragedy":

My child, don't lose sight of good planning and insight. Hang on to them. —Proverbs 3:21, NLT

God met me more than halfway, he freed me from my anxious fears. —Psalm 34:4, MSG

God is our refuge and our strength, always ready to help in times of trouble. So we will not fear, even if earthquakes come and the mountains crumble into the sea. —Ps. 46:1-2, MSG

Give all your worries and cares to God, for he cares about you. —1 Peter 5:7, NLT

Summary

1. You are now capable of easily identifying the presence of the Voice.

2. You have learned to distinguish between healthy and unhealthy emotional pain.

3. You have learned how to find some minor lies (the pests) coming from the Voice.

4. You have learned how to interrogate the Voice so that you can smoke out the major lies, namely the vermin keywords.

5. In this chapter you now know how it all ties together. One thought category leads to one emotion category that leads to one behavior category. Psychologists call this "cognitive specificity."[1]

6. By understanding the packaging of thoughts, emotions and behavior, you can more easily find all the pieces. If you only know one piece, you can quickly determine the other two. For example, you know you are feeling guilty but not certain about what the Voice is saying or why you are doing what you are doing. The guilt tells you the Voice is bombarding you with "should" messages. You, also, can see more clearly that your actions are an attempt to punish yourself for making this cosmic, terrible mistake.

Assignment

Use the information in this chapter to continue your two-column Voice Interrogation Log. As you fill in the left column (Voice) you will interrogate it in the right column (you). Look for the vermin. When you spot one, circle the keyword in the left column and write the Truth word-for-word in the right column.

We will repeat ourselves again: Only by writing can you expose the Voice enough to make significant changes in your life. You are trying to capture those "automatic thoughts" that we all have just on the edge of awareness. They are fleeting, barely perceptible statements that the Voice says to you throughout the day. Although they are fast and thus hard to

---

1   Ingram, R. E., Kendall, P., Smith, T. W., Donnel, C. & Ronan, K. (1987). Cognitive specificity in emotional distress. *Journal of Personality & Social Psychology* 53(4), 734-742.

detect, they directly generate feelings that are quite often self-defeating in nature.

Writing Tip

The problem is not that the Voice talks and lies to you. It is deeper than that. The handicap is that when the Voice lies to you, you automatically agree with it and believe its message. To get at this deeper level of lies and distortions, you need not only to find the vermin keywords but also to understand how they are a lie.

Each lie has a counter-truth. At this point you do not need to be concerned if you cannot believe the truth yet. That will come with experience and practice. For now, just try to understand intellectually how the Voice is lying and the truth of what you are saying when you respond.

Belief always comes *after* understanding, not *before* as the Voice would have you believe. For many difficult ideas, humans need to have some understanding before they can commit to believing something. Without the understanding, the belief does not have a solid foundation.

As you use the canned truth to respond, the Voice may say to you, "You can't say that because you don't believe it." Since you may not believe it yet, this may stymie you and stop you in your tracks. This is just another sloppy trick. As usual, it is backwards. It is not true that you can only say something after you believe it. The truth is that by saying it often enough, you will eventually believe it.

One finally thought. As you write the truth, do it slowly and thoughtfully. Rather than doing it by rote, think about the implications of what this truth means and how your life will change when you can accept it into your life.

Chapter Seven
Five Steps Toward Grace

Summing it all up, friends, I'd say you'll do best by filling your minds and meditating on things true, noble, reputable, authentic, compelling, gracious — the best, not the worst; the beautiful, not the ugly; things to praise, not things to curse.
— Philippians 4:8 (MSG)

Now it's time to use all your skills to defeat the Voice for good. In this chapter we show how to directly attack the Voice and its Big Lies. We boil it down to five simple steps. The accompanying flow chart (Figure 7-A) guides you through the entire process. It may look a little confusing at first. Just start at the top and read off each step in progression. Each step adds a new level of clarity. The final step of the "replacement truth" (which was explained in chapter 6) is a step that needs to become a way of life from here forward. This is where you get to recreate a new and better "you" in a more godly and rewarding life.

Your eventual goal is to create new interpretations for all life situations that have troubled you in the past. This means creating new beliefs about how God's world works. Changing your thoughts can have dramatic results in your life. In his book, *Your Best Life Now*, Joel Osteen[1], pastor of Lakewood Church in Houston, offers seven different ways this can take place. Psychologists and pastors agree on the importance of changed thinking for spiritual growth.

---

1 Osteen, J. (2004). *Your best life now: 7 steps to living at your full potential.* Lebanon, IN: Warner Faith.

Remember that the replacement truth may not be a pleasant thought. Healthy emotions are not necessarily pain-free, but they do get you moving in a healthier direction. We supply a limited amount of replacement phrases and Bible verses to get you started (See Appendix 2). Your challenge is to ultimately create new phrases for yourself. Take some time. See how many new thoughts you can come up with on your own. We want you to make these replacement thoughts relevant, credible, and optimistic.

In one of his most famous verses, Paul of Tarsus teaches us that "God causes everything to work together for the good of those who love God and are called according to his purpose for them" (Rom. 8:28, NLT). It's important to note that Paul writes this in the present tense! He is not talking about some unseeable event in an unknown future. Changing the way you think will make you feel good about life in the here and now. Using the five steps we're introducing in this chapter, you'll be able to reinterpret your most painful life events. You'll be able to replace old interpretations with new ones—new thoughts and beliefs that lead you to living without toxic emotions.

Practicing this skill of developing new thinking leads to a much better life. We're not saying that life will no longer be difficult. We will never control those painful life dominoes that invariably fall on us. However, writing, interrogating, and using the Five Steps will make your life more productive, mature, and Christ-like.

The Basics of Fighting the Voice

Looking at Figure 7-A (the flow chart or "road map"), you can see that the starting point is knowing what the Voice is saying to you. Since you have been doing this for quite awhile, this part is easy. Once you have that information, follow the arrow to the left. The next step is to see if you have a keyword or phrase. If you find a semblance of a keyword then go directly to the five steps (This will explained in more detail later in this chapter.):

1. What unhealthy emotion are you experiencing?

2. What action are you engaging in or heading toward?

3. What is the Voice saying to you?

4. What is the Replacement Truth?

5. Fight back three times. Use one of our prepared phrases or scripture verses from the appendix, or create your own.

If, as you are examining your thinking, you don't discover any expressions that look like keywords, follow the left arrow down to the three interrogation techniques ("So what if you think____?" "Why should I____?" and, "None of your business!"). Ruthless interrogation will force the Voice to give up a term that has the meaning of a keyword. When you sense the presence of a keyword, start fighting using the five steps.

After fighting the keyword or using an interrogation response, follow the arrows once again. The next step is to answer the question, "Is the Voice still hassling you?" If the answer is "yes" you go back the to top and ask what the Voice is saying to you. (A word of caution here, sometimes the Voice shuts up just to confuse you. If this happens, listen quietly. It cannot stand it when you try to control your thinking. If the Voice is lurking in the shadows, it will eventually blurt out something.)

In the event the Voice is still hassling you, answer the question, "Is it saying anything different?" The odds are good that the answer will be yes. If this is true, go again to the top to find out what it is saying this time. You continue in the loop until one of two things happens: either the Voice has left the mental arena, or it is beginning to repeat itself. If the Voice stops harassing you, you need to take a break. Distract yourself, go on to another project—enjoy your life.

Using Repetition

Once the Voice repeats itself—and eventually it will—follow the arrow downward and use our example or another of your choosing. We recommend using a phrase that is very strong and nasty—something you would not say in polite company. After all, this is a life-and-death struggle with the Voice, not a debate. When you have chosen your own Repetition, repeat it three times. It may look like this:

Table 7-A: Using the Repetition Technique

Voice	Me
You really should apologize to your friend.	You already told me that, so "Get out of my life!"
You didn't even hear what I said.	Oh, I heard you all right. "Get out of my life!"
What is this "Get out of my life" garbage? Is that all you can say?	This is the last time I'm telling you, "Get out of my life!!"

This strategy has been adopted from the assertion training technique called the Broken Record. This phrase does not make much sense anymore since very few people listen to LP records for their music. Younger people may not even know what an LP is. These LPs were made of vinyl and could crack or get scratched. When this happened, the needle on the turntable arm "skipped" when it hit the crack. In other words, instead of continuing to play the music, the tone arm would go backwards and repeat the last few notes or words that you had heard just before the crack. This would continue forever unless someone moved the tone arm. The "broken record" would cease all forward movement because the needle would be stuck in one groove.

Your use of Repetition is meant to work like the crack in the vinyl record and stop the forward progress of the Voice. This is important because when the Voice suspects you are winning, it will try to tire you out and wear you down by saying the same old thing until you just give in. When the Voice starts repeating itself by using the same keywords, you use your chosen Repetition. Use it every time without variation. This technique is your way of saying, "I've fought the Voice and now it is time to take a break."

After the third Repetition, you walk away. You are in charge of when to fight the Voice and when to stop. This decision really irritates the Voice good! Take a break because you deserve it. Later, you can come back to beat up the Voice some more. You notice on the Road Map that you have two ways of walking away: distraction and replanting. For now, just use the first one, distraction. Do something pleasant, soothing or enjoyable. It is your choice. You will learn how to use replanting statements in chapter 9.

When you decide to re-enter the fray, begin at the top. We have covered all details of the Road Map except the gray heart in the upper left. This contains the "heart" of fighting the Voice. To fight back, you must strictly follow the five steps (See Figure 7-A).

1. What unhealthy emotion are you feeling or could you be feeling?

2. What destructive action are you engaging in or heading toward?

3. What is the Voice saying to you?

4. What is the Replacement Truth?

5. Fight back three times.

Using a Template For Fighting the Voice

This format simplifies the five steps. We provide this in the "Pest Control Kit." You can create your own from Appendix 3 in this book, or order one from us at support@TheWorryFreeLife.com. Here is how the template works, step by step:

1. *"Voice, you are making (trying to make) me feel* _____."
   You merely fill in the missing emotion. This will always be one of the six unhealthy emotions (Guilt, Resentment, Irrational Fear, Helplessness, Depression, Unhealthy Anxiety).

2. *"You are trying to get me to* _____." In this blank, place the action or behavior the Voice wants you to do.

3. *"You are telling me that* _____." As in your Voice Log, you will put its verbatim message in the blank.

4. *"The truth is* _____." Insert the Replacement Truth here.

5. The last step involves putting some added force behind the Replacement Truth you have stated in Step 4. Once you have established that the truth is more powerful and realistic than the lie, you want to hammer the message home. Until now, the fights have never been fair. Even if you level the playing field by replacing each lie with a replacement truth, it won't be enough. The Voice is still too strong. This is why, along with each truth, you elaborate it with three additional forward-moving statements. This gives you a favorable ratio of four to one in your favor; the Voice lies once, you strike back with *four* powerful truths—the replacement truth plus three supporting or expanded truths. Every time

you do this you continue to weaken the Voice. Eventually, you will be stronger, have the upper hand, and will be in charge of your life. Some people even like to add a verse from Scripture to cap it all off. We've provided some examples. Notice how Helen and Russell each handled situations they faced.

Example #1

Helen was fuming because her husband had done it again. He arrived home late from work and apologized, explaining that he did the best he could but the boss kept him late again. Helen felt really irritated. The Voice tempted her to let him have it. She had been planning this special dinner all week and now it was cold. The excitement she had felt earlier was gone and she was left with disappointment, frustration, sadness, and a good dose of resentment. Her Voice Fighting log looks like this:

Voice to Helen	Helen to the Voice
How dare he try to explain this away after all you've done for him!	So what if you think I've done a lot for him?
Why did you even marry such a man?	It's none of you business!
He will never change.	So what if you think he will never change?
He always does this to you.	So what if you think he always does this to me?

You should really let him have it.	Hah! I caught you -- that is the should keyword. Voice, you're trying to get me to feel guilty. You just want me to punish myself. You are lying when you tell me that I should let him have it.
	State the Truth: Well, the Truth is that I am a responsible adult and can make my own decisions.
	Then hammer the Voice three more times with additional forward moving statements:
	A) I am going to substitute the words "will" or "choose" for the word "should."
	B) I am a responsible adult and can decide for myself what is right and wrong.
	C) Guilt is one of your tricks to keep me dependent upon the unrealistic expectations of other people.
	Scripture: The Lord directs the steps of the godly. He delights in every detail of their lives. Though they stumble, they will never fall, for the Lord holds them by the hand. (Psalm 37:23-24, NLT).

After fighting back against the keyword "should," Helen notices another keyword pop up:

Voice	Helen
Okay, okay, so you're a big girl and can make your own decisions.	So what if you think I'm a big girl and can make my own decisions?
He still screwed up your beautiful dinner.	So what if you think he screwed up my beautiful dinner?
He does this all the time.	So what if you think he does this all the time?
He didn't even call to let you know he would be late.	So what if you think he didn't call me to let me know he would be late from work?

124

That just proves what a rotten, uncaring jerk he is.	Gotcha again! That is the worthless (them) keyword.
.	1. Voice, you're trying to get me to feel resentment. 2. You just want me to retaliate against my husband. 3. You are lying when you tell me that my husband is a rotten, uncaring jerk. 4. The Truth is that no matter how he treats me, he still has infinite worth! Then again, hammer the Voice three more times with additional forward moving statements: A) I can be angry without being resentful and full of hatred. B) You lie when you tell me that the way to get things done with him is to retaliate so he won't hurt me again. C) I can be angry with my husband without being resentful. Scripture: A stone is heavy and sand is weighty, but the resentment caused by a fool is heavier than both (Prov. 27:3, NLT).

Notice that the Voice had first tried to convince Helen to get even with her husband so that the Voice could make her feel guilty about it later. When that did not work, the Voice took a more direct approach and accused her husband of being a worthless human being.

Example #2

Some friends invited Russell to a neighborhood party. This had never happened before. He decided to put his best foot forward and bring his favorite casserole. After he arrived, he found out that he did not know anyone. Worse than that, it seemed that no one was willing to chat with him for long. When he left after about half an hour, he noticed that his casserole had hardly been touched. After he returned home, he felt totally rejected, worthless, and depressed. His Voice Fighting log looked like this:

Voice to Russell	Russell to Voice
This just proves again what a loser you are.	So what if you think I'm a loser?
Your life is over.	So what if you think my life is over?
What kind of fool are you to think that perfect strangers could warm up to you?	That's none of your business!
Just look at yourself.	Why should I look at myself?
You are fat and ugly and they hated your casserole!	So what if you think I'm fat and ugly? So what if you think they hated my casserole?
You might as well just give up and eat a gallon of ice cream tonight.	Why should I give up and eat a gallon of ice cream tonight?

Because you are worthless and that is what worthless people do.	Okay, there is the worthless (me) keyword. 1. Voice, you're trying to get me to feel depressed. 2. You just want me to become lifeless by eating a gallon of ice cream. 3. You are lying when you tell me I am worthless because no one interacted with me at the party. 4. The Truth is that no matter how other people treat me, I still have infinite worth! Hammer the Voice 3 more times with forward moving statements: A) No matter what I do, I am still a worthwhile person. B) I allow myself to feel depressed only by agreeing with you when you tell me that I am a no-good person. C) I am a wonderful, delightful, and a lovable person merely because I am alive. Scripture: "You surely know that your body is a temple where the Holy Spirit lives. The Spirit is in you and is a gift from God. You are no longer your own" (1 Cor. 6:19, CEV). I do not want to shove a gallon of ice cream into this house of the Holy Spirit.

Are you following this process? Using this format is how you will become proactive with the Voice and begin to take the offensive. It is a struggle that requires effort and diligence on your part. Don't expect this to work the first time you use it. If you do this daily, give yourself a week or two before expecting to see results. Like any new skill, it will take time to master. Everyone is different, so it's impossible to determine how long such mastery will take you. But you can be sure of this: the more pages you write, the sooner you'll be able to take control of your life away from the Voice.

Pessimism

Society does not make this any easier. Pessimism is the norm in our society. Murphy's Law ("Whatever can go wrong, will go wrong.") has become the anthem for the Baby Boomers and their offspring. With the social pressure surrounding us to expect the worst, we have become used to dreaming vaguely and dreading vividly. But from now on, you are going to start doing just the opposite. By capturing your peripheral thoughts, evaluating and re-creating them, you can develop a perspective on life that allows you to dream vividly and dread vaguely.

When you first start changing your thinking, the Voice will still try to sway you to believe the "so-called" evidence for supporting a gloomier outlook. This tendency to accept evidence that supports your old self-destructive beliefs and ignore evidence that is more optimistic is called "confirmation bias." Finding evidence to support more courageous, hopeful and loving thoughts will be unnatural and difficult at first, but it is hugely rewarding. This is the essence of character building and spiritual growth.

When Pat first started to practice this technique of replacement thinking, he struggled at first. Nevertheless, this is where he found his new faith and regular church attendance to be helpful in very powerful ways. He knew his old thinking was corrupted, but he did not have much with which to replace it. As a thinking person, empty platitudes and simple positive thinking were not helpful. Yet the faith that the characters from the Bible displayed was hugely inspirational. The living examples he witnessed in the lives of his pastors and fellow believers were pivotal in his accelerated growth and recovery from the pit into which he had fallen.

Moral Beacons

The tenacious faith of Job, the courage of Deborah, the healthy skepticism of Jacob, the purposefulness of Esther, the loyalty and passion of David, the devotion of Mary Magdalene—all such stories can become moral beacons.

For Pat, especially helpful was the example of the all-consuming purpose burning inside St. Paul. Pat found such biblical heroes and heroines to be great sources for gleaning and adopting new, realistic beliefs, thoughts and interpretations that he could apply in constructive ways to his own life. If you are seeking, as he was, you may be struggling with the *act* of faith itself. Perhaps like Pat, you are wondering about the validity of such beliefs. Does God really exist? How can I know for sure? How can I trust God when life treats me unfairly? What if it is not true? Pat struggled with all these questions and finally came to the conclusion that faith is a choice. It is not something that hits you like a lightning bolt and then changes you instantly and automatically. The very definition of faith is to believe in something for which there is no proof. If we based our Christianity on proof, it would no longer be a faith-based system. As Hebrews 11:1 tells us, "Faith makes us sure of what we hope for and gives us proof of what we cannot see" (CEV). In *The Message* paraphrase of this verse, faith is called "our handle on what we can't see."

Pat tells the following story: "I can remember being confirmed in the church when I was twelve years old. The ceremony terribly disappointed me. My dismay was so great that I decided I was done with church and religion for good. You see, I was expecting that ceremony to be the magic moment when I would finally know the truth, and God would reveal himself in all his glory. It was nothing more than unrealistic thinking. Now I *choose* to believe in God, in eternal life, and in the power of love to redeem human suffering. To do so is healthy and powerful for me. It works to believe these things. When I have doubts, I fight it off as an attack from the Voice and do everything I can to reaffirm my beliefs. I do this by finding or creating thoughts that are credible for me. I cannot prove the existence of God and do not even think it is possible or necessary. More important, my faith empowers me. Thoughts, beliefs, and interpretation based on faith make life better. It gives me strength and hope through the tough times and incredible joy, exhilaration and passion in the good times."

Using Resources

We encourage you to find other great sources for developing your personal replacement beliefs. Reading any good quality literature and non-fictional works are a gold mine of new healthy beliefs. Developing new relationships in healthy social circles can be very helpful. Joining small groups and serving in church can provide healthy environments. Devoting part of your life to helping those who are hungry, poor, or suffering can enrich both yourself and others. Faith is a process of growth that is never-ending.

To mature personally, emotionally, and spiritually, expose yourself to new and rejuvenating ideas within your faith. If you find challenging new ideas frightening, it is a red-flag that the Voice may be at work in your thoughts. Many Christians never let their faith grow beyond the time when they first entered it. Paul tells us that growth is natural. "When I was a child, I spoke and thought and reasoned as a child does, but when I grew up, I put away childish things" (1 Cor. 13:11, NLT). As a child, Paul was afraid of what he did not understand and would avoid ideas that ran against his childish beliefs.

J. B. Phillips, a contemporary of C. S. Lewis, wrote a book called *Your God is Too Small*.[2] He outlines over a dozen ways Christians have limited understandings of God. In the chapter entitled, God-in-a-Box, he explains how so many of us think that our version of God can be the only possible correct version. He reminds us that no version of God "has a monopoly of God's grace, and none has an exclusive recipe for producing Christian character. It is quite plain to the disinterested observer that the real God takes no notice whatever of the boxes; 'the Spirit bloweth where it listeth' and is subject to no regulation of man." Christian growth occurs when we look back and understand that the path we have chosen fills us with joy and surprise.

A Tool to Guide You through the Five Steps

We have created a tool that encapsulates the entire Five Steps to Grace. The main concern people have when they begin fighting the Voice is what to use for the three final pieces of Step 5. To make it easy for you we have included sample fighting pieces and Scripture verses for each keyword in the appendix. We highly recommend putting this material into a set of wire-bound index cards. We call this our Pest Control Kit. You can create your own from the material contained in appendix 3, or you can order

---

2   Phillips, J. B. (1960). *Your God is too small*. New York: Macmillan

the kits from our web site at www.TheWorryFreeLife.com. We recommend that you keep the Pest Control Kit with you always. When the Voice is beating you with overpowering lies and emotions, remembering what to do is extremely difficult. The Pest Control Kit will walk you through the process step-by-step.

Many people have a backup Pest Control Kit because they rely on it so much that misplacing it can throw them off track. Terry tells of the time when one of his clients called him in a panic because she had lost her purse. As he began asking the typical questions about how much money it contained, driver's license and credit card information, and the like, she stopped and said, "You don't understand. My Pest Control Kit was in my purse. It is gone. Now what do I do?"

The Pest Control Kit allows you to have, in the palm of your hand, all the information you need to defeat the Voice. It is a powerful and effective tool. Using the Pest Control Kit as a reference in real time is extremely helpful whenever the Voice strikes. Waiting until evening to recall and use fighting skills against the Voice will decrease your effectiveness.

Summary

You have finally moved through a series of skills and arrived at the point where you can begin taking your life back. Everything you have learned so far has been directed toward fighting the Voice aggressively. The skill in this chapter is probably one of the most effective procedures in all of psychology. It is a direct descendent of what psychologists call "cognitive restructuring." By using it correctly and often, you will begin to notice a marked improvement in your inner life: your thoughts, your emotions, and your stress level. This skill must eventually be part of your everyday mental life. To have long-term effectiveness, it must become a lifestyle.

Unfortunately, the Voice will often go into hiding once you become strong in combating it. Ironically, it will bide its time until you are feeling great. It will do this because your personal pain has been a great motivator to learn this material. Unfortunately, as you lessen the pain, you will also weaken the motivation to continue using your skills. We see this all the time. With less motivation, you might use your skills less often with no adverse effects. Then, just when your skills are becoming a bit rusty, the Voice will strike violently and you will have a monstrous setback. Never fear. Just pick up your materials and start over. Use it as a learning experience so that next time the Voice tries the same trick, you will be ready for it.

Fighting the Voice needs to become as much of a habit as all your other faith behaviors—such as daily prayer, Bible study, and fellowship. Once it has become a habit, you will not need to do as much writing, because much of it will be in your head. However, do not be fooled. The time will come when fighting back in your head will not be strong enough. It is during these times when you will go back to writing just long enough to gain control again.

Assignment

Now the work begins. With these Voice-fighting tools, you'll want to put this assignment at the at the top of your personal commitments for the next few weeks. Even though you may only fight the Voice for a few minutes at a time, try to get in at least an hour's worth every day.

Begin using the five-step Voice-fighting procedure immediately. You can do it in writing, speaking it aloud, or going over it in your head. It should come as no surprise that, this early in the game, writing is the only effective procedure. One advantage of writing (using a two-column format) is that you can go slowly enough to learn the procedure. You will catch your mistakes and can learn from them. You need to begin fighting the Voice by having the Pest Control Kit next to your Voice Fighting Log. As you move through the procedure, you will merely copy the information from the Pest Control Kit to your Voice Fighting Log.

You simply cannot use this skill too much. At this point, the Voice will put enormous resources into getting you to do as little as possible. Our long experience in teaching this technique has shown us again and again that there is a direct relationship between how well people do and how many pages they write daily. If you do a page or two a week, you will wait a long time for good results. If you do several pages a day (or more!), you will begin to experience success much sooner.

Writing Tip

Determine to work at this skill as you have never worked to learn a skill before. Defeating the Voice is a matter of emotional life or death. Christ came so that you might have the abundant life. You now have the tools to make the process happen. Until now, you had to deal with Voice indirectly by asking for God's help. Now you can continue to do that and also take more responsibility for the results. You will be in direct combat. You do the work, and God will give you the courage and fortitude to succeed.

Chapter Eight
Christian Affirmations

You welcomed me as if I were an angel of God, as Christ Jesus himself.
What, then, happened to your positive attitude? — Galatians 4:14-15 (ISV)

Now that you have the tools to chase the Voice out of your garden, it's time to rebuild the landscape. Rebuilding your garden landscape produces new self-confidence and increases your personal power. Since the Voice has taken so much of your mental capacity, you may have empty spaces to fill as you continue to move it out of your life. Using Christian Affirmations will help you to backfill the emptiness left behind as the Voice continues its retreat. The more you can fill, the harder it will be for the Voice to attempt a comeback.

Since this may be an unfamiliar activity, you will need to be especially intentional about this skill. As with all other skills you have learned, the more practice and repetitions you can do, the more effective the affirmation will be for you.

The Christian Affirmation Bank

Christian Affirmations are statements about you that are positive, strong, and unbelievable—yes, *unbelievable*! The more you *disbelieve* a Christian Affirmation, the better its potential. For example, if you were to say to yourself, "I have red hair," and you actually *have* red hair, the statement would have little impact on you. However, if you were to say to yourself, "I am a wonderfully special person" and you found that statement utterly impossible to believe, then that statement would make an effective Christian Affirmation.

You can use Christian Affirmations to serve two purposes. First, as we have already mentioned, they fill the vacancy left by the Voice as it is moved out of your garden. Since our brains do not like vacuums, you had better put something in that mental space or else the Voice will return to fill it.

Second, Christian Affirmations serve as self-fulfilling prophesies. We all know that if we hear something long enough and often enough, we tend to believe it. Using Christian Affirmations works the same way—to our benefit. Using them is a form of reprogramming our mental state with the beliefs and perceptions that are best for us.

To start, you need to develop a storehouse of strong, positive sayings. You can make up your own. Some people find good examples from reading the Bible, hearing a powerful idea from a sermon or speech, listening for them in an adult life skills class, or being alert to pithy sayings or phrases that jump out at you as you read good books and articles. As you keep your heart and mind open for examples of memorable positive sayings, the number you'll come up with will amaze you.

Perhaps the most effective method for discovering dynamic and forceful Christian Affirmations is to listen carefully to the Voice. (Yes, you read that correctly!) This idea may sound strange since you now know that the Voice always lies. But by turning these lies upside down and converting each one into a Christian Affirmation, you use the Voice's power against it. For example, if the Voice keeps telling you are a loser, you flip it over and say, "I am a winner." If it tells you that you are unlovable, you use the opposite: "I am a highly lovable person."

Some affirmations can come directly from Scripture—perhaps a verse you memorized as a child—or from *allusions* to certain Bible passages or perhaps a hymn. The Voice tells you that you're incapable of succeeding, that you can't do *anything* right. But you turn that around and make the words of the Apostle Paul your own words: "I can do all things through Christ who strengthens me" (Philippians 4:13). The Voice tells you that you are not worthy of God's attention and love—that God has no time for you. You turn that around and say, " I am important to God. God isn't going to forget me any more than a loving mother would forget her baby" (from Isaiah 49:15) Or "I matter to God. God has counted even the hairs on my head" (from Luke 12:7). The Voice says, "You can't handle what life dishes out to you. You're a weakling." You counter with the words of 2

Corinthians 12:10, "When I am weak, then I am strong." You can find more such examples in your own Bible reading.

Making Your List

You're probably wondering how to begin making a list of Christian Affirmations. Check out the box below and look at some affirmations from our graduates. That can help you get started in making your own list.

- I am able to attract a mature, well-balanced and kind person to be my lifelong lover and special friend.
- I am attracting infinite happiness and unlimited abundance.
- I am whole and perfect as God created me.
- I love me just as I am.
- I have unlimited abundance.
- I have infinite worth and unlimited potential.

When you have at least a dozen items on your list, you can begin using them. As time goes by, continue adding to the list. This process is open-ended because the number of Christian Affirmations you can use is unlimited. We call this list your Christian Affirmation Bank. You'll be making both regular deposits and withdrawals from this "bank account."

Retraining Your Mind

At the beginning of each day, pick a Christian Affirmation to take with you for that day. Choosing from a list instead of having to think of one on the spot will save you time. Each day, as you withdraw a Christian Affirmation from your bank, put the date beside it so you can tell when you last used it. Each month you need to review your Christian Affirmation Bank. And be sure to keep making new deposits, adding new, relevant affirmations to your account regularly The more each Christian Affirmation disagrees with what the Voice has been telling you, the better it will work.

You're aim is to choose (or create) an "affirmation of the day" that speaks strongly and uniquely to you for that particular day. You might want to write it on an index card and carry it with you. You can practice your Christian Affirmations three different ways: mentally, verbally, and graphically.

Mental Christian Affirmations

Mental Christian Affirmations are probably the easiest to use because you can be completely inconspicuous when you practice them. You may think this is too much effort, but it truly turns out to be very little time at all. Try to repeat your affirmation every waking hour. If you want to be systematic, practice at the top or bottom of each hour and more than once at a time. You can also repeat it over and over as you walk along, or stop at a traffic light, or sandwiched in between all the busy moments of the day, or when you take a quick moment to close your eyes or look out the window or pour a cup of coffee.

You could call this use of Christian Affirmations the steam roller technique. It is unquestionably tedious and simple-minded. The repetitious use of the same Christian Affirmation repeatedly, however, will begin to burn into your memory those beliefs that are necessary for a better life. After all, this is the very method the Voice has used with you for many years. It kept telling you all sorts of negative, destructive notions until you eventually believed them. That is what worrying is! It is now time to reverse this process by putting the lid on worry thoughts and replacing them with these powerful, positive statements. Someday you will sincerely believe them.

Verbal Christian Affirmations

Another way you can make your Christian Affirmations work for you is to say them aloud. Saying your Christian Affirmations aloud has the advantage of increasing your sense of personal power by letting you hear them. Undoubtedly, you would only want to do this when you are alone—in your car or in your house would be excellent times to do this. Our clients have found two methods for doing this which are quite successful: the mirror technique and the recording technique. If you can think of other ways to practice verbal Christian Affirmations, by all means do so. If you find another way that is effective for you, please e-mail us (support@The-WorryFreeLife.com) so we can pass on your good idea to others.

The mirror technique. Stand in front of a mirror and try to convince the person in the mirror how important it is for him or her to believe your Christian Affirmation. You need to point out to the person in the mirror the significance of the Christian Affirmation. This works best if you can become emotionally involved in trying to influence the mirror image to believe what you are saying. Pretend you are an actress or an actor playing a part. Use every available acting trick you can think of to convince this image how outstanding and sensational this Christian Affirmation is. Do this several times a day.

The recording technique. Using an old fashioned mini-cassette tape recorder or an iPod, record your Christian Affirmation for as long as you can. If you decide to use a tape recorder, use an endless loop tape. This way, when you have finished recording your Christian Affirmation for the length of the loop, it will continue endlessly until you stop the tape. If you use an MP3 player let it run for a minute or two. As you listen to your recording, the sound of your voice will startle you at first and fully grab your attention. Don't be concerned if you don't like the sound of your voice because no one else will hear it. Do this as often as you can.

Written Christian Affirmations

The method of written or graphic Christian Affirmations is probably the most vigorous method of the three. It is also the most cumbersome. This technique will take about one to two hours to complete. Begin by making three columns on a piece of paper. Label each column from left to right: "Christian Affirmation," "The Voice," and "Me" You write your Christian Affirmation in the left-hand column using the formula, "I, (your name), [Christian Affirmation]." When you own this statement, the odds are very high the Voice will try to overpower your acceptance of this statement and try to make a nasty response back to you. Write its response in the middle column. When you have done this, write your retort in the last column. It might look like this:

Table 8-A

Christian Affirmation	The Voice	Jane
I, Jane Doe, am a winner.	You? What a laugh!	Just wait to see who has the last laugh.

Your retort is different from the fighting technique you learned in the previous chapter. Do not concern yourself with whether the Voice is using a keyword, statement, demand, or question. You are not on the defensive when you use this method. You are taking your strength to the Voice, confronting it on its own turf.

Do you notice the sequence? You make a strong statement; the Voice tries to intimidate you; you stand your ground and come back with a counter statement that can sometimes be witty or cutting but always strong. Positive affirmations thus surround the message of the Voice, both before and after it reacts. The last word goes to you. Finish the exchange with a smart aleck remark. Pulverize the dumb comment from a weakened Voice that is trying its feeble best to rattle you.

When you have completed these three columns, you do it again—write the same statement underneath the first statement in column one. The Voice will probably say something different this time—write it down. Give a different response. Do this a total of twenty times.

First Repetition

When you have completed this set of twenty repetitions of your chosen Christian Affirmation with the varied responses, you will do another set of twenty. This time you will change the formula slightly. Change the pronoun "I" to the pronoun "you." For example, instead of using the statement, "I am a winner" twenty times, the next step is to write it as, "You are a winner" twenty times. You make it feel like someone who cares about you is saying it to you.

Table 8-B

Christian Affirmation	The Voice	Jane
I, Jane Doe, am a winner	You? What a laugh!	Just wait to see who has the last laugh.
(repeat 19 times)	(whatever the Voice says)	(19 new retorts from you)
You, Jane Doe, are a winner	You don't believe that.	Every day that passes, I will believe it more than today.
(repeat 19 times)	(whatever the Voice says)	(19 new retorts from you)

Finally, after you have done twenty "you" statements, change the pronoun again from "you" to "she" or "he" (whichever is appropriate). This time, you want to experience the statements as listening to your friends talk about you in a way that they really believe. It will look like this:

Table 8-C

Christian Affirmation	The Voice	Me
I, Jane Doe, am a winner.	You? What a laugh!	Just wait to see who has the last laugh.
(Repeat 19 times)	(Whatever the Voice says)	(19 new retorts from you)
You, Jane Doe, are a winner.	You don't believe that.	Every day that passes, I will believe it more than today.
(Repeat 19 times)	(Whatever the Voice says)	(19 new retorts from you)
She, Jane Doe, is a winner.	They pretend to believe that, but they really hate you.	Nobody hates me as much as I hate you.
(Repeat 19 times)	(Whatever the Voice says)	(19 new retorts from you)

You will find this written Christian Affirmation technique very forceful, although it is laborious. It has maximum power if you can complete all sixty Christian Affirmations in one sitting. If you cannot do this, the next best thing is to complete the Christian Affirmation in three sittings. You could do the first twenty (the "I" statements) in the morning, the second twenty (the "you" statements) in the afternoon, and the third twenty (the "she or he" statements) in the evening.

Do a set of written Christian Affirmations daily for about a month. Each day, of course, you will have a new Christian Affirmation to use. You will use that Christian Affirmation mentally, verbally, and on paper each day.

Success Journal

In a separate journal, record your positive experiences and successes at the end of each day. Include things that you did well that day: specific victories against the Voice, and positive experiences with your family, friends, and loved ones.

Professor Martin Seligman has developed a wonderful format for recording daily success that we want to share with you. It is based on his research in Positive Psychology, and you can read more about it and how to apply it to your life at his website: www.reflectivehappiness.com

Seligman's extensive research shows proven ways people can actually become much happier. His method for increasing happiness includes this simple writing exercise: *each night write down in your Success Journal three things that went well that day, and why they went well.* That's it! Do this every night for two weeks and you will notice a significant buoying up of your mood. Try to emphasize things you did well. If you cannot think of three things, then identify some things that happened to you that you enjoyed.

Research bears out that most people spend far more time thinking about how they can correct something that has gone wrong (or is about to go wrong) than they do basking in what has gone right. This reduces life satisfaction and maximizes anxiety and depression.

Noticing and analyzing what goes well in our lives builds the skills of remembering good events and not taking them for granted. It builds gratitude as well. Analyzing why events go well encourages a consciousness of blessings and molds optimism about the future.

The important part of this exercise is the "why" part. As you explore what it is about you that causes these good things to happen, you will begin to discover some of your signature strengths (We have more on this in chapter 11). By realizing what you are best at, you can intentionally look for opportunities to exercise these strengths more often, creating more of the feelings of "mastery" and "flow" in your daily life.

Summary

As you begin to move the Voice and its debris farther away from your garden, you will have room to fill in the space left behind. Some people think that a healthy garden is one cleaned up and left that way. This is a tricky deception. The Voice will *never* stop putting pests and vermin back into your garden. You cannot get rid of the Voice entirely. You can only minimize its influence in your life.

In the vacuum left by the Voice you must replant your garden. Your first step is to begin using Christian Affirmations as a preliminary step to having a replanted, well-nourished, and healthy garden. In the remaining chapters we will teach you additional skills for nurturing and tending your garden.

These new skills are not only new for you but are new to the field of psychology. They are the result of one of the most exciting things to happen to the profession. In 1998, former president of the American Psychological Association, Martin Seligman, whose research we mentioned above, gathered together other prominent psychologists and founded the movement called Positive Psychology. Using scientific research as his methodology, he began to discover personal tools and skills for enhancing one's life and personal growth. And in the following chapters, we'll be sharing more of what this Positive Psychology movement has been discovering about life satisfaction and fulfillment and how you can apply these findings in your own life.

Assignment

Begin to reprogram your thinking through the practice of Christian Affirmation as a tool to *replace* (not destroy) the Voice's vermin. Do not forget to use your Pest Control Kit and the Voice fighting tools along with this skill. As you move on in using Christian Affirmations, continue to fight the Voice.

Writing Tip

After you have used Christian affirmations for a month, you need no longer do them every day. Instead, you may decide to use them when you are having a "good day." Each day of your life for at least several years, you need to be either fighting the Voice or using Christian affirmations. You may use both in the same day.

One of the most common mistakes is to use Christian affirmations instead of fighting the Voice. Until all of the skills in this book become automatic, the rule of thumb to use is this:

- On bad days, fight the Voice.
- On good days, use Christian affirmations.

The two skills are most effective when used together. When your life is not going well, fight the Voice. When you are having good days, use your Christian affirmations. This powerful combination will bring forth a beautiful and satisfying garden.

Chapter Nine
Replanting Your Garden

. . . if you plant in the soil of your spiritual nature, you will harvest everlasting life
— Galatians 6:8 (GW)

As you begin to throw out all the mental obstacles that keep you from living fully, you want to begin replacing them as completely as you can. In the last chapter we showed you how to begin adding new thought patterns into your life. In this chapter you will learn how to identify five common illusions the Voice uses to distort the meaning of your Christian life.

Weeding Out the Voice's illusions

Illusion number 1: Christians have no right to have rights.

The Voice wants you to be confused about core issues of your faith. We are not talking about doctrinal statements that change from denomination to denomination at various times, but rather about certain Christian ideals that can be easily distorted. Because of the Biblical metaphor of the Suffering Servant, for example, some Christians believe that good Christians have no inherent rights to their humanity. "As a Christian," says the Voice, "you don't have the rights other people have." The Voice may even tear scripture verses from context and distort their intended meaning, such as hammering you with a passage such as 1 Peter 2:21: "After all, God chose you to suffer as you follow in the footsteps of Christ, who set an example by suffering for you" (CEV).

Illusion number 2: You must always put the needs of others ahead of your own.

When some Christians entertain the idea that they may have human needs and rights just like anyone else, they may worry that such thinking will mean they are selfish and uncaring and that claiming their rights violates Christian principles. This is another distorted lie from the Voice. Perhaps they grew up hearing that JOY is spelled by putting **J**esus first, **O**thers second, and **Y**ourself last. They may have taken it to extremes in thinking they have no rights and can care for their own needs only after they have tried to meet everyone else's needs. Many women especially fall into this trap. Remember: God has given you stewardship over your life. No one else in the world has the ultimate responsibility for what direction you take in your life. Caring for yourself *before* you care for others is necessary, as we'll discuss below. We call it "Christian selfishness." This type of selfishness is different from worldly selfishness where people care for themselves *instead* of caring for others.

Illusion number 3: Forget personal responsibility; it's all up to God

Another distortion is the belief that living the pious Christian life will somehow compel God to grant us riches and abundance—that we have no responsibility in the making of wise or unwise decisions that affect our lives. However, God chooses not to interfere in some areas of our lives. We know from Chapter 1 that God has granted us stewardship over our behaviors, our emotions, our sensations, and our thoughts. God has granted us sovereignty over these parts of our lives. Only we can take action in these areas. They fall under the category of "personal responsibility."

Illusion number 4: Preaching the gospel matters more than living the gospel.

This third illusion spotlights the importance of social responsibility, something the Voice may try to downplay. Protecting your own views, friends, family, and interests, while combating those who are not supportive of Christianity is the Voice's way of keeping you from loving your neighbor. We can actually distance ourselves from our neighbor at the same time we claim to be loving our neighbor because we are focused mainly on the mandate to take the Gospel into "all the world," as important as that is. Historically, some Christians have interpreted this to mean that all we need to do is *preach* the Gospel rather than *live* the Gospel. Social responsibility has two sides to it. The first is to keep your property lines clear and always visible so that you are not taking responsibility for the feelings of other people; those feelings are *their* responsibility. The second side is the Christian's response to human suffering; and that response is *our* responsibility.

Social responsibility is related to compassion for other people. Compassion was one of the outstanding characteristics of Jesus. As Brennan Manning says in his book, *A Glimpse of Jesus: The Stranger to Self-hatred*, he is the "... Son of God because he's compassionate in a way that eludes human comprehension and possibility. ..."[1] Christians sometimes forget that they must be known, not for being right, but for being compassionate.

Illusion number 5: You don't have to forgive; some things are unforgivable.

The Voice tells you that some sins are not forgivable. It encourages your righteous indignation, and urges you never to allow yourself to forgive those who wronged you. Some Christians think the Sermon on the Mount does not apply to certain situations because some people are so evil they are somehow outside the human community. When you cannot experience forgiveness for those who have wronged you, the Voice can keep you from completing your spiritual journey.

After Weeding Out the Illusions, It's Time to Replant

An awareness of each of these five illusions perpetuated by the Voice will help us not to be fooled by them. But we need more information so that we can replace the lies, replanting the garden. Let's look at the truth behind each distortion.

Christian Rights

Take the matter of our right to have rights. We Christians sometimes act as if other people have rights but we do not. For example, we sometimes believe that we do not have the right to protest unfair treatment or criticism because it would violate Christ's standard of turning the other cheek. Sometimes we feel guilty when we feel too happy or when life is going too well for us. Perhaps the least appreciated right among Christians is the right to make mistakes. We find it all too easy to feel guilty when we mess up.

---

1   Manning, B. (2004). *A glimpse of Jesus: The stranger to self-hatred.* (Reprint ed.). San Francisco: HarperSanFrancisco.

The grace-filled perspective is to recognize that God wants us to live an abundant life, and that includes basing our life on God-given human rights. God wants us to access our humanity at the deepest level possible. Here is a list of some of the rights that have been given to each of us.[2]

I have the right to make my own friends.

I have the right to protest unfair treatment or criticism.

I have the right to be illogical in making decisions.

I have the right to be appreciated as a person in my own right, not considered as an appendage or extension of someone else.

I have the right to be acknowledged as a person who contributes to society, no matter how small that contribution might be.

I have the right to put myself first, sometimes.

I have the right to waste time.

I have the right to joy—to play and refresh my strength.

I have the right to choose not to respond to circumstances.

I have the right to avoid injury and sickness.

I have the right to love and be loved—to give and to get.

I have the right to make mistakes and be responsible for them.

I have the right to think and feel according to my convictions.

I have the right to ask for help or emotional support.

I have the right to protect my privacy.

I have the right to be happy!

I have the right not to take responsibility for someone else's problems.

I have the right not to justify my behavior to others.

I have the right to rest my mind and repair my body.

I have the right to say: "I don't know," "I don't understand," "I don't care" and "No!"

I have the right to choose my own marriage partner.

Christian Selfishness

When are you at your peak for helping others? When you have your own needs met and allow God to fill you with His grace. This is almost impossible when you spend your life continually giving to others without taking care of your own basic needs. As we pointed out earlier, this "Christian selfishness" is in stark contrast with uncaring "worldly selfishness," which

---

2 Adapted from Seabury, D. (1990). *The art of selfishness*. New York: Pocket Books.

is wrapped up in its own desires, needs, and rights in ways that pay no regards to the rights and needs of others.

If you've ever flown, you're probably familiar with the standard instructions the flight attendant gives before the plane takes off. The "airplane oxygen mask lecture" surprises people when they hear it for the first time. Flight attendants tell passengers that if a decrease in the airplane cabin pressure should occur, passengers should cover their own mouth and nose with the oxygen mask *before* attending to the needs of someone who needs their help. A mother has to make sure she is wearing her oxygen mask before giving the lifesaving oxygen to her baby. If instead she did what seems instinctual but opposite to the instructions, both mother and baby would perish.

When you say "no" to a person's request because you have an immediate need to care for yourself, it is because to do otherwise would be a violation of God's mandate to be a good steward. This is not God's only mandate, of course. We are also to take care of the sick, the poor and marginalized people of the world. But to do this adequately means you need to have something to give to others. If you don't take time to fill your own well, you won't have enough water to give away to others.

You may find that several items in the above list are difficult for you. If this is the case, then you need to take the time and effort to incorporate these rights into your life. The Voice will work hard to keep you from doing this with as many plausible sounding lies as possible. This might surprise you. However, the Voice is constantly trying to keep you from knowing and exercising your rights. If you have worked your way this far into the book, you may be doing much better on your original problems. The Voice may be more silent and seem far away. However, incorporating these rights into your life will surely provoke the Voice out of hiding. Being aware of this and being willing to confront it will help you to be successful in owning and practicing these rights.

Personal Responsibility

We experience responsibility two different ways: personally and socially. Let's look first at personal responsibility. This is related to personal rights. Rights and responsibility must go together for effective living. God not only expects you to be aware of your rights but to exercise them in a responsible way. The definition we use for personal responsibility is the following: *Being willing to accept the consequences of your actions without blame or excuse.* This is not always easy. It seems to many people that personal responsibility is becoming less common in civilized society. As author Charles Sykes points out in his book, *A Nation of Victims*,[3] we have gradually given up personal responsibility for our mistakes and transgressions. He believes that the rallying cry of modern America is, "I am not responsible, it's not my fault." This mentality has become so automatic that people often play the victim without even knowing they are doing it. They automatically blame their environment, their past, or other people for their difficulties. This is not the way of God's grace. Each of us needs to initiate a "moratorium on blame" by accepting the part we play in initiating and maintaining pain in our lives.

Victim or Victor?

Christians need to begin changing from being a victims to being victors. After all, Paul reminds us of the promise, "But thanks be to God, who gives us the victory through our Lord Jesus Christ" (1Cor:15:57, GNT). Victims have a recognizable pattern of behavior: seeing themselves as helpless and not in charge of their lives, feeling that other people are more capable than they themselves are, having a dim outlook on their future, believing that nothing can be done to change the course of their lives, and waiting for something magical to occur to make their lives different. When you compare the different attitudes between victims and victors, you get a good sense of which style of life is the one you want. You can see the difference between being a victim and being a victor by looking at the following chart.[4]

---

3 Sykes, C. J. (1993). *A nation of victims: The decay of the American character*. New York: St. Martins Griffin.
4 Sandbek, T. J. (1993). *The deadly diet: Recovering from anorexia and bulimia*. Oakland, CA: New Harbinger.

Table 9-A

THE VICTIM	THE VICTOR
. . .sees few or no choices available.	. . . sees life full of choices.
. . . sees problems as hopeless barriers.	. . . sees problems as challenges to be solved.
. . . believes people who get ahead are just lucky.	. . . believes that people who get ahead do so primarily out of their own efforts and preparation.
. . . is resistant to change and unwilling to seriously consider other options.	. . . is open to change and willing to change for a good reason.
. . . believes destiny is determined by external circumstances beyond control.	. . . believes destiny is determined by personal efforts.
. . . feels unable to influence the future.	. . . feels empowered to influence the future.
. . . is uninvolved in personal development.	. . . is totally involved in personal development.
. . . gives little consideration to personal desires in relationships.	. . . gives serious consideration to personal desires in relationships.
. . . allows others and outside events to make personal decisions.	. . . actively makes personal decisions.
. . . has either no personal objectives or sets unrealistic goals.	. . . sets realistic and achievable personal objectives.
. . . avoids future life planning.	. . . carefully plans personal future.

Taking personal responsibility for your life by accepting the consequences of your actions is the first step toward living the victorious Christian life. The difficulty in doing so occurs because personal responsibility has two sides: choice and consequence. Most people like to make their own decisions but get annoyed when others try to "control" them. However, people often experience a disconnect between their choice and their willingness to accept the consequence when things do not go right. People want to make their own choices but want someone else to be accountable for mistakes. They want to blame something or someone else when things go wrong. To accept the consequences of your behavior does not mean you have to like those consequences. You may feel frustrated, disgusted, or even angry over the consequences. Nevertheless, you must accept them as they are. Only when you become fully responsible for your life can you have the freedom to learn from your mistakes and grow into Christian maturity.

Acting and thinking like a victim can lock us into ineffective ways of solving life's problems. To avoid this, we may find it helpful to think about our approach to two "s" words: *sources* of problems and *solutions* to problems.

Models for Understanding Personal Responsibility

We can assign the source of our problems either to ourselves or to the outside world. In the same way we may find solutions within ourselves or from the outside. This understanding gives you four ways to assign responsibility for managing your life. A study by Philip Brickman and his associates at the University of Michigan called these four attitudes toward personal responsibility, "Models of Helping and Coping."[5] We have adapted these models for understanding the different ways you can take personal responsibility for your life and have changed some of the model names in ways that better serve our purposes here. Figure 9-A illustrates how problems and solutions interact with each other. We explain the four models below.

Managerial Model of Responsibility

Maybe you run your life as if you can solve any problem. You may not accept responsibility for having a problem—only for solving it. We call this lifestyle the Managerial Model because it is often how poor managers run their business. They assume they can solve all their problems but will blame others when they cannot solve problems.

The Managerial Model of Responsibility is one of the models the Voice uses to make you less whole. Operating within this model, the Voice wants you to believe you are responsible only for *solutions* to problems, but that all your problems are caused by everything outside you. Although you may appear strong to others, you may also tend to complain and grumble more than other people.

Roger. Roger was a successful stockbroker and did not seem to fit into our class. Many of the other members looked up to him and some even put

5 Brickman, P., Rabinowitz, V.C., Karuza, J., Coates, D., Cohn, E. & Kidder, L. (1982). Models of helping and coping. *American Psychologist* 37(4), 368-384.

him on a pedestal. His lifestyle could be described as stressfully successful. He referred to himself as both a workaholic and a "playaholic." No matter what he did, he was always going at top speed. Even when he was calm on the outside, his mind never slowed down. Eventually, he found it difficult to stay connected with people. His family and friends saw him as growing ever more distant. During one class period, he told his small group that he believed that if he ever slowed down even slightly, the world would run over him and crush him.

Once the Voice locks you into this life model, you, like Roger, will always have a gnawing sense that you will never get on top of your difficulties. Even when you are very successful, you might still feel powerless to come to terms with a world that cannot be controlled. This sense of not having total control over your life causes tremendous stress, and so you keep striving to gain such control. Since the Voice is behind this model, it can easily fill your garden with millions of busy-busy pests (See chapter 4 for the definition of this bug).

Medical Model of Responsibility

Individuals who manage their lives according to the Medical Model of Responsibility are similar to people who utilize the Managerial Model except for this characteristic: they not only take no responsibility for having problems, they also give up responsibility for solving their problems. This means they locate both the source of their problems and the solutions outside themselves. Troubles that come into their lives are considered something like a viral or bacterial attack on the body, requiring a call to a doctor to seek a cure. They feel helpless in dealing with their problems and expect others to solve them for them. Besides using friends, family, and neighbors, they put too much reliance on experts, whether in the fields of medicine, finance, childcare, or any other human endeavor.

Patty. Few people envied Patty because she seemed so dependent on others. Although a sweet and charming person, she was surrounded by people who could help her make decisions. Her mother was her best friend and helped her get through school, get a job, and run her family. Patty would talk with her mother several times a day and valued her input and advice. Her friends described Patty as clueless in understanding her contribution to her struggles. She never understood that she had the potential to make her life either better or worse.

When her mother died from leukemia, Patty was undone, not from the grief, but rather because she was a ship adrift without an engine or rudder. Her loving husband was too busy to micromanage her life. Her friends finally tired of continually coming to her aid for problems they often saw as trivial. This was a perfect place for the Voice to step in and take over. It seemed as if all the vermin began to take up residence in her garden: guilt, depression, helplessness, unhealthy anxiety, irrational fear, and even resentment.

As you can see, the downside of this model is that the more you rely on others for living your life, the less you will learn how to run your own life. You may find yourself in a situation where your chronological age is outpacing your maturity age. Christian growth is only possible when you can learn from your mistakes. If you are neither responsible for the problems in your life nor the solutions to them, then you cannot make mistakes from which to learn. The Voice can even trick you into thinking that complete and absolute dependence on God for mundane decisions is indicative of spiritual maturity. The more you act as if God is a cosmic vending machine, the more the Voice can cloud and distort your relationship to God.

Machine Model of Responsibility

In ancient Greek and Roman drama, when plots sometimes became so entangled that there seemed no possible way out of a difficulty, one of the gods might intervene and resolve the dilemma in a spectacular though implausible way. To dramatize this type of solution, a statue of a god would be lowered to the stage by machinery. Such a plot resolution came to be known as a *deus ex machina* ("god from a machine") literary device, and though not unusual, has usually been frowned upon as an artificial and improbable "quick fix" to a complicated situation in novels and plays.

Some people deal with their own lives with such expectations. Thus, we call the third way of handling life the Machine Model of Responsibility. This life approach is one in which you believe you are responsible for your problems, but only others can come up with solutions. You're willing to accept yourself as the source of your problems, but you can't seem to believe that you have the ability to solve them. You need someone to rescue you from the corner you've backed yourself into. Consequently, you need to find another source to run or fix your life, such as a "higher power." This approach will bog you down by constantly talking about your problem without doing anything about it.

Mike. Mike came to class eager to learn what we could teach about him about having a better life. He had tremendous insight and was an encyclopedia of information about mental health in his small group. He had completely traced his difficulties back to his family of origin. He had cataloged all his transgressions for the last forty years. Over the years, he had seen many therapists, attended a variety of support groups, and read innumerable books. Our class was just the latest part of his journey to find the magic bullet "out there." He was waiting for the statue of the "god from the machine" to be lowered from the ceiling.

The Voice wants you to see this lifestyle as a reasonable approach to life. Unfortunately, it can sap the lifeblood of self-care from you. This attitude makes it easy for you to live a life that is full of struggles and overwhelming emotional exertion. Others may even admire your continued attempts to stay out of "denial" and work on your problems. You may find that you are constantly focused on your problems while waiting patiently for "something" to happen that will make your life better. Some Christians with addiction issues try to use this model for dealing with their personal problems. They look for answers from their church, their support groups, addiction programs or their friends.

Even if a person can change the addictive behavior, the emotional pain and destructive talk of the Voice that drove the addiction will likely still be present. You never have total freedom until you can take responsibility for the total solution, namely, ridding yourself of the influence the Voice has in your life and successfully tending your garden.

Moral Model of Responsibility

This is the approach the Voice especially wants you to avoid. It is the model of personal strength, spiritual growth and maturity, and Christian grace. By far the most effective attitude toward problems and solutions is to accept responsibility for both having your problems and working out the solutions to these problems. Accepting personal responsibility for your problems does not mean you always cause them. Many difficulties in life are beyond your control and always will be. On the other hand, to be entirely blameless for any of your problems is unrealistic.

A serious illness that is highly related to your genes passed on to you by your ancestors might be inevitable for you. Even so, you can take responsibility for living a healthy life. You can do this by learning what you can about the expected illness (problem) and then take the most effective steps for dealing with the illness when it occurs (solution).

The word "morality" is often distorted within Christianity. It is most often used exclusively to refer to sexual behavior. Morality is much larger than issues of sexuality. It includes our entire being and how we care for God's creation which includes ourselves and others. It means "striving for self-possessed maturity." We sometimes refer to this way of living as Moral Centeredness. It is related to Christian selfishness (see above) by taking care of yourself before taking care of others.

You want to develop an attitude that maximizes your ability to care for yourself. In this way you can be an effective human being living in the fullness of God's love for you. When you become responsible for your problems and solutions, your relationships improve (or you leave those relationships that are toxic to you). You become a new creature. Salvation is not merely an assent that Jesus is Lord; it is not merely your acceptance into the body of Christ. Christians often wonder what the Apostle Paul meant when he instructed us to "work out your own salvation" (Philippians 2:12) or when James wrote that "faith without works is dead" (James 2:17). Salvation is a process, not a moment in time when you accepted Christ. Your salvation is a continuous, daily experience of taking responsibility for your life—accepting responsibility for your problems and taking appropriate action for the solutions. Taking personal responsibility by using the Moral Model frees you from the tyranny of living in a sinful world. This way of being a Christian allows you to "live fully, love wastefully, and be all that you are capable of being."[6]

Social Responsibility

We've examined in detail some ways that taking personal responsibility is an important flip side of one of the illusions the Voice uses to trick us. *Social* responsibility is likewise important and flows from the practice of personal responsibility. When you have allowed God to fill your spirit with

6   Spong, J. S. (2002). *A new Christianity for a new world.* San Francisco: HarperSanFrancisco.

goodness and grace by taking full responsibility for your humanity, you will be overflowing with a desire and longing for the rest of God's creation. You can give of yourself in a way you never thought possible. Because you have become a "new creature" others may comment on something "different" about you. You radiate the goodness of the Holy Spirit and can give love in ways inconceivable to many people. This was the enigma of the life Jesus led. His complete God-filled life brought compassion beyond the cultural boundaries that were norms for his contemporaries.

Social responsibility is one core constituent of psychological and spiritual wellbeing. People whose life is greater than their own needs have a better quality of life than those whose goals do not include the wellbeing of others. This idea goes back to the Greeks. They taught that people who live in ways that realize their true potential are living by more enduring values. People who live for short-term happiness, the little "h," very seldom move to a higher morality. Jesus devoted his entire life to the higher purpose of caring for others. He taught us that this is the surest way to be in a right relationship with God. Research also supports that having a purpose in life that values the lives of others is one of the major ingredients of the Big "H."[7]

Hurting People's Feelings

There is a downside to caring for others. Your gentleness, sensitivity, and kindness will attract many people, some of whom will want you to take care of them. These people will be your "friends" but will want to take everything you have. Out of Christian love, you may be tempted to give and give. Most of these emotionally needy friends will be operating from the Medical or Machine Model of Responsibility and will be looking to you to make their lives better. The most morally authentic action you can take is to compassionately insist these people take responsibility for their own lives. Do you remember the chapter on Property Lines? These people have wandered into your beautiful garden and want you to let them live there. This just does not work. Each person must learn to tend and maintain his or her own garden. You can show them how to do it, but you cannot make

---

7   Ryff, C. D. (1989). Happiness is everything, or is it? Explorations on the meaning of psychological wellbeing. *Journal of Personality and Social Psychology* 57(6), 1069-1081.

them do it. You have only limited emotional and time resources. If others are bleeding you dry, move them from your life and give of yourself to others who are more receptive to establishing a growing relationship rather than a dependent one.

One of the most common hooks that can drain you is "hurting other people's feelings." Christians are notorious for taking or avoiding an action because of how others will feel. You now know that this is an illusion. You cannot hurt another person's feelings because feelings come from thoughts. Since you cannot control another person's thoughts, you cannot hurt their feelings. Only the other person's thoughts can generate the feelings they are experiencing. The distinction you want to make is between taking responsibility for another person's feelings and your actions toward that person. You are responsible for what you do to another person. You cannot be responsible for how they feel about it. Not being responsible for another person's feelings does not mean you do not care about someone's feelings. Though you refuse to accept responsibility for their feelings, you can still be empathic, loving, and caring.

This may be difficult for Christians who follow the premise that agape love is always doing for others regardless of the consequences to oneself. Mark tells us in his gospel that Jesus told his disciples to leave a village—"shake off its dust from your feet" (6:11)—if they refused to engage the disciples appropriately. Even Jesus needed relief from ministering to people. He would go off by himself to recharge his soul even when others needed his healing grace.

Love Your Neighbor
The big question is deciding with whom to share your garden. Although the Bible tells us to "love our neighbor," we are fairly restrictive about who that neighbor happens to be. Most of us are comfortable with those like ourselves. We fall into the trap of making only these people our neighbors. The Bible teaches us otherwise. Christian love has no boundaries on who our neighbors are. Christian love compels us to open our garden to those who do not have a healthy garden. This openness is the larger picture of social responsibility.

Writer Brian McLaren, pastor of the Cedar Ridge Community Church in Spencerville, Maryland, believes that the church is often confused about

Jesus's "secret message."[8] He teaches that doing God's work is to become a peacemaker and put our effort into loving others. The Bible tells us social responsibility is based on justice, equality, and peace toward all humanity. Some Christians gloss over these ideas as high-minded. But remember, God does not just love us—God is Love (1 John 4:16). If we ask what is love, the answer screams out to us from the Bible. The prophet Micah tells us to "do justice, love kindness, and walk humbly with your God" (Micah 6:8). The continually unsettling demand is that there are no restrictions on identifying our neighbors. That's what the familiar story of the Good Samaritan is all about. Check out Luke 10: 29-37. Human nature wants to exclude certain people from being our neighbor, often supporting our decision with Bible verses (taken out of context).

If we need further reminders of how to express our Christian freedom to exercise our faith through love and social responsibility, Jesus tells us in Luke 4:18 (ASV), "The Spirit of the Lord is upon me, because he hath anointed me to preach the gospel to the poor; he hath sent me to heal the brokenhearted, to preach deliverance to the captives, and recovering of sight to the blind, to set at liberty them that are bruised."

One of the great spiritual prophets of our time is the founder of *Sojourners* magazine, Jim Wallis. He has shown Christians that a faith without social justice is an incomplete faith. He found that the second most common theme in the Old Testament is about the poor and God's response to injustice. He discovered several thousand verses devoted to this theme. "One of every sixteen verses in the New Testament is about the poor or the subject of money (Mammon, as the gospels call it). In the first three (Synoptic) gospels, it is one of ten verses, and in the book of John, it is one in seven!"[9]

Another type of social justice is the matter of forgiveness of those who have hurt you. One of the Voice's most potent lies it that it's necessary to harbor hatred, bitterness and resentment toward those who have caused us pain. You have already learned that the opposite of these toxic feelings is

---

8   McLaren, B. (2006). *The secret message of Jesus: Uncovering the truth that could change everything.* Nashville: W Publishing Group

9   Wallis, J. (2005). *God's politics: Why the right gets it wrong and the left doesn't get it.* San Francisco: Harper.

anger. Anger will keep you from being revengeful and will motivate you to either confront the abuser or protect yourself from further onslaughts.

Forgiveness

The next step to complete your journey in grace is to learn to forgive those who have hurt you. Lewis Smedes, late professor of theology and ethics at Fuller Theological Seminary, was a leader in the field of forgiveness. He emphasized that forgiving someone was not for their benefit but for ours: "When we forgive, we set a prisoner free and discover that the prisoner we set free is us."[10]

One of the most helpful resources for learning to forgive has come out of the Human Development Study Group at the University of Madison, Wisconsin. Its founder and guiding light is Dr. Robert Enright who is the unquestioned pioneer in the scientific study of forgiveness.[11] His research-based suggestions for true forgiveness are not meant for "the casual reader seeking hints for self-improvement." The research shows that complete forgiveness of another person is only possible when one is fully committed and immersed in the four stages of forgiveness—self discovery, deciding to forgive, working on forgiveness, and deepening the forgiveness.

Phase One: Self Discovery

Completion of this phase allows you to progress through the next three phases of forgiveness. This phase is a writing phase. The more difficult this phase is for you, the more writing you need to do. Since you have come this far by writing copiously, you have experienced the advantages of writing.

Self discovery begins by recognizing that a wrong has been done to you. Although this seems obvious to most people, it is not always obvious to the injured party. Social constraints may keep you from fully acknowledging the wrong and allowing you to feel the full extent of the pain. This can happen, for example, if you have been abused in your past. People who are supposed to love us—family and friends—complicate our lives when

---

10 Smedes, L. B. (1997). *Art of forgiving*. New York: Ballantine Books.
11 Enright, R. D. (2001). *Forgiveness is a choice: A step-by-step process for resolving anger and restoring hope*. Washington, DC: American Psychological Association.

they abuse us. If you have not allowed yourself to fully comprehend a past situation where you have been wronged, the following steps will help you to get in touch with it.

What exactly happened to you?
When did this happen?
How often did it happen?
Who was unfair?
Why do you think that the person was unfair?

You must examine the past unfairness from a rational point of view without the help of the Voice, which wants to cloud your memory and confuse you with resentment and bitterness. Mingled with the resentment might be some healthy emotions, for example, anger. Feeling angry is reasonable because someone has violated your rights.

Other healthy, painful emotions could also accompany or follow anger such as shame. Remember that shame is an emotion that happens when you have violated public standards. This differs from remorse where you have violated your own personal standards.

As you already know, any of the six Vermin can deplete your energy for living. If you have allowed the resentment Vermin to be in your life, you will want to get revenge for the wrong done to you. It is even possible the incident may have occurred twenty years ago but still consumes your need for retaliation today. If any of the resentment Vermin are present, use your Pest Control Kit to convert the resentment to anger. When you have done this, allow yourself to be angry but do it in a mindful way—experiencing and owning the anger. It will be your anger, and it will be appropriate. As with all healthy emotional pain, it cannot continue forever and it cannot damage you.

As you manage the memories of the past iniquity, the Voice may try to sneak its way back in, again, by comparing your life with that of the offender. Kevin told us he and his family were now poor because the small company he had started with a partner was bankrupt. His partner had embezzled all the cash and assets from the company and left the company. One of his most recurring damaging images was envisioning the former partner living in a French villa. Meanwhile, he and his wife had to move to a small apartment and struggle each month just to stay alive. The Voice continued to have the upper hand until Kevin could forgive the heinous wrong committed by his former business partner.

Sometimes you may realize that something has altered your life and it will never be the same again. Judy lost her child because of a drunk driver. A major source of pain for her was the realization that no matter what happened to the offender, her child would never return. At first, coming to this understanding felt like giving up hope. As she allowed herself to accept the reality of this pain, she began her first steps to leaving her emotional plateau. Facing the realities of your painful experience unconditionally will allow you to move to the next phase.

Victims of traumatic injustice, says Beverly Flanigan, Professor at the University of Wisconsin, alter their view of how the world works.[12] If you have experienced trauma, you may now see the world as a dangerous and cruel place. If the trauma involved another human being, you may now believe that you cannot trust other people.

After completing this self-discovery phase and feel you are ready, proceed to the next step: the Decision Phase of forgiveness.[13]

Phase Two: Decision

By now you realize that your old ways of dealing with the trauma have been unsuccessful. Much of this ineffectiveness has been the result of the Voice's telling you how to manage your wounds. Overcoming this means recognizing the necessity for finding new ways of dealing with and putting to rest your past hurts. Until this is done, your distress will be in the hands of the Voice.

Your first step is to consider, finally, that forgiveness of the abuser might be a realistic option for you. To help you in this consideration, you need to understand carefully what forgiveness is. Forgiveness is the combination of abandoning resentment (which is a natural response) while adopting friendlier attitudes toward the abuser (which is a very unnatural and distasteful response). Doing this takes time. Allow yourself patience to

---

12 Flanigan, B. (1992). *Forgiving the unforgivable*. New York: Wiley.

13 If this step is extremely painful or difficult for you, you may want to talk to a psychologist who will offer you a safe place to bring up these past hurts. With professional help, you will be ready to go on to the next phases of forgiveness.

make the switch in this part of your journey. Eventually, you will be able to embrace this unnatural attitude.

Several obstacles may stand in the way of accepting the need to forgive. Some people find it difficult to even think about forgiveness because they believe they might be excusing, forgetting, or even condoning the transgression. Others have the impression that forgiving the abuser will turn themselves into a "doormat"—that doing so will allow the abuser to abuse them again. Some men believe that to forgive someone means they are weak persons. Trying to hold on to the hatred seems more brave and strong. This is a lie from the Voice that keeps men in the pit of despair and hurt. However, if forgiving someone who does not deserve it is harder than not forgiving them, then only a strong person can do it. A final obstacle may be the interaction between forgiveness and justice-seeking. Everyone has a sense of fair-play. A stronger version of this is called justice. Unfortunately, justice is often associated with retribution and retaliation. This is still another strategy of the Voice to keep you from moving beyond your pain and anguish. If you are encountering any of these obstacles, writing about them and talking with trusted friends or even a psychologist might be helpful.

The last step in this Decision Phase is to make a commitment to forgive the offender. This is different from actually forgiving the person. Once you make the mental commitment for forgiveness and feel the forgiveness in your heart toward the offender, you can move on to the next domino, behavior.

Phase Three: Working on Forgiveness

This can be a difficult phase but eventually a highly rewarding one. It is like removing the shackles that bind you to pain and suffering. When you have finished, you can experience a sense of freedom and a new humanity in grace. If you find this phase too difficult, then you need to go back to the previous phase and spend more time getting ready.

Reframing. The first step in the Working-on-Forgiveness Phase is called *reframing*—a process in which you reconsider the entire painful event within a new and fresh perspective. This is an exercise that the Voice will work hard to keep from happening. The goal of this first step is to perceive the abuser as a human being rather than as Evil incarnate. Dr. Enright suggests answering and pondering the following three questions:[14]

- ❏ *"What was it like for the offender as he or she was growing up?"* Understanding the background is different from condoning or excusing the offense. The point of this question is to reframe the humanity of the abuser. It is possible that the person is or was someone who lived with fear, confusion, or vulnerability. They may have had an overwhelmingly powerful Voice guiding and directing their actions. You make no judgments from this information. It is merely to begin a new way of understanding the situation.

- ❏ *"What was it like for the offender at the time of the offense that you are considering?"* As with the previous question, it does not excuse the behavior ("He only did it because he was unable to control his rage."). The answers to this question brings an additional layer of perception for you.

- ❏ *"Can you see him or her as a member of the human community?"* You do not give the offender status by assigning him to socially acceptable categories such as mother, father, pastor, etc. Instead, understanding that the offender is one of God's created creatures is necessary for you. The offender is a person whom God also loves, as difficult as that may be to accept. You already know the Voice wants you to believe that some people do not have infinite worth and do not deserve your respect. If you need to brush up on this, re-read chapter 6.

Empathy and compassion. As you seriously and thoughtfully consider these questions, you may begin experiencing empathy and compassion for the abuser. Some people find it difficult to put themselves inside the other person's shoes because their past experience makes them feel unsafe to do so. Empathy will not be possible if you have not completely dealt with the previous material. Making the transition to this step may take time—which is okay. Again writing and talking to others will enhance the journey. Many

---

14 Enright, R. D. & Fitzgibbons, R. P. (2002). *Helping clients forgive: An empirical guide for resolving anger and restoring hope.* Washington, D.C.: American Psychological Association.

people find that experiencing empathy for the offender needs to begin in microscopic doses. This is perfectly acceptable and will allow you to continue to longer moments of empathic experience. As with mindfulness, empathizing with another person has no moral judgments attached. Once empathy begins to occur more naturally and frequently, you will feel compassion toward your offender. This emotion is the antidote that will cure the emotional cancer of resentment that has been slowly destroying your ability to have healthy and stable personal relationships. You know you have conquered resentment when you begin to feel compassion because compassion and resentment cannot coexist. The Voice will pull out all the stops to keep you from experiencing compassion for "that evil person."

Letting go of pain. The next step in phase three a transitional step that involves your letting go of fighting the pain and hurt. As with all healthy emotional pain, complete acceptance of the emotion will cause it to pass. All healthy pain is temporary and short-lived and this is no exception. To bear the pain means that you accept the painful event as historical fact and then you let it go. You cannot change it. You accept the past while working on learning to cope with the present. Some people have explained that it took much courage to complete this step because they did not think they could do it. You, too, may need to be courageous in completing this step.

Expressing forgiveness. The last step in this working-on-forgiveness phase is to give a moral gift. If forgiveness is to be complete, it must be expressed. If the offender is not available for contact, this will not apply to you. If the person is available, then you may wonder if you should try to reconnect with the abuser. This is a decision that is probably best done with the help of other trusted people in your life. Some people want to feel so free from the bonds of resentment that they move too quickly at this point. To sense a need for reconciliation is different from assuming the person is different or that they will be happy to reconnect with you. You have to be very careful that you move at the proper speed at this point. A trusted friend or helper can be enormously helpful here. Even if your offender is available, you may decide there is too much risk or danger to complete this step.

Phase Four: Deepening the Forgiveness.

People who suffer from events not of their making have a need to find meaning in their suffering. Meaning can be found in many different places. Some people find it in the Bible (the Book of Job, the concept of the Suffering Servant, some of the Psalms, and other passages on this theme). Others find such meaning in recognizing how their suffering changed their lives in a positive way ("Now that I can look back on it, I realize I am a better and stronger person for its having happened.").

For some, knowing that they are not alone in their suffering is helpful. This is the reason for the explosion of support groups and self-help books in the latter half of the twentieth century. Knowing that you are not the "only one" can be a source of hope and comfort. Many of our clients find that when they have reached this place in their personal journey, they want to help others who are just beginning the journey. Finally, allow this experience of forgiveness to become a transformational experience in your life.

Summary

No matter how successful you have been thus far in taking back your life from the Voice, you can never completely destroy the Voice. Although vigilance is important, being proactive is even more important. The skills in this chapter show you another way to take direct action for filling the mental and emotional vacuum left by kicking the Voice out.

You can stay ahead of the Voice by fully understanding your God-given rights. Using your list of rights as part of your morning preparation for the day will give you many solid returns. The Voice may have stripped you of your rights by convincing you that these rights were unavailable to you. Having and expressing these rights is fundamental to your ability to move forward into a more mature Christian life. Now is the time to build them into your life.

Taking personal responsibility for your actions will make you stronger in your walk with the Lord. The Voice wants you to find as many excuses as possible for getting you stuck in your personal growth. You want to identify these excuses and destroy them. Amazingly, some people even use portions of the Bible to maintain their lack of personal responsibility.

Reaching out to the marginalized of our society and staying on the side of the Biblical teachings on justice, peace, and equality is integral to being part of a strong and God-like community of believers. Unfortunately, some Christians ignore these issues or, at most, pay lip service to these Christian principles. Our faith should never wallow in narcissism—being concerned only with our own well-being or that of those who agree with us. We have all had the unfortunate experience of listening to people calling themselves Christians while at the same time being filled with hatred and bitterness toward others. Unbelievably, some Christians even advocate killing other humans for the cause of their beliefs. As a Spirit-filled Christian, you need to be part of the Christian community committed to following the Bible's examples of peace and justice.

Forgiving those who have hurt you the most is essential to keeping the Voice at bay. It is the least you can do to follow Christ's example of forgiving those who killed him. This may be one of the most difficult and painful parts of your personal journey. Everyone who has done it before you bears witness to the freedom and life-giving consequences of engaging in this process.

Assignment

Moving forward by learning and using these Christian strategies often takes personal courage. We have worked with many people who do not believe they are courageous. Everyone, even you, have had moments of personal courage in life. It is easy to forget these events as the Voice tries to blot out your memories. The passage of time allows the Voice to choose what it wants you to remember.

Try to remember some of your personal courage events. Maybe you delivered food to a sick neighbor even though their dog threatened you in their yard. Do you remember a speech you gave which gave you stage fright, yet you went through with it anyway? Perhaps you stood up for someone who was being bullied or verbally abused even though you were scared about getting involved.

As you recall those times of bravery, remind yourself that you are capable of being more courageous than you think you can be. Only one courageous act in your entire life means that you have the capacity to act this way. With the Voice withering away, you can fill up your being with healthy characteristics such as courage.

Writing Tip #1

One technique that has been helpful for those we have worked with is to make your rights a morning ritual. From the list of rights near the beginning of this chapter, identify those that are difficult for you and put them on a separate piece of paper. Tape this list of your personal rights to the bathroom mirror (or any other place you go when you wake up in the morning). Before doing any of your other morning routines, repeat these rights, thoughtfully and carefully, aloud to yourself. Do this daily for one month and then write a few paragraphs on what this exercise meant to you. If it was helpful, you will want to continue it by adding and deleting items as you see fit. If it was not helpful, move onto another exercise.

Writing Tip #2

Think of ways in which you have acted irresponsibly (remember the definition of responsibility) and by doing so gave up your personal power. For any of these acts of irresponsibility, have you ever blamed:

- your childhood?
- your inherited genes?
- your medical condition (brain chemistry)?
- peer pressure?
- your environment?
- other?

If you answered yes to any of these, write a small essay (for your eyes only) for each "yes" answer. Write about how the Voice has gotten you to act irresponsibly and what it has cost you.

Writing Tip #3

Identify someone in your past who has been the source of deep wounding for you. If you are ready to clean out that part of your life and move forward, read the forgiveness section again to make certain you are ready to begin. Take as much time as you need for each of the four steps. Going too slowly is better than moving too quickly. This project will probably overlap with your continuing to finish this book. However, you may find that you want to put the rest of the book on hold until you have moved through forgiveness. Do not let the Voice talk you out of this. You are now far enough along in your journey to make your own decisions regardless what other people—and especially the Voice—believe.

Chapter Ten
The Behavior Domino

Like the Holy One who called you, be holy yourselves also in all your behavior.
—1 Peter 1:15, NASB

We have concentrated, up to this point, on the first three dominoes: life events, thoughts, and feelings. You have learned that the interaction between these three dominoes is automatic. Life events trigger destructive thoughts before we are even aware of them. The resulting emotions seem instantaneous. When the thought domino is changed, the emotion domino is changed, too. The change might not be immediate, but it will happen automatically given enough time and practice.

However, changing this third or emotion domino does not always cause change in the next domino, the behavior domino. This is because the *consequences* control our behaviors. Although this might not make sense immediately, we will explain this more fully later in this chapter.

Difficulties with the Behavior Domino

Many people believe that once you have made significant changes to your internal self—have become a new person—that you will start acting differently. But all one needs to do is to look around with open eyes to know such an assumption calls for caution. How often have you heard about someone's life-changing experience only to see the person revert to old behaviors within a week or two? Have you ever heard someone tell you that once you use their remedy (religious or secular) your self-destructive habits will disappear? Why is it so hard to change your ways even though you have prayed and prayed for help? Have you ever felt that the "new you" is right around the corner, only to discover that the emotion you felt was only a temporary mask for the "old you?"

Although we can sometimes change our behavior after a change of heart, this is not always the case. The *myth* of insight has been long-standing in the professional mental health community. This myth assumes that once we know "why" we are engaging in unhealthy behaviors, an automatic change will take place. This notion is encouraged in movies, TV, and pop psychology books. Yes, sometimes this happens, but the sad fact is that an automatic metamorphosis is much less common than believed. In this chapter, we will teach you some motivational skills for making behavioral changes .[1]

Target Behaviors

One of the most difficult problems with changing behavioral habits is that they are so stubborn. When you begin the journey to change lifetime habits, the effort can be daunting. You will be using all the skills you have already learned to make this chapter work for you. The Voice will increase its efforts to keep you from taking action because changing your behavior is the final step in the demise of this enemy. The Voice will encourage you to continue focusing on your internal self (thoughts, emotions, sensations) so that you can neglect this last, crucial step for change.

Think about this. You have changed your thoughts to healthy ones. You no longer experience destructive emotions, and your stress level is lower. Nevertheless you may still blow up at people or treat people based on prejudice. You may even lie and manipulate others. You may still be inhibited in social settings, overeat, abuse drugs or alcohol, smoke, spend compulsively, or do any number of things that have destructive consequences—all because you're trying to manage your discomfort. Any of these behaviors sounds an alarm that you are still radically incomplete. It's important now to target the behaviors you'll want to work on.

1　You may want to look at one of the classics in the mental health field on this topic: A book by David Watson and Roland Tharp called *Self-Directed Behavior: Self-modification for Personal Adjustment* (Brooks/Cole).

Selecting a Goal

The first step is to decide to prioritize what you need to change. What behavior or habit do you want to change first? In making your decision, it will help to identify two categories of behaviors. One set of behaviors is composed of positive actions that are *not being done*, and the other set is made up of negative actions that *are being done*. Psychologists have names for each of these categories.

Deficit behaviors. Deficit behaviors are disregarded, neglected, or undone healthy, constructive behaviors—behaviors that don't happen often enough. You know you need more sleep, but you stay up too late and don't get enough shut-eye. You know the importance of paying bills on time, but you pay them at the last minute or even late, thereby risking credit card penalties or damaging your credit rating. You're aware of the importance of spending time in activities that refresh your soul, but you neglect to participate in them. Deficit behaviors could also involve not working on social skills. We have all known difficult people who contributed to our discomfort. Often we respond by simply trying to avoid these people, because nothing we do seems to work. Psychologist John Townsend's book, *Who's Pushing Your Buttons?: Handling the Difficult People in Your Life*[2], is a great resource if you tend to "give up too soon." His book shows you how to develop new skills in dealing with others, such as healthy confrontation, negotiation, and setting appropriate limits.

Excessive behaviors. The second set of behaviors are those things that you do or say that are destructive either to yourself or to others. Psychologists refer to such behaviors that happen too often as *excessive behaviors*. The goal is to decrease their frequency and intensity. Examples would include addictive behaviors, temper tantrums, and spending money unwisely. Commonly, most people concentrate on this set of behaviors because they are so obvious and annoying. The problem with this typical strategy (the use of what psychologists call *reduction methods*) is that the skills you need to decrease the frequency of these behaviors are not very effective. Even when they work, the results are often temporary and loaded

---

2   Townsend, J. (2004). *Who's Pushing Your Buttons?: Handling the Difficult People in Your Life*. Franklin, TN: Integrity Publishers.

with problems.[3] Therefore, we will not be showing you how to decrease destructive habits. Instead, we will show you something more effective.

Replacement Behaviors

You might at this point feel that a quandary has been posed. If decreasing your self-destructive behaviors is important for you but you cannot use typical strategies to decrease them, what are you supposed to do? Psychology has identified a very clever way to do this by using something called *replacement behaviors*. Replacement behaviors are based on the notion that all destructive behaviors have incompatible, opposite behaviors that can be used for your target or goal behaviors. Sometimes these replacement behaviors are easy to identify and sometimes they are more difficult. With some thought and maybe ideas from friends, you can always find the replacement behavior for your self-destructive behaviors. By definition, a replacement behavior is one that you want to do more often and is incompatible with the unhealthy behavior. Therefore we can use the same behavior change procedures for your destructive behaviors (increasing their *opposite* replacement behavior) as can be used for your constructive behaviors (getting such positive actions to happen more often).

Identifying your target behaviors. Begin by making two lists: destructive behaviors you want to decrease (for example, snarling at your spouse) and constructive behaviors you want to increase (for example, getting more sleep). You may want to use input from family and friends. When the list is complete (you can always add new items later), convert all of your destructive behaviors to constructive target (replacement) behaviors that are incompatible with the destructive behaviors. Table 10-1 has some examples:

---

3   The technical word for describing these reduction methods is called *punishment*. However, this use of the word punishment does not assume that it must be aversive to the person being punished. Psychology uses the word much more broadly. Since we will be avoiding these techniques, we will not spend time explaining their use.

Table 10-A: Destructive Habits to Be Replaced

EXCESSIVE BEHAVIOR	REPLACEMENT BEHAVIOR
Snarling at my spouse	Telling my spouse how I feel when he or she does something that upsets me
Spanking my children	Learn positive parenting skills
Drinking a six-pack after dinner	Limiting myself to only two drinks after dinner
Overeating; i.e., more than 2500 calories/day	Recording how many calories I eat each not to exceed 2500
Paying bills late	Pay all bills by the 15th and 30th of each month

The first column names those undesirable things you do too often.; the second column identifies what you would like to do more. Even though you want to decrease the left side behaviors and increase the right side behaviors, you are going to set your target for increasing behaviors. (In other words, your goal will not stated in terms of stopping the behavior on the left, but rather as *doing* the column on the right.)

Identifying and replacing destructive behaviors. We humans have an almost limitless amount of destructive behaviors at our disposal. To set a target behavior for our excessive behaviors, you will need a change of perception. Instead of the replacement behavior describing what "not to do," you want to find an action that you can *do*—doing the target behavior "instead of" the destructive behavior. You will also notice that we try to put numbers on some of the target (replacement) behaviors. Some people may find this too frivolous or difficult. The advantage of using numbers is that it gives you more clarity and definitive boundaries—an action that is concrete and specific. This is more effective than setting goals based on vague and nebulous language that are too easy to circumvent. To finish this step for identifying target replacement behaviors you need to:

- Clearly identify the destructive behavior.
- Find an incompatible replacement behavior using specific language: who, what, where, when, how often.
- Be as specific as possible for the constructive behavior you want to increase.

Table 10-B: Constructive Behaviors in Which You Have a Deficit and Want to Increase the Behavior

DEFICIT BEHAVIOR	TARGET (NEW) BEHAVIOR
I avoid talking to people I don't know well	Learn how to initiate conversation with strangers
I don't get enough sleep	Go to bed 8 hours before I need to get up
I don't spend enough time in Bible study	Read and study for 30 minutes before 9AM three times a week
I am not expressing positive feelings towards my spouse often enough	Twice a day, tell him or her what I enjoy about our relationship
I don't exercise enough	M, W, F go to gym at 5 o'clock and exercise for 30 minutes

The left column indicates an area of insufficiency, whereas the column on the right lists the target behavior you want to increase to making up for the deficit by "depositing more' in that 'behavior bank account."

Identifying and increasing constructive behaviors. You saw in Table 10-1 that the target behaviors are fairly specific in replacing the destructive behaviors. You want to do the same for your constructive target behaviors (Table 10-2).

For some of your deficit behaviors you will actually have to learn *how* to do them. The first example in Table 10-2 describes a behavior that does not exist—something that is lacking. To learn how to do this skill (initiating conversation with strangers) you need to break it down into several steps that can be practiced and learned one at a time as in the following sequence:[4]

- Begin by making contact with a person by giving eye contact, saying "hi" and maybe shaking hands.
- Check to see if the other person is responding.
- Get the other person to talk about herself by using small talk, asking open-ended questions and listening for free information.
- Try to pick up on that free information with something about yourself—a related experience you have had or something you have read that will connect with what the other person has said.

---

4   Psychologists call this process *task analysis*

- Expect pauses in the conversation and try to relax when this happens. You may also have to fight the Voice about being a poor conversationalist.
- Finish the conversation when you are ready by thanking the person for talking with you and then using a canned response for termination. "I gotta run now. It's been nice chatting with you."

Making Observations

Although you may not need to do this for all your target behaviors, many people find this part extremely helpful because it makes your goal more specific by clarifying what you want to accomplish. You are much more likely to keep moving toward your goal if it appears reachable. Using numbers makes it possible to gauge your progress, and such objective measures can override any subjective impressions. In addition, objectivity is a strong, effective tool for combating the Voice's vague lies and taunts as it attempts to discourage you.

Remember, this is different from recording your thoughts, emotions or physical sensations. We're talking here about the fourth domino—*behavior*. In a sense, it's easier to observe behavior because your actions are public. They are not hidden like Domino Two (thoughts) and Domino Three (feelings). Others can see and hear your behaviors, too.

You will begin your observations by tracking and recording the frequency of both your destructive behaviors and your replacement behaviors (how often each behavior occurs). To record how you interact with your family you can track how often you snarl at them and also how often you speak to them pleasantly. Keep this behavior log for a about a week—long enough to get a sense that your observations are representative.[5]

Using Motivators

The next step is to connect these target behaviors with your personal motivators.[6] In the mid-twentieth century, psychologists discovered

---

5   Merely, watching your behaviors will have an effect on their frequency. If you think this would not give you an accurate picture, then have someone else track your behaviors as unobtrusively as possible.

6   Our use of the word "motivator" is what psychologists call a *reinforcer.*

that humans are powerfully affected by the personal consequences of their actions. This finding was not well received at first. Ancient human experience, and later, science, showed that a cause preceded an effect. If you hit a glass with a hammer, the swinging of the hammer takes place before the glass breaks. This concept was so basic that people accepted it as a truth for the entire universe of human experience. When the field of mental health began, everyone assumed that human beings operated under the same guidelines. Namely, if you wanted to know "why" someone did something, you looked back in time for a cause. Freud and his followers made this idea part of our daily language and understanding.

When we discovered that what *followed* our actions was more of a cause than what preceded our actions, it did not seem to make sense. After decades of research and innumerable hours of clinical experience, we now know, beyond any doubt, that consequences control our behavior.[7] These consequences can be external (extrinsic) or internal (intrinsic). You will learn to manage your behavior by effectively managing the consequences of your behavior.

Remember, there are two types of consequences: Reinforcers (rewards) and reducers (punishment). Reinforcers are consequences that increase behavior; reducers are consequences that decrease behaviors. Research has proven that reinforcers are more effective and predictable than reducers. Since we want you to work on increasing behaviors (target behaviors for your deficit behaviors and replacement behaviors for your excessive behaviors) you will concentrate on using reinforcers. In this chapter, we will use the word "motivator" for reinforcement.

Motivator Menu

Before you can begin to use motivators, you will need to find which ones work for you. Everyone responds differently to motivators. Some people can change behavior by using intrinsic motivators. For example, simply telling yourself how proud you are for having exercised or reminding yourself of the benefits for having done so can make it more likely you exercise again soon.

---

7   We are oversimplifying this for the purposes of this book. The application of these ideas is called Applied Behavior Analysis.

Others need more concrete, extrinsic, motivators. Some people put aside motivator money they get to spend as they complete their target behaviors. Sometimes, having other people say something or do something for you can also motivate you to take action.

Your first step is to identify what motivators would work for you. To help you get started in gathering this information, answer the following questions:

- What kinds of things do you like to have?
- What are your major interests?
- What are your hobbies?
- Which people do you like to be with?
- What do you like to do with these people?
- What do you do for fun when alone?
- What do you do to relax?
- What are some of your fantasies?
- What makes you feel good?
- What would be a nice present to receive?
- What kinds of things are important to you?
- What would you buy if you had an extra $50? An extra $100? An extra $500?
- On what do you spend your money each week?
- What commonplace things do you do every day that are enjoyable?
- What pleasant things do you say to yourself that are motivating?

Using Your Motivators

From your answers to the above list, decide what motivators you think might work for you. If you have decided to use mostly extrinsic motivators, then you can combine your motivators with your target behaviors. One possibility is to assign point values to your target behaviors and a different set of points to your motivators.

Each time you engage in one of your target/replacement behaviors you could earn a specific amount of points. For example, each day you stay within your calorie limit you could earn ten points. Or, you might earn three points each time you smile at someone at work. By keeping track of the total points you have earned you can then spend them on the motivators you have chosen.

You can spend any number of these points on any of the motivators you have chosen. If you decided that going to a movie was worth 350 points, then you can do this when you have earned enough points to do so.

Table 10-3 is an example of a Motivator Menu. In this menu, the motivators are not assigned to the behaviors to their left. These are really two lists in one. Any motivator on the right can be used for any behavior on the left. As you earn the points on the left you can "buy" any of the motivators on the right if you have enough credits.

Table 10-C: Motivator Menu

TARGET/ REPLACEMENT BEHAVIOR	# POINTS EARNED	MOTIVATOR	COST FOR USING THE MOTIVATOR
Stay within my calorie limit	10 points/day	Go to a movie (rent a movie, etc.)	350 points
Smile more at my family, friends, co-workers, etc.	3 points for each instance	Take a drive in the country	40 points
Get to work on time	5 points/day	Play a round of golf	75 points
Give my spouse 20 minutes of my attention when I get home from work	7 points/day	Have lunch with a friend	25 points
Eat a "forbidden" food	20 points for each instance	Turn off the phone, TV and read a book	1 point/minute
Drive over the Bay Bridge	50 points for each instance	Have a pedicure	45 points
Take time for myself (minimum of 15 minutes)	3 points for each 15 minutes	Take a vacation (weekend, week, 2 weeks, etc.)	200 points/day of vacation
Confront my boss	10 points	Buy frivolous clothes	100 points
Finish my homework before 10 pm	3 points	Sleep in and have breakfast in bed	60 points

Speak to a stranger	4 points for each instance	Spend time on my hobby	50 points
Spend time talking to (my mother, etc.) on the phone	1 point for each 5 minutes	Veg out in front of the TV	50 points
Spend 30 minutes exercising	10 points for each 30 minutes		
Get at least 7 hours sleep (not counting naps)	8 points/day		

This plan works just like your bank account. When you engage in a target behavior you earn points to be spent toward one or more of the motivators. Try to make this project fun. Natalie and her husband had been talking about going to Hawaii. Neither had ever been there and were now able to go. Instead of using many motivators, we helped Natalie to set up a point system for her target. Each time she did one of these behaviors, she earned a certain amount of points depending on the behavior. To earn the trip to Hawaii with her husband, she had to earn a minimum amount of points before a set date. Any additional points earned beyond that time would go towards money for shopping. Both Natalie and her husband wanted her to succeed so they agreed to add one additional part to their Hawaii project. They decided that her husband would definitely be going, but she could only go if she had earned enough points. At first she was reluctant to add this part. With more thought, Natalie realized that the stronger they made the consequence the more she would be willing to work for it. They both made it to Hawaii—with plenty of spending money.

Some people think this approach is demeaning because it looks like a program we would use with our children. It is true that a system of rewards (minus certain kinds of punishments, because punishments don't work well) is very effective with young children. However, the principle of reinforcement works with people of all ages. The trick is to find a way of doing it that works for you.

Some people find that using points is helpful because it adds structure and an objectivity to their program for self change. Others find it too rigid and would rather make it more simple by tying specific motivators to specific behaviors.

An example of a less structured method is one we used with Jerry who was planning to switch jobs. He needed to send out resumes to prospective employers. He knew exactly what to do but kept procrastinating and putting off this task. Instead of spending time exploring his "reasons" for avoiding these tasks, we had him tell us what his wife could do for him that might motivate him. When he hesitated, his wife immediately volunteered that her husband loved to eat. She was a good cook and a great dessert cook. We first identified several special desserts that he loved but didn't have very often. Then we set up a simple program where he would get one of these special desserts every time he completed at least one task related to future jobs. Three days later, his wife contacted us and told us that he had been successful three days in a row. She told us that she had been quite skeptical this would work, but delighted that it did.

The Premack Principle
David Premack, currently emeritus professor of psychology at the University of Pennsylvania, discovered something amazing. He found that the person receiving the motivator *does not have to like* the motivator. For example, when Dr. Sandbek worked in a psychiatric hospital years ago, they were having difficulty motivating one of the patients to attend group therapy meetings. No incentives they could offer seemed to work to get the person to go to group therapy. The staff then observed the patient for a week and found that he spent most of his time just looking at old magazines. When asked what he enjoyed reading, he said he didn't like reading them. When they offered to buy him new ones, he expressed no interest. Nevertheless, he continued to look at old magazines most of his waking hours. The staff finally collected all the old magazines in the hospital ward that he was on.

The next day, prior to the next therapy meeting, he was shown some of the old magazines and was told he could look at them if he went to the meeting for 10 minutes. He decided to do it and received the magazines immediately after he left the meeting. Over the weeks, he had to stay longer in the meetings to earn his magazines. All the while, he continued to insist that reading these old magazines was no fun because he already knew what was in them.

By the time he was attending all the meetings, we collected old magazines that he had not seen. These "new" magazines were then used as motivators for getting him to participate more fully in his skills training therapy program.

You can use the same principle. If you find two behaviors that you want to increase and one of them occurs more often than the other, then you can use this principle. All you need to do is rearrange your life so that the high frequency behavior occurs *only* after the low frequency behavior. If you do this diligently, the low frequency behavior will eventually occur more often.

Neal found that he would come home from work and vegetate in front of the television. When we asked him what he enjoyed about watching TV, he admitted that it wasn't really enjoyable, just a habit. He had done well in Voice fighting about his depression but was stuck with this do-nothing behavior. He did not want to exercise but we found that he used to have some hobbies that he enjoyed. He admitted that he would like to start doing them again.

He used to like reading, playing his guitar, and chatting with people online. He started by doing either of these three things for thirty minutes as soon as he came home. To help him remember, he had a note attached to the dashboard of his car reminding him of the hobby he was to do when he got home. When he walked through the door, he either had his guitar or a book on the hall table or another sign reminding him to go immediately to the computer. He set a timer for thirty minutes. After thirty minutes, he went to the TV and vegetated. Within a week, he was watching only the shows he enjoyed and was spending all the rest of his after-work time doing activities that brought him enjoyment.

Shaping

In the previous example with Jerry and the desserts, he did not have to wait until after all the resumes were completed to receive an initial reward. His first special dessert came after he had completed a first step—the collection of all the information needed to complete his resumes. Next, he was rewarded when he found the computer program he wanted to use to make the resumes. The third dessert came when he had completed only one resume. This continued until he had finished all of his resumes and had sent them out to prospective employers. His wife was so pleased when he was finally finished that she booked them into a romantic hotel for the following weekend. Needless to say, he enjoyed the weekend.

Shaping is a very powerful procedure. If you find that the motivators are not having the impact you want, then perhaps you need to break down your goal into smaller steps and reward yourself for the completion of each small step. The Voice will try to tell you how stupid this is, "Why do you have to be such a wimp and do these little baby steps? Just go ahead and get it done!" This is a sure formula for failure. Use your shaping procedures and you will be guaranteed of success.

Trevor decided he could not drastically change from six beers a night to one a night. He decided to work on his target behavior gradually. He moved his goal from a baseline of six beers a night to five a night. This meant he would get his motivator points by drinking five beers a night—an improvement worth rewarding. When he established this new standard (five beers/night, five days in a row), he then received his motivator for only having four beers. Although this technique does not work for everyone, for others the gradual approach is very helpful.

Contracting

Sometimes, having a contract can be a useful part of your action plan. As you have already experienced, writing is an essential step in your life-changing process. Making a written contract with yourself also makes the skills in this chapter much more effective. Social psychology has taught us that we humans need to be consistent between our beliefs, words and actions. Writing and signing your contract will make your commitment more powerful and long-lasting because it ties your action of writing into your thoughts and emotions. You may even want to share your written contract with someone you trust. The contract needs to include the following items:

- Your target behaviors spelled out in specific terms, including time limits.
- The specific motivators you will be using and how you will earn them.
- Who, if anyone else, will be involved in your plan.
- Specific times for you to monitor your progress and how this will be done.

181

The Voice's Tricks

As you can imagine, the Voice won't be happy with your using the skills in this chapter. It would be more than content if you just worked on improving your emotional state and your thoughts without ever translating them into action. Many psychologists are familiar with people telling them how much some experience has changed their lives because they *feel* so much better. Upon closer examination, their behavior had not changed.

This step—the behavior domino—is sometimes the lengthiest step in the entire change process. The length depends on how many behaviors you want to change and how deeply ingrained they are. Since you have come this far in your progress, forgetting the Voice is easy. But it will always be there and will always try to win back control. As you begin the end phases of your life-change program, the Voice will use various means to sabotage your progress.

Procrastination

When you started your program, emotional pain was a powerful motivator for learning your new skills. Unfortunately, the farther you travel from the original emotional pain, the less power this pain will have in motivating you. The Voice may tell you that now that you are doing so well, you can slow down a bit and enjoy the fruits of your labor. You may start slacking off and procrastinating the development of necessary skills for reaching your goals. With pain diminishing in your life, it's important therefore to use your *new* motivators (rather than the pain that started you on your journey) to change and maintain your actions.

Half-Hearted Attempts

The Voice will tell you that if you insist on working on your behavior you can do so with minimal effort. Now that you have worked so hard to get where you are, you don't need to spend so much effort learning these new skills. "You are so strong and happy now. Wasting time perfecting new skills when there is so much life to enjoy does not make sense."

Overload

If the previous advice does not work, the Voice will try to convince you to work on all the other problems you have, urging you to give all of them your attention simultaneously rather than concentrating on only one or two at a time. "You are strong and have been very successful," the Voice will tell you. "Why not multitask and make progress even faster?" Although this might work for some people, you must insist on running the show. Proceed at your own pace. Good advice from the Voice is worse than bad advice from yourself.

Think Big

The Voice—that slimy little Lord of Lies—will try to tell you: "Don't let the small successes define improvement for you anymore. You are way beyond taking those baby steps you took at the beginning. It is demeaning for you to progress at such a slow pace. Real winners move quickly and decisively." The Voice is no doubt congratulating itself for being so clever! Keep your eye on the big picture and reaching your goal step by step. Don't be fooled.

Become a Generalist and Practice Eclecticism

Although the skills taught in this book may have changed your life, the Voice will tell you to try another way. This statement contains some truth, but be careful. Psychologists have determined that our culture has more than five hundred different life change methods available to people. The research shows that out of this large pool, only a handful have any scientific validation. The vast majority of mental health panaceas are, at worst, akin to snake oil and, at best, neutral.[8] By all means keep reading a variety of materials and learning more about how to improve your life. But be cautious about what methods you select.

Two Sides of the Coin

The Voice will tell you it wants you to have a "balanced" approach to life—again a half-truth. Some research has shown that negative thinking

---

8   Eisner, D. A. (2000). *The death of psychotherapy: From Freud to alien abductions.* Westport, CT: Praeger Publishers. This author has conservatively estimated that there were between 400 and 500 different brands of psychotherapy when he conducted his research. There are many more therapies today since the number continues to increase at a steady pace. Since the vast majority of psychotherapies have not been subjected to rigorous empirical evaluation (e.g., randomized, controlled trials), you have no way of knowing whether such change procedures are effective, ineffective, or harmful. And if they are effective, you have no way of knowing whether to attribute the effectiveness to luck, spontaneous remission, or the placebo effect.

people may be more "reality-oriented" than positive thinking people. We now know that healthier people overestimate the degree of control they have over the environment. They also see themselves in an overly positive light and are generally unrealistically optimistic about the future. As with most lies from the Voice, you do not have to make a choice between realistic and optimistic. Psychologist Sandra Schneider at the University of South Florida[9] has described something called "realistic optimism." As she puts it, "We each have the opportunity to guide the direction of our own lives and subjective experiences, both in our day-to-day choices and in our long-term plans . . . .The illusion of the good life is likely to break down for those who lull themselves into complacency with self-deceptive beliefs, but the illusion is likely to become reality for those who are optimistic within the fuzzy boundaries established by the active engagement in life."

Summary

Have you ever known someone who has been in therapy for decades and loves to tell others how much therapy has changed his or her life? Upon closer examination, you discover that this person still engages in destructive behaviors while failing to learn new growth behaviors. In the final analysis, changing yourself on the inside is not good enough if nothing changes on the outside. Faith without good works is dead, in spite of the noise it makes (See James 2:14-26).

It is possible that your mastery over the Voice has been enough for you to make the behavioral changes necessary for your life. Nevertheless, growth and change are never-ending. At some point in your journey, you may need these behavioral motivation skills, so keep them handy.

These "behavioral contingency" skills can work very rapidly if you strongly devote yourself to using them. They can also be effective on habit skills that are leftover remnants of the past influence of the Voice. However, when you begin working on habits, the Voice will probably show up with some of its vermin in an attempt to keep you from changing.

---

9   Schneider, S. L. (2001). In search of realistic optimism: Meaning, knowledge, and warm fuzziness. *American Psychologist* 56(3), 250-263.

Before you go to the final chapter, make sure you have been experiencing success with the skills in this chapter. Chapter 11 is based on research from the newest movement in mental health, Positive Psychology. The material is not merely someone's ideas of what might help people. Like all the skills in this book, they have been subjected to scientific scrutiny. These skills have proven to be successful with people who manage to make them part of their daily lives.

Writing Tip #1

There are two kinds of target behaviors: Replacement behaviors and new behaviors. Both kinds or behaviors are meant to increase and happen more often. The replacement behavior is one that is incompatible with a too-frequent destructive behavior. Incompatible means that when you engage in the replacement behavior the original destructive behavior cannot occur. By increasing the replacement behavior, you automatically decrease the destructive behavior.

The new behavior is one that either happens too little or not at all. You want it to also increase with time. Both types of behaviors are increased through the use of carefully chosen motivators.

Writing Tip #2

As with previous skills, good record keeping is essential to changing your behavior. In fact, it might even be *more* important than it was for changing your thoughts and emotions. We have all gotten into disagreements with others about whether or not we did a particular behavior. Often it ends up as "they said, I said." When you have an accurately written record of your behavior, you have evidence for yourself and others. We all have blind sides to our behaviors because the Voice can convince us that we have behaved differently from what actually happened. Your written goals and motivators are a powerful way to keep you focused on your plan for self-improvement.

Pat has a beautiful leather-bound journal that he uses to permanently record his successes and observe his new healthier behaviors. Being able to look back and see how far he has come is tremendously encouraging. Having this record is especially powerful when the Voice tries to tell him that he has not really changed—that he is the same loser he always was.

Chapter Eleven
Accepting God's Grace

Grace to you and peace from God our Father and the Lord Jesus Christ.
— Romans 1:7 (ASV)

Jesus never promised that salvation would automatically bring us peace and joy. We can see this in our churches today, where many pious, God-centered people are experiencing emotional pain. The Christian life is a journey that may start with our new relationship to Christ, but, like any journey, it must keep progressing. "Coming alive" to God is a concept Tony Campolo talks about in his book, *Carpe Diem*.[1] He is speaking of a way of being —a way of moving forward in our Christian journey. It is something you can experience as you master the skills we've presented in this book. The skills you've been learning so far were designed to show you how to remove the obstacles on your path. Now that you have removed most of them, it's time for some additional skills to help you progress further.

Rebuilding the Positive

Replacing old habits with new ones needs to be done deliberately and intentionally. The Voice's influence and the resulting emotions and behaviors were your old habits. Your new habits allow you to have the worthy objective of becoming more realistic about life. As you learned earlier in this book, the Big "H" style of happiness is the end goal of life. Little "h" is too transitory to be the foundation on which you stand. Big "H" brings a peace of mind that comes from having a sense of meaning

---

1   Campolo, T. (1995). Carpe Diem. Nashville: W Publishing Group.

while you are engaging the world around you, just as Jesus was engrossed in the world around him. In the words of John Spong, this means "loving wastefully and living purposefully."

As a psychologist, Terry discovered long ago that when people can release themselves from their emotional pain, they do not automatically experience the Big "H". Earlier in this book, we introduced you to Martin Seligman, psychologist and past president of the American Psychological Association, who began a new movement in mental health. This research-based movement, called Positive Psychology concentrates on what makes people thrive and experience fulfillment. It is changing the way we approach our quest for obtaining a Christian quality of life. The goal of positive psychology is to teach people how to achieve the elements of the Big "H": hope, wisdom, creativity, future mindedness, courage, spirituality, and responsibility. These goals dovetail nicely with the goals of Christianity.

This chapter will help you to take specific steps for increasing your HQ—your *happiness quotient*. The more you have been successful in defeating the Voice, the more effective these new behaviors will be for you. Near the end of this chapter, we'll share with you some of Dr. Seligman's exercises for learning to live the abundant life.

Happiness Revisited

Christianity is about so much more than avoiding immoral behavior. Yet, you wouldn't know that if you attended some churches, where people in the pews are bombarded constantly with directives about what they are *not* to do. For centuries, all too many churches have focused on sin more than grace, on fear more than courage, on limitations more than freedom, on judgment more than love, on punishment more than compassion. Knowing what *not* to do, however, does not automatically tell us what to do. Instead, obsessively dwelling on the "don'ts" fosters a climate of negativity and suspicion —the very qualities so effectively use by the Voice.

Scientists describe happiness as a global satisfaction with relationships, recreation, and work. Truly happy Christians experience a degree of fulfillment in their most important needs, goals, and wishes. It's a happiness that embodies what Paul called the "fruit of the Spirit" and includes such qualities as love, joy, peace, patience, gentleness, goodness, and faith. Jesus practiced this type of living and expects us to model it, too. Such a lifestyle is a process that makes full use of our talents, capacities, potentialities. Just as Christ transcended the ordinary and mundane aspects of life, we, too, can focus on the brighter side of life: looking forward instead of backward, reaching beyond ourselves, and accepting personal progress as a "receding horizon." When we have learned fully to walk in the steps of Jesus, we become more aware of our personal assets as we systematically get our needs met. Being filled with the Holy Spirit means being willing to accept ourselves for who we are, while continually expanding our range of experiences and increasing our autonomy and self-sufficiency.

Happiness Research

Although many people, for years, have repeated the refrain that scientists cannot study matters such as love, happiness, and hope, this is simply not true. At the end of the twentieth century, research into happiness exploded. If you were to conduct a search for articles on happiness in the psychology journals, you would find 150 articles published in 1979, 780 articles in 1989, and more than three thousand articles in 1999 —an increase of more than 1,900% in just twenty years. In 2000, the *American Psychologist* journal devoted an entire issue to the research on happiness.

David Myers, a psychology professor at Hope College in Michigan, found that happy people share several characteristics.[2] Happy people like themselves, feel a sense of personal control, are usually optimistic, and tend to be extroverted. If some of these qualities are lacking in your life, the Voice may still be lingering at the outskirts of your property line. You can also contribute to the building of these qualities by working on the exercises in this chapter.

One myth about happiness is that it is the opposite of sadness.[3] A National Institutes of Health study of the brain found that negative and positive emotions are independent of each other.[4] In other

---

2 Myers, D. (1992). *The pursuit of happiness: Who is happy —and why.* New York: William Morrow.

3 Rafanelli, C., Park, S. K., Ruini, C., Ottolini, F., Cazzaro, M. & Fava, G. A. (2000). Rating wellbeing and distress. *Stress Medicine* 16(1), 55-61.

4 George, M. S., Ketter, T. A., Parekh, P. I. & Horwitz, B. (1995). Brain activity during transient sadness and happiness in healthy women.

words, decreasing negative emotions will not automatically increase positive ones. Your positive emotions affect a different part of your brain than your negative emotions do. Happiness is more than the absence of emotional pain. As Dr. Seligman points out, it is not enough to go from minus seven to zero, but we must be able to go from zero to plus seven.[5] Happiness, as psychologists write about it, goes by many different terms: "quality of life," "subjective well being," "psychological wellbeing," and "flow."

Quality of Life

Quality of life includes both internal and external components. Things outside of us that can contribute to quality of life include satisfying relationships, a healthy environment, and political freedom. In this chapter, we are emphasizing those internal qualities that contribute to a good quality of life such as personal satisfaction, setting personal limits, exercising personal rights, and self-confidence.

Michael B. Frisch, professor of psychology at Baylor University has found that increasing your quality of life can have major positive consequences for you.[6] A better quality of life can result in living longer, it can increase your problem-solving ability for life's annoyances and even contribute to helping people find and keep better jobs. Most importantly, people who have a solid quality of life find their social lives are stronger and more satisfying.

People who are more satisfied with life will likely be more energetic, forgiving, and generous than others who are less satisfied with their lives. Increasing your quality of life can even make you less susceptible to disease.

Obtaining a good quality of life is where you want your life to go after you have minimized the influence of the Voice in your life. For some people, getting rid of the Voice does not automatically improve quality of life. This final chapter points you in the direction for how to obtain a better quality

American Journal of Psychiatry 152(3), 341-351.

5   Seligman, M. E. P. (2004). *Authentic happiness: Using the new positive psychology to realize your potential for lasting fulfillment.* New York: Free Press.

6   Frisch, M. B. (1998). Quality of life therapy and assessment in health care. *Clinical Psychology: Science & Practice* 5(1), 19-40.

of life. The information in this area is increasing dramatically. An excellent reference on the topic of well-being is the book by Daniel Kahneman and his colleagues. Although quite scholarly, for those wanting to dig deeper into the subject, this book will cover topics such as conceptual issues, moods and emotions, personality differences, and social and biological influences.[7]

Subjective Wellbeing

You can observe another perspective to apply to your Christian walk by peering through the research lens of Ed Diener, psychologist at the University of Illinois. He believes that how satisfied you are with your life—your subjective wellbeing—is based on how you describe and evaluate your own life. It is not based on the perceptions or observations of others, even experts.

Your level of subjective wellbeing is a measure of how happy you are. Almost universally, people rate happiness more important than any other aspect of life, including money. Science concurs that happiness is highly desirable because of the outcomes it produces. Others in the field have collaborated to find out what benefits are derived from subjective well-being. Psychologists Sonja Lyubormirsky, Sonja King, and Ed Diener discovered that people who see themselves as happy:

- have stronger immune systems and may even live longer
- are better citizens at work
- are more creative
- tend to be more successful in their particular society
- do better in social relationships
- cope well in difficult situations
- like themselves more than unhappy people do[8]

One conclusion from Dr. Diener's research is the absence of a specific "key" to happiness. Although this may be difficult to accept for some

---

7   Kahneman, D., Diener, E. & Schwarz, N. (Eds.). (1999). *Well-being: The foundations of hedonic psychology*. New York: Russell Sage Foundation.
8   Lyubomirsky, S., King, L. & Diener, E. (2005). The benefits of frequent positive affect: Does happiness lead to success? *Psychological Bulletin* 131(6), 803-855.

Christians, all one needs to do is carefully observe the many unhappy people within our churches. It is true that some studies show that religious people are generally happier than nonreligious people. However, the difference is not great. Since the Bible is not a psychology textbook, nor a manual on successful relationships, many of today's churches include professional counseling as part of their ministry to their congregation. As you will see in the next section, many ingredients are available for being happy. It seems that the more ingredients you have available, the more likely you will be happy.

The happiest people studied in Dr. Diener's lab always had at least two qualities: good mental health and good social relationships.[9] When these two qualities are combined with spirituality, the circle is complete. They become the three legs of the stool upon which we sit.

As the Bible teaches, relationships are critically important for living the Big "H." Married people are generally happier than unmarried people. On average, divorced people are less happy than either of these two groups. Understandably, many widows have a drop in their happiness level for several years after their partner dies. Widowers experience the same drop, but the happiness drop generally does not last as long. This is partially because women's brains are hard-wired to grieve longer than men—an average of two years instead of the six-month grieving period for men. Society can also exacerbate the problem of grieving for women. Many widows are left in precarious financial situations. Since most societies have operated from a patriarchal perspective, widows have had fewer opportunities for finding new situations that can contribute to their happiness.

As with all generalizations about human behavior, however, there are many exceptions to the extent of male grieving. For example, the former Israeli prime minister Menachim Begin never got over his beloved wife's death and resigned his position a year later to live his remaining eight or nine years in seclusion. C.S. Lewis was devastated by his wife Joy's death. He wrote a book about the experience, *A Grief Observed*. It was so personal and filled with such emotional agitation that he did not dare to give his own name as the author.[10] Writer Calvin Trilling's book, *About Alice*, was

---

9   Diener, E. & Seligman, M. (2002). Very happy people. *Psychological Science* 13 80-83.

10   Although his name is now associated with the book, it was originally

written in tribute to his wife who died of cancer and heart disease. A further example is seen in poet laureate Donald Hall's many writings about the pain he endured over the loss of his wife, Jane Kenyon, who was also a renowned poet and such a part of him.

Happiness research has been worldwide instead of confined within the borders of the United States. Dr. Diener and Dr. Myers teamed up to analyze information from more than 900 surveys that involved more than one million people from forty-one nations.[11] These surveys represented people of all ages, sexes, and races.

They found a surprising consistency of happiness within the human population. To measure this, they devised a test based on a 0-to-10 scale. Zero was the low extreme that characterized people who were very unhappy or completely dissatisfied with life; a score of five was neutral and a score of ten represented people who were extremely content with their quality of life. When one considers the vast chasm between wealth and poverty, freedom and totalitarianism, and differences in health conditions around the world, the results were astonishing. They found that most people in all countries were happy—the average score was 6.75! Age, gender, or race did not affect these results.

They did find some differences based on environmental conditions. Groups of people that reported less happiness included hospitalized alcoholics, newly incarcerated inmates, new therapy clients, South African blacks under apartheid, and people living under conditions of political suppression. As expected, significant differences occurred in happiness between very wealthy nations and very poor nations.

You can take the simple questionnaire that they call the *Satisfaction With Life Scale*.[12] It is a short, 5-item instrument designed to measure the

---

published under the pseudonym of N.W. Clerk. He did this because he did not want readers to think that his grief indicated a lack of faith on his part.

11 Myers, D. G. & Diener, E. (1996). The pursuit of happiness: New research uncovers some anti-intuitive insights into how many people are happy and why. *Scientific American* 70-72.

12 Diener, E., Suh, E. & Oishi, S. (1997). Recent findings on subjective wellbeing. *Indian Journal of Clinical Psychology.*

global satisfaction of your life. It only takes about one minute to complete. You will find it in the Appendix 4.

Psychological Wellbeing: The Six Ingredients

Another approach to understanding the Big "H" has found that happiness is composed of six fundamental ingredients of psychological wellbeing: autonomy, environmental mastery, personal growth, positive relations with others, purpose in life, and self-acceptance. Carol Ryff, psychologist at the University of Wisconsin, Madison, began studying psychological wellbeing in the latter half of the twentieth century.[13] She has developed the Scales of Psychological Wellbeing to measure how well a person does on each of these six dimensions. Her research has practical implications for Christians who are seriously interested in deepening their walk with God and showing evidence of the fruit of the Spirit. Working on improving each of the six dimensions or ingredients of psychological wellbeing can be an important part of the process.

Increase Autonomy
Christ told us that since he has set us free, we "shall be free indeed" (John 8:36). Freedom can be burdensome. Freedom means we can no longer hold others accountable for our mistakes because freedom means we must take full responsibility for our lives. Freedom also means we are free from the rules that constrict our lives and constrain our spiritual journey. This was a major struggle in the early church between law and grace. Living under law somehow feels safer and less risky. Living the abundant life is much riskier than living the Christian life based on rules and restrictions.

Psychologist and philosopher Erich Fromm addressed this issue in the middle of the last century by stating that a totalitarian lifestyle may attract people specifically because of the lack of freedom.[14] Denying freedom of choice can keep people from feeling they must risk a wrong decision and thus having to feel guilty for having sinned. The decisions have been made for them by someone else; all they have to do is follow the rules and not think about it.

---

13 Ryff, C. D. (1989). Happiness is everything, or is it? Explorations on the meaning of psychological wellbeing. *Journal of Personality and Social Psychology* 57(6), 1069-1081.

14 Fromm, E. (1941). *Escape from freedom*. New York: Rinehart.

Because autonomy fosters questions and independent thinking, some Christians are suspicious of it. They believe the solution lies in eliminating all doubts about faith and demanding an unswerving obedience to the version of truth that proponents of modern-day legalism hold. But by not allowing Christians to ask questions or entertain doubts, such proponents are inadvertently demeaning them and denying their human dignity as bearers of God's image and as people made free in Christ.

Our faith is anemic when stripped of the dynamic process of doubting. Questions and doubts are characteristic of the healthy spiritual journey. Stories of faithful doubters permeate the Bible. The writers of the Psalms were always wondering why God failed to take action when they thought he should have. They also questioned why it seemed God's promises weren't kept. Many prophets questioned God's actions—even argued with God. (Read the book of Job, for example.) One of the greatest theologians of our day, Paul Tillich, tells us that doubt is essential to being alive.[15] We do not need to protect God from our questions and doubt. As our faith moves through various valleys of doubt, we become stronger with each visit. Devout Christians often base their deep sense of honesty and integrity on doubt. When this is honored, we can grow in grace and become all that God wants us to be. Rob Bell, pastor of Mars Hill Bible Church in Grand Rapids, Michigan encourages and accepts people into his church who have serious doubts about Christianity and faith.[16] Rather than meeting them as an apologist for the faith, he encourages a dialogue, much as Jesus did with people of his day.

From her research on psychological wellbeing, Dr. Ryff has concluded that autonomy is related to self-determination. It's important, then, to free ourselves from those parts of life that can stifle our autonomy. Rather than letting the outside world control us, we need to regulate our behavior from within and not let our decisions and actions be determined by others. Sometimes the "outside world" can be a distorted aspect of Christianity. We need to be wary of these forms of Christianity that have become a mirror

---

15 Tillich, P. (1967). *Systematic Theology*. (Vol. 2). Chicago: University of Chicago Press.
16 Bell, R. (2005). *Velvet Elvis: Repainting the Christian faith*. Grand Rapids, MI: Zondervan.

of our culture. History shows us that a dynamic and energetic Christianity is one that is continually pushing on the cultural and historical limitations. When Augustine wrote (and was later quoted by Martin Luther), "Love God and do as you please," he meant that when love of God comes first, your actions will not only be pleasing to you but also to God. New Christians have a difficult time understanding this concept. As you gain spiritual autonomy, you will find that Christian freedom to love unconditionally is at the heart of spiritual maturity.

Even the often used word "love," can be difficult to get our mind around. Leonard Sweet, currently the E. Stanley Jones Professor of Evangelism at Drew University, Madison, NJ, in his book, *The Three Hardest Words in the World to Get Right*,[17] uses 256 pages just to talk about the three words in the phrase, "I love you." There is so much to learn about love.

Strengthen Environmental Mastery

Some Christians who find themselves in toxic environments find it difficult to leave and move on. The Voice can use your environment in ways to inhibit your walk with God. Strengthening your environment means you need to be able to choose the surroundings that promote your personal growth. Your life has the potential of being continually enriched through active engagement with the world around you. If your sphere of life is narrow, you may want to consider expanding it to experience more of the richness of God's creation. A healthy, nurturing psychological environment is as important for people as the physical environment is for plants. And a toxic environment spewing poisons from negative people into the air, whether at work or in other situations, can be unhealthy and damaging.

Kimberly finally realized that her relationship with Desiree, her sister, kept robbing her of living a rich, full life. As much as she loved her sister, the relationship had always been full of friction since they were teenagers. Kimberly felt Desiree always resented her every time something positive happened. She could no longer share happy events because Desiree always found something negative to say. Although they used to talk daily, Kimberly dreaded hearing the phone ring, fearing that it might be her sister. Time had only made things worse. They even had a long talk about how Kimberly felt

---

17 Sweet, L. (2006). *The three hardest words in the world to get right.* Colorado Springs, CO: WaterBrook Press.

regarding the amount of negativity coming from Desiree, but Desiree was not at all receptive to Kimberly's efforts to see if they could work together to change the situation. Instead, Kimberly was accused of putting down her sister, never appreciating her, and generally being responsible for the misery in Desiree's life. Midway through our class, Kimberly realized that her love for her sister was not enough to help Desiree. She had to make the painful decision to have no more contact because the relationship was negatively affecting her children, her family, and her job.

Sometimes, as you close doors on relationships that are unhealthy for you and that strengthen the Voice's efforts to damage your garden, you can leave the door open for renewed contact at a later time should the other person begin to change. Mastering your environment means that you can have some influence over these complex situations that may come your way. As you master the middle dominoes (thoughts, emotions, sensations, and behavior), you can begin to work on the life domino. Facing new and unfamiliar challenges can also help you develop new and effective coping strategies that will help to bolster your self confidence.

Encourage Personal Growth

"We must try to become mature," admonished the writer to the Hebrews, "and start thinking about more than just the basic things we were taught about Christ" (Hebrews 6:1, CEV). Since the Christian walk is a continuous growth process, we must be open to new experiences. Some Christians have a world view defined by fear and anxiety. Jesus, by his life and words, taught us to go beyond our hesitations and indecisiveness to embrace the fullness of life. Many early Christians believed they must continue to practice the religious rituals and laws of the Hebrew Bible (especially the Torah—the first five books of what Christians call the Old Testament). The apostle Paul was continually preaching the good news that the New Life is more than laws and restrictions. By being open to new experiences, you can continue to develop into the mature Christian that God wants you to be.

As a new Christian, Sam was confused about the rules and regulations he found in different versions of Christianity. He knew that he was expected to avoid sin. He even wondered if Christian growth simply meant avoiding as many sins as possible. Was a true Christian one who avoided the most sins? Would this mean that the longer his sin list, the more things he could avoid and therefore the more pure he would be? As he learned about how the Voice works, he came to the conclusion that this "status by negation" was one of the Voice's tricks. The truth slowly dawned on him: growth was not about avoiding the negative but rather embracing the positive.

Change is the hallmark of personal growth. It does not mean more of the same. Older Christians, who have journeyed far down their Christian path, can look back and see the changes. Had they retained their earlier version of Christianity, they would still be Christian babies living on breast milk (1 Peter 2:2; Hebrews 5:12-14, NEV).

A common mistake is to think the Christian walk is about being absolutely obedient to someone else's version of Christian standards. This type of spirituality reduces Christianity to a set of rules for the benefit of other Christians rather than for the benefit of your relationship to God. As J. B. Phillips put it, "Some . . . modern enthusiastic Christians . . . tend to regard Christianity as a performance. But it still is, as it was originally, a way of living, and in no sense a performance acted for the benefit of the surrounding world."[18] That "surrounding world" can often include other Christians who can hinder our growth by trying to persuade us that they know what is best for us.

Develop Positive Relations with Others

Although we must avoid letting others determine how we should live our lives, it's important to learn how to develop positive relations with other people if we are to experience psychological wellbeing. Timothy had always been shy. As he grew into adulthood, he accepted his shyness as a way of life. He convinced himself that he did not need other people and could live a full life by himself. He was uneasy about this part of his life (the avoidance of social connections) when we explained the psychological importance of other people. At first, he fought this new information. The cognitive dissonance made him uncomfortable, and he considered dropping out of class. But in his small group one week, he decided to bring this matter up and was astounded when someone told him this sounded like the Voice. Maybe he was not doomed to a solitary life after all. As he toyed with the idea of overcoming his shyness, he recognized that his new skills could help him shed this lifestyle. Today, he is a different person. His friends are amazed that he was not always friendly and so much fun to be with.

---

18 Phillips, J. B. (1960). *Your God is too small*. New York: Macmillan.

197

The cornerstone of the Christian life is firmly embedded within our relationships to others. One of Christ's greatest lessons was the breaking of restrictive barriers put on him by religious leaders. Talking to a Samaritan woman at a well seems a bit innocent with today's perspective. Jewish prejudice against Samaritans was stronger than our nation's prejudice against blacks was a hundred years ago. A Jewish traveler would take a longer, out of the way walk from Galilee to Jerusalem just to avoid breathing Samaritan air if he were to take a more direct route. Jesus broke the tribal boundaries of his day so that you can tear down the barriers of your day—even those built by religious leaders.

As you work out your salvation, your warm, trusting relationships with others will eventually extend across all human restrictions, whether they are political, geographical, cultural or religious. Having feelings of empathy and affection for all human beings will take you further on your spiritual journey. Embracing those in our own circle is easy; doing so with those who are different from us is not so easy. The irony is that religion should be the device that melts away all human social impediments. Unfortunately, history shows us that religion can be the source of violent and hate-filled reactions toward those outside a particular religious circle or tradition.

Being positive only toward those who are just like us takes no effort at all. Jesus reminded us, however, that this is not sufficient: "I assure you, when you did it to one of the least of these my brothers and sisters, you were doing it to me" (Matthew 25:40, NLT). Think of the most undesirable, unlovable, or terrifying humans alive and you have an idea who Christ meant by the "least of my brothers and sisters." These are the ones we are to love.

Identify Purpose in Life

In recent years, there has been a renewed emphasis within the Christian community on the fifth component for strengthening Christian maturity: the importance of purpose. This has been largely through the efforts of Rick Warren, pastor of Saddleback Church in Southern California, who wrote *The Purpose Driven Life.*[19] In researching the components of psychological wellbeing, Dr. Carol Ryff came to the conclusion that having a sense of purpose and meaning in your life will contribute substantially to your

19 Warren, R. (2002). *The Purpose Driven Life.* Grand Rapids, MI: Zondervan.

overall wellbeing. This, in turn, we would emphasize, contributes positively to your walk with God. A sense of directedness is not a passive experience but one filled with intentionality, thoughtfulness, and determination to move forward in your Christian journey. It is what the apostle Paul had in mind when he wrote, "I have not yet reached my goal, and I am not perfect, but Christ has taken hold of me. So I keep on running and struggling to take hold of the prize. My friends, I don't feel that I have already arrived. But I forget what is behind, and I struggle for what is ahead. I run toward the goal . . . "(Philippians 3:12-14, CEV).

Katy had always let her environment determine her direction in life. She attended the college of her father, married the man most admired by her mother, and only chose new friends who were approved by her older friends. She only came to our class because her best friend encouraged her to come. She was diligent in her homework because we told her to do so. The idea that she could discover for herself a purpose and meaning to her life was foreign and confusing. As she began to find out who she was, she learned she only defined herself within the presence of other people. This section, identifying purpose in life, helped her to discover who she was apart from others. This made her relationships stronger because she was able to have her real self connect to others.

Having a sense of purpose is also important for filling those voids in your life that can drain your joy for living. Individuals without a purpose in life often experience alienation and depression.[20] Benny had spent most of his weekends on the couch in a depressed state. His friends had moved on because he no longer enjoyed their company, nor did his friends have fun when he was around. Fighting the Voice helped Benny relieve the intensity of the depression, but he still felt a deep void in his life. He tried to pray, but it did not seem to help. Reading his Bible was like reading the telephone book. When we began teaching about the importance of purpose, something clicked on for him. He realized that his life had always been built on just getting by. Although bright and talented, he never had a sense of where he was going in life. By middle age, it all seemed so hopeless and empty. He has now found purpose in several different areas: working with young children in Sunday School, becoming physically fit by running

---

20 Brickman, P. & Coates, D. (Eds.). (1987). *Commitment and mental health.* Englewood Cliffs, NJ: Prentice-Hall.

marathons, and volunteering to work with homeless people. As a result, his children are happier, he has had several promotions at work, and his wife also feels rejuvenated.

For some Christians, one of the stumbling blocks to finding purpose is their loss of what John Eldridge calls *desire*—that longing for a richer, fuller experience of all that God has to offer them. Life's disappointments and hurts have taken their toll and have muted their soul's cry for something more. In his book, *The Journey of Desire*, Eldridge—founder and director of Ransomed Heart Ministries in Colorado Springs, Colorado—expresses his belief that igniting desire will awaken the ability to live life fully.[21] You will know when your life is fired up with desire and is filled with purpose because you will be spending a considerable portion of your time being involved in more activities that are consistent with your values. Purposeful activities are those that you have chosen freely, which you can approach flexibly, and have fully integrated into your daily life.

Foster Self-acceptance

The final skill for enhancing your Christian walk, based on the six ingredients that Dr. Carol Carol Ryff has shown are essential for psychological well being, is the ability to accept yourself as you are now. Acceptance of one's self includes both the good and the bad. Some Christians can accept the negative parts because they acknowledge themselves as sinners. These same people sometimes find that accepting the positive aspects of themselves is more difficult. Self-acceptance means accepting all of you. Accepting your healthy attributes does not make you less humble.

To not accept all of yourself is to erect a barrier between you and God. We know that God accepts you just as you are. If you do not to the same, you are saying "no" to God. You are telling God that his creation, *you*, is unacceptable. This weakens your spiritual formation.

Sasha was a strikingly beautiful young woman who could not accept her defects. She overemphasized them in a way that interfered with her life. She was so convinced that her face was imperfect that she desperately tried to convince cosmetic surgeons to make her more beautiful. She was dismayed that they would not help her. Eventually, she realized this behavior

---

21 Eldredge, J. (2000). *The journey of desire: Searching for the life we've only dreamed of.* Nashville: Nelson Books.

was promoted by her sense of worthlessness. The Voice had told her that she was only acceptable if she looked perfect. After she began successfully fighting the Voice, she was able to find a place within herself for accepting every part of who she was.

Self-acceptance does not mean you no longer need to make any changes. Change is in everybody's future. While working on self improvement, accepting yourself with all your flaws and emotional warts is still important. One of the Voice's favorite targets is your self-acceptance. If it can weaken this part of you, all other parts of your life are much more accessible to the Voice's tricks.

Franklin loved talking about himself as a sinner. He had a large catalog of past misdeeds. Being a forgiven sinner was his life. Accepting any goodness about himself was very difficult. The Voice had convinced him that if he admitted having any good qualities, he would immediately become full of pride and violate the standard of Christian humility. He struggled for a long time and took our class again. During this second class, be began to realize that God was not embarrassed or uncomfortable with his good qualities, so why should he be ashamed to accept them? The gradual acceptance of his complete being spilled over into all the areas of his life, and he became a new person.

Not only must you accept yourself in the present, you must also accept your past. You cannot change your past. You cannot control your future. Only the present is available to you for mastery. As you have already learned, this means concentrating on your successes. If the Voice can get you to forget your successes, then each new one seems like the first one. It would be as though none of the earlier successes had ever occurred. Or, to put it another way, it would be like trying to build a stone fence, but every time you laid down a stone, someone took it away.

Flow

We've seen that psychologists write about happiness using many different terms: "quality of life," "subjective well being," "psychological wellbeing," and "flow." We now come to the fourth of these terms relating to life at its fullest. Psychologist Mihaly Csikszentmihalyi, who directs the Quality of Life Research Center at the Claremont Graduate University in California, uses the term "flow" to describe those times when a person is so totally immersed in an experience that he or she seems to lose all track of time in the sheer exhilaration of the moment.[22] At such times, creativity can flow with ease, the activity in which one is engaged seems effortless, and zest and energy surpass anything experienced in ordinary moments.

His research found that about 15% of people never experience flow while the same number experienced it at least once a day. Everybody else will find flow in their activities in differing degrees.

Flow can be found in different areas of life, for example sports, music, painting, writing, friendships. The experience is often described as "being at one with the moment." An athlete in this state would not be aware of anything outside herself. She would not notice the crowds, referees, the stadium or even the equipment being used. She would only be aware of the moments of competing and the accompanying feelings. In sports, this state of ecstasy is often referred to as "being in the zone."

The awareness that occurs in flow is often different from the normal awareness we experience. Sometimes people feel as if they are an outsider watching themselves engage in an activity. This does not happen in flow. The awareness of the activity and the activity itself are the same experience.

Flow is felt when you are doing something you enjoy that can bring a sense of accomplishment: woodworking, solving a puzzle, making a quilt, or any pastime that can bring enjoyment. A clear sense of what you want to accomplish within an activity is one of the prerequisites for being in flow. Having a strong sense of inner clarity about your expectations is common. This would mean what you are and are not capable of accomplishing.

As in the example above, an ability to deeply concentrate on your activity is one of the hallmarks of flow. You do not have to cope with a wandering mind when in flow. This focused attention brings the added benefit of inner serenity and a feeling like you have gone beyond the boundaries of your everyday self.

Flow also brings about a distorted sense of time. "Where did the time go?" is a question often asked when an activity ends that has been saturated with flow. Somehow, flow interrupts our brain's ability to track time during the activity.

---

22 Csikszentmihalyi, M. (1997). *Finding flow.* .New York: Basic Books.

To better your chances at experiencing flow, you need to do activities that are neither too easy nor too hard. This balance can increase the likelihood that an activity can be a flow activity. Activities that you do just for the sake of doing them can also produce flow. This happens when an activity is its own reward. Personal control also enhances the opportunity for flow. You want to do things that do not make you anxious or produce boredom. Having a strong sense of confidence in what you are doing makes it more likely that you can have and enjoy flow.

Emotional Intelligence

Happiness is more often found in people with high emotional intelligence (EI). This term was first coined by two Yale psychologists, Peter Salovey and John Mayer.[23] They defined emotional intelligence as a combination of effective self expression and emotional regulation. They believe that high EI can contribute significantly to an improved quality of life. When you have a high EI Quotient you are more able to experience your own emotions and communicate them effectively. Your relationships are able to be more satisfying because of your emotional engagement.

Like any set of skills, you can learn emotional intelligence. This set of skills not only gives you more rewarding relationships with people but also allows you a richer and more intimate relationship with God. In his book, *Emotional Intelligence*, Daniel Goleman —a psychologist by training, but working as a journalist —describes the ingredients that make up EI.[24] As you look at each of these qualities, you'll notice a similarity to other aspects of psychological wellbeing.

Self Awareness

Being self-aware means observing yourself more realistically. The Voice urges you to see yourself unrealistically —as not having good qualities or being loaded with bad qualities. Being realistic means you can recognize the difference between your healthy emotional pain and your unhealthy emotional pain. As you gain competency recognizing the difference, you build a larger vocabulary for your feelings. An expanded vocabulary helps

23 Salovey, P. & Mayer, J. D. (1990). *Emotional intelligence. Imagination, Cognition & Personality* 185-211.

24 Goleman, D. (1995). *Emotional intelligence: Why it can matter more than IQ*. New York: Bantam Books.

you experience the richness and emotional wealth of life. As you increase your emotional intelligence, you also increase your awareness of the relationship between your thoughts, feelings, and behavior.

Personal Decision Making

Just being persons of faith doesn't automatically and continually make us wise decision makers. As you have learned from the section on guilt in the emotions chapter, living a guilt-free life depends on the basis from which you make choices. God does not desire that we act as automatons. You need to make decisions by fully understanding the consequences of your potential choices.

Tiffany had always believed that the best decisions were ones supported by Scripture. Although Scripture was a strong foundation for her, she began to realize that today's culture is vastly different from Biblical times. So many issues that cropped up regularly for her seemed to have no reference in the Bible. As she became more familiar with the work of the enemy Voice, she discovered that it can turn good things into bad. The Voice had convinced Tiffany to use the Bible as a fortune cookie. The more she became aware of the Voice's devious lies, she knew that God wanted her to be a mature adult by using her intelligence. She began to live life by making her own decisions and accepting the consequences of these decisions.

Her new course of action meant she began looking at consequences she liked and wanted and the ones she did not like or want. Tiffany began to pick the consequences that were the best for her under the circumstances. The Voice tried to keep her from doing this by telling her she was offending God and becoming a marginal Christian. The Voice even tried to bolster its arguments by quoting Bible verses and snippets from sermons she had heard in church.

If the Voice tries to block your making decisions that are based on responsible choices, you need to negate its life-destroying influence. By getting you to live by rules rather than choices, the Voice's instructions can hold you back from the freedom of living in Gods grace.

Managing Feelings

This is another emotional intelligence skill you are now very good at performing. Since you can tell the difference between healthy emotional pain and unhealthy emotional pain, you can quickly monitor the Voice's messages and decide which feelings and behaviors are associated with particular keywords. Additionally, you have a variety of effective skills for dealing with healthy painful emotions.

In the past, every time Norman felt emotional distress, he would do anything he could to get rid of it as quickly as possible. Instead of crying, he would go outside and play basketball by himself or any buddies who were available. Stress was effectively managed by a six-pack. He would walk out of the house when he and his wife had disagreements. He was amazed to discover in the class that not all painful emotions are unacceptable. He discussed with his other small group members how he had missed God's alarm clock by not paying attention to his painful feelings. Resentment was his most frequent vermin. One day during his daily Bible reading he came across the following in Romans: "And it shall be, that in the place where it was said unto them, Ye are not my people, There shall they be called sons of the living God." (9:26, ASV). It was like sitting next to a large gong being struck. God opened Norman's eyes by revealing to him that all of creation belongs to God. If God loved all people unconditionally, Norman realized that he could no longer devalue another human to the point it ended in resentment.

Handling Stress

Stress is caused by worry (the Voice) which activates your sympathetic nervous system. You have two solutions to minimizing stress in your life. Fighting the Voice is an excellent way for preventing stress since the sympathetic nervous system is often activated by worry. Spiritual Direction—the organization that helps people "develop a deeper relationship with the spiritual aspect of being human"—encourages people to use meditation as a corrective for stress. There are many types of meditation from prayerful meditation (advocated by C. S. Lewis) to walking meditation.

We encourage people to use three skills which are very effective for reducing stress: natural breathing, mind-calming, and muscle relaxation. Natural breathing occurs when you breathe in and push out your diaphragm at the same time. This must also be done slowly: inhaling on a slow count to five and then immediately exhaling at the same speed. Slowing your breathing means a complete natural breath will take about ten to twelve seconds. Additionally, you need to pause after each exhale. Start the inhale whenever it feels natural to do so.

Muscle relaxation is systematically tensing and releasing various muscles in your body. We often start people by having them do this with fifteen different muscles. Each group of muscles, from their feet to the top of their head, takes about a minute. The total process takes about seventeen to eighteen minutes.

When the muscle relaxation is complete, you want to begin a mind calming technique. Some people attempt to merely "empty" their mind. Others need to think of something pleasant. This is done for about two to three minutes. Mind wandering is common at the beginning but need not be discouraging. With time you will be able to concentrate and stay locked on a calm mind.

Remember, that these three skills are like any other skill. They need to be practiced on a regular basis. Many people think they are only to be used when they are stressed. That is like learning to swim after you fall out of the boat. We encourage people to over-practice these skills so that they become automatic.

Making these methods a part of your natural routine and developing a healthy lifestyle can fulfill your role as a good steward for the life that you have been given. Good nutrition, exercise, and sufficient sleep can also contribute to a healthy life and less stressful life.

Empathy

As you become centered on supervising your thoughts, emotions, and behavior, you can find more time for others. Moving your focus from "me" to "not-me, but-human-just-like-me" is a way to become more empathic to your "neighbors"—even those who may repulse or intimidate you. By understanding others' feelings and concerns and taking their perspective, you can forgive others easier.

Jodie began to realize near the end of our class that she was becoming "narcissistic." Her entire life, for as long as she could remember, revolved around making herself better. She had a shelf full of self help books. Every support group in town knew her on a first-name basis. The money spent on decades of counseling would have paid for a new exotic foreign car. In a flash, she realized that the Voice had even used her attempts at self improvement to keep her at a plateau. She told us during the last class that she had gotten rid of all her books, scheduled volunteer work during support group times, and talked to her counselor about terminating her therapy. To her surprise her therapist agree that would be an excellent idea.

Empathy helps you to become less fearful of what others might think or say. It also helps you to move away from prejudice and being judgmental as you grow in your appreciation of the differences between all of God's people.

Communication

Emotional intelligence includes the ability to relate to another person at more than superficial levels. Doing this depends on finding the right balance between being a good talker and one who can listen and ask meaningful questions.

Roy was struggling with the communication problems his wife kept talking about. He thought he was a good talker but had to admit that he became tongue-tied and confused around women. We taught him how to use "female-speak" and he began practicing with his wife. He had to listen by being present and using appropriate body language. Understanding that women process information aloud (men tend to do it internally), Roy was able to realize that his wife's talking demonstrated her desire to connect with him. He had thought she talked in order to pass information to him. It was all about relating emotionally, and if she presented him with a problem, she did not expect him to solve it but simply to listen to her in a caring way. Eventually, he was able to share his own feelings with her, tentatively at first, then with more depth and substance.

Good communication is all about being present with the person who is speaking and trying to stay connected even when you become distracted. Communication is the very essence of good relationships. It is about having a sincere interest in knowing about the other person at a personal level. Effective communication allows you to disagree or even argue without taking it personally or becoming frightened.

Self-Disclosure

Christians with high emotional intelligence tend to value openness not only among other believers but with people who do not share their values. Some Christians remain close-minded to the rest of the world because they think their only purpose in life is to save souls. Consequently, their only allowable motivation for contact with non-believers is to proselytize them and "bring them to the Lord." In this frame of mind, befriending an unbeliever or reaching out to someone who is hurting or living in poverty is not acceptable merely as an act of Christian love but rather as a means to an end—getting that person converted or persuading him or her to come to our church. The late Dr. Edward J. Carnell, former professor and president of Fuller Seminary, sarcastically described that attitude in his comment, "Handing out tracts is much more important than founding a hospital."[25]

Although having a well articulated set of Christian beliefs is important, the Bible is very clear that loving our neighbor is more important than how our beliefs differ from those of our neighbor. Self-disclosure helps us to build trust with others. It means taking the risk of getting close to those who are unattractive and undesirable by the world's standards or who do not share our attitudes toward life.

Insight

All humans live with internal contradictions and patterns of acting that do not make sense to others. Christians are no different. How often have you noticed the disparity between a person's public prayers and his or her private life? Identifying inconsistent patterns in your emotional life and behavior is part of your faith journey. With the Voice reduced to an occasional annoyance in your life, you can scrutinize your life with less fear and apprehension. One of the most continuous comments our students make is how much more they know about themselves after learning the material. They begin to see themselves as others see them.

Joyce had always had difficulty accepting compliments from others. Her first reaction when getting a compliment was to negate it either silently to herself or verbally to the person talking to her. During the class, she realized that this reaction was linked to the Voice's continually having her

---

25 Carnell, E. J. (1959). *The case for orthodox theology*. Philadelphia: Westminster Press.

focusing on her faults. When she became proficient at fighting the Voice and indicated a desire to work on this problem, she used an exercise we call, "Your Faults Are Not Your Fault." She learned the difference between having human faults and condemning herself for having them. Her goal was to realize that she was more than her faults. She began by acknowledging that she was able to tolerate the faults of others but had been using a different standard for her own faults. The exercise began by having Joyce respond thoughtfully to the following statements:

- ❏ Name people you know who have similar faults to yours.
- ❏ Think of those you have cared about whose faults were more severe than yours.
- ❏ Consider people who you know who are not perfect.

When Joyce had spent several days carefully thinking about other people's flaws, she discovered that she was able to care about them. Finally, her last step was to ponder her flaws and faults through the eyes of other people. As she thought about people who loved her, she began to comprehend at a deep level that people who loved her would do so whether she changed or stayed the same. The more she concentrated on what people loved about her, the more she was able to strengthen her buffer between herself and the Voice.

You can imagine that the Voice released its vermin at her full force. The stranglehold it had on her was about to be broken and it would lose dominance over her. She would have been unable to complete this exercise prior to learning the Voice fighting skills. When she began to weaken the power of the Voice, she was able to build up her own strength.

Insight is more effective when you have the skills and tools to change what is interfering with your Christian growth. As you see unhealthy patterns in your life, you can begin to approach them with honesty and integrity. The stronger you become in your Christian walk, the easier you can accept feedback and criticism for your own evaluation. Insight is crucial for continued growth. A major component of insight is being able to find your personal dreams and life's passions. Bruce Wilkinson has written a helpful story about a "Nobody named Ordinary" who lived in the Land of Familiar.[26] This story is a fable about pursuing one's dreams. We

---

26 Wilkinson, B. (2003). *The dream giver*. Sisters, OR: Multnomah

have worked with people who struggled with the Voice and seemed to be limited in their progress. When they identified a dream buried deep within their soul, they came alive once they began to pursue what God had placed within them.

Spiritual insight is often clouded by a Christianity that is too familiar and narrow. Philip Yancey, editor at large of *Christianity Today*, has written a book titled *Finding God in Unexpected Places*.[27] He shows us how traces of God can be found in the most surprising and astonishing circumstances and locations. Insight means looking beyond the every day and discovering God where we least expected God to be.

Self-Acceptance

As we already discussed above in describing Dr. Carol Carol Ryff's ingredients for psychological well being, some Christians have a problem with self-acceptance. They believe that pride is a sin and therefore harboring any positive thoughts about oneself is something to be avoided. But only *false* pride is unacceptable. False pride is a style of self-disclosure tainted with boasting and bragging about one's accomplishments without grasping its impact on the listener. Such pride is motivated by insecurity and competitiveness. But true pride is a matter of personal honesty. It requires you to recognize *both* your strengths and weaknesses. It is a mistake to deny your strengths while thinking that a declaration of weakness is a sign of saintliness.

You have the God-given right to feel satisfaction in what you do and seeing yourself in a positive light. By seeing yourself in a balanced way, you'll find it much easier to live with your spiritual warts and human flaws, because they are balanced by so many fine qualities. That doesn't mean you have to deny your deficits or proclaim them as a mark of an impure heart. Instead, you can laugh at yourself for being imperfect. Laughing at yourself is not the same as putting yourself down. It is a way of connecting with the deep parts of yourself as a human being, As the Christian writer, Anne Lamott, has said, "Laughter is carbonated holiness.[28]

Publishers.

27 Yancey, P. (2005). *Finding God in unexpected places*, New York: Doubleday.

28 Lamott, A. (2005). *Plan B: Further thoughts on faith*. New York: Penguin Books.

Acceptance needs to embrace your total person—thoughts, feelings, actions, and appearance. In our visually oriented society, accepting our visible flaws can be difficult. Jenny was so critical of her physical imperfection she would avoid mirrors whenever possible. When she would see her reflection, she immediately began a long litany of self abuse. When she understood this was merely the Voice trying to rob her of her wellbeing, she decided to focus on changing this part of her life. After she became proficient in fighting the Voice, we gave her an exercise to help her become more objective about her physical appearance. She would stand in front of a full length mirror without clothes. As she looked at all the parts of her body, she was to write down answers to the following questions:

- What do you like? What do you not like?
- What is changeable? What is not changeable?

Instead of beginning from the premise that she should have a perfect body, we had her begin from the fact that no one has a "perfect" body. She began by looking at her hair and scanned her body down to her toes. She listed the parts of her body she saw in the mirror. For each part, she indicated whether she liked or disliked that part using a scale from one to five. She used the same scale to indicate whether she could change that part or not. As she did this exercise many times—continuing to ward off the Voice, which tried to discourage her from doing the exercise—she began to gain more clarity about loving and accepting herself as God did.

Personal responsibility

The final ingredient on the list of what characterizes emotional intelligence is personal responsibility, a quality we have already covered in chapter 9. Personal responsibility involves the acceptance of the potential consequences of your actions without blame or excuse. Maintaining this attitude toward life allows you to become spiritually alive and mature. Personal responsibility also includes knowing when to depend on our own resources or to ask others for help.

Social Relationships

Emotional intelligence does not exist in a vacuum. It cannot exist apart from other people. Having a supportive and caring social network is vital to maintaining a solid level of happiness and spiritual wellbeing. Everyone differs in their degree of need for social contacts. God has made some people content with a minimal number of close friends, while other people were created with a need for many friends.

If the Voice has thwarted your need for more friends, then it is now time to begin a process for increasing your social support network. You can begin by completing the following Interpersonal Life Chart that focuses on six aspects of your relationships with other people: How often do you see or otherwise contact these people? What qualities are acceptable and unacceptable for each of your contacts? What are some common interests you share with each of these people? What are the satisfaction levels? And, in what ways can you improve these relationships?

When this exercise is complete, you can use all the skills you have learned to devise strategies for making your interpersonal relationships better. As with all gardens, some plants need to be culled and others nurtured. You will want to practice these strategies in your real world. You can monitor them in your journal to see how effective they are. The monitoring process will help you figure out ways to alter or to make changes for a particular strategy to make it work better for you.

Begin by describing your current social network. You can use the following table (use more paper if you need to) or make your own.

Table 11-A: My Social Network

	CONTACT FREQUENCY	ACCEPTABLE QUALITIES	UNACCEPTABLE QUALITIES	COMMON INTERESTS	SATISFACTION LEVEL	IMPROVEMENT AREAS
Loved ones						
Best friends						
Work or Social Contacts						
Regular Friends						
Acquaintances						
Comments:						

When you have completed the preceding chart, you can begin working on your Interpersonal Action Plan. Identify a specific person from the previous chart you would like to deal with better. It could be a person who makes your life miserable or it could be a person you want to know better. The Voice may try to make either situation more difficult by worming its way back into this exercise. If this happens, deal with the Voice first and then complete the exercise. At this point in your life, you have a large toolbox full of skills that you can apply to this exercise.

Table 11-B: My Interpersonal Action Plan

TARGET PERSON	SITUATION
What do I want to accomplish?	
MY STRATEGIES	
How will I deal with the Voice?	
How will I soothe myself?	
How can I be mindful?	
What will I do differently?	
What will I do if its doesn't work?	
Which emotional intelligence skill will use?	
My own questions?	

Hope

Hope is also one of the great themes of Christianity (1 Corinthians 13:13). In the history of the Christian church, it has been a major adaptive response to times of stress and desperation. Christians have found hope to be a necessary ingredient for emotional survival during times of disastrous circumstances such as severe loss or incurable and terminal illnesses. Some scholars make a distinction between wishing and hoping. They believe that wishing is more concrete and directed toward specific outcomes (a suitable mate, gaining a special reward). Furthermore, hope is more global such as hoping to be set free, to be understood and recognized, or to be reconciled to other people.

Ancient Jewish culture established an entire genre of hope in their apocalyptic writings. It was full of symbolism and fantasy images for a better future. It brought hope to the Jewish people through God's future action in times of present oppression. The writings saw a time in the future when God would overthrow the oppressors and the people would be exalted and free of persecution.

In the New Testament, fifty-eight verses speak of hope. Saint Paul gives us a stunning description of hope: "For it was by hope that we were saved; but if we see what we hope for, then it is not really hope. For who of us hopes for something that we see? But if we hope for what we do not see, we wait for it with patience" (Romans 8:24-25, GNT). In other words, he does not base salvation on certainty but on hope and faith. Some Christians expend enormous amounts of time and energy trying to convince themselves and others of the certainty of God and the Christian faith. Certainty is the province of science and mathematics and that is why scientists have nothing to say about the certainty of religious faith.

Nevertheless, hope has been the subject of much research. Rick Snyder,[29] a psychologist at the University of Kansas, is a leading scientist who studies hope. His research has found that hope is composed of two components: *agency* and *pathways*. What he means by agency is your sense of determination in meeting your personal goals. A pathway refers to your perceived ability to find and use ways to reach your goals.

Sometimes people see hope as a passive waiting for something good to happen. From his research, Dr. Snyder shows that hope is more than wishful thinking. It involves a willfulness and resoluteness along with a direction for getting to a goal. The writer to the Hebrews talked about such an attitude, too. "We who have run for our very lives to God have

29 Snyder, C. R., Harris, C., Anderson, J. R., Holleran, S. A., Irving, L. M. & Sigmon, S. T., et al. (1991). The will and the ways: Development and validation of an individual-differences measure of hope. *Journal of Personality and Social Psychology* 60(4), 570-585.

every reason to grab the promised hope with both hands and never let go" (Hebrews 6:18, MSG).

Additional research has shown the practical benefits of having a high degree of hope. A study of college athletes found that hope predicted athletic outcomes in female cross-country athletes.[30] Another study looked at 111 mothers of 5- to 18-yr-old children who had serious illnesses such as cerebral palsy, spina bifida, or insulin-dependent diabetes mellitus. The researchers found that hope served as a resilience factor against distress in mothers of children with chronic physical conditions. Mothers who had high perceptions of hope found that hope acted as a buffering effect when their stress was high.[31]

In a 6-year study, individual differences in hope for entering college freshmen predicted overall grade point averages in spite of differences in entrance examination scores. More students with high hope scores graduated than students with low hope.[32] Hope can act as a safeguard against feeling overwhelmed in stressful situations. People with high levels of hope evaluate difficult circumstances as challenging but not overwhelming. It can also act as a powerful protective factor against depression.

Hope is another skill you can learn. With practice you can increase hope in your life.[33] The techniques are similar to what you have already learned. The following is a checklist for the tools you need to increase hope.

- Identify the Voice that attempts to dampen hope
- Accurately name your emotions
- Be clear about what problem you are dealing with and who owns

---

30 Curry, L. A., Snyder, C. R., Cook, D. L., Ruby, B. C. & Rehm, M. (1973). Role of hope in academic and sport achievement. *Journal of Personality & Social Psychology* 73(6), 1257-1267.

31 Horton, T. V. & Wallander, J. L. (2001). Hope and social support as resilience factors against psychological distress of mothers who care for children with chronic physical conditions. *Rehabilitation Psychology* 46(4), 382-399.

32 Snyder, C. R., Shorey, H. S., Cheavens, J., Pulvers, K. M., Adams, V. H. I. & Wiklund, C. (1994). Hope and academic success in college. *Journal of Educational Psychology* 94(4), 820-826.

33 Nezu, A. M., Nezu, C. M. & Perri, M. G. (1989). *Problem-solving therapy for depression: Theory, research and clinical guidelines.* New York: Wiley.

it (property line issues)

- Generate a variety of alternative solutions to a specific problem
- Systematically evaluate the consequences of each potential solution
- Evaluate and monitor the outcomes of your actions

Those of you who have already filled several notebooks with your writing assignments have, more than likely, already experienced more hope in your life.

Increasing Happiness Skills

Now that you better understand what the ingredients of happiness are, you can begin some happiness-building exercises for applying them to your Christian life. By far, the best available resources on happiness are those produced by Dr. Martin Seligman. We encourage you to read and apply the wisdom found in his books, which we have listed in the references section at the end of this book. In addition, you will gain even more valuable tools by going to his websites and taking what Dr. Seligman has to offer. One website is called Authentic Happiness,[34] the other is Reflective Happiness.[35] The first one gives you access to eighteen (as of this writing) free questionnaires.

By joining the second one for a small fee, you will be kept up-to-date with new happiness tests and questionnaires, a newsletter, a community forum, and question-and-answer sessions with Dr. Seligman. The most exciting part of the website is the monthly happiness-building program you will receive. Remember, the field of positive psychology is quite new. By using these resources, you can stay abreast of the new techniques that continue to emerge for building your life and sharing it with others.

Seligman's Gratitude Visit

In his book, *Everybody's Normal Till You Get to Know Them*,[36] Dr. John Ortberg, psychologist and pastor, tells us that one of the most profound aspects of a healthy relationship is something he calls heartfelt gratitude.

---

34 http://www.authentichappiness.org
35 http://www.reflectivehappiness.com
36 Ortberg, J. (2003). *Everybody's normal till you get to know them.* Grand

This quality is important for Christian community. Science recently developed a method for reaching out to others in gratitude. It is an exercise created by Dr. Seligman. He calls it the Gratitude Visit and it is taken from his book, *Authentic Happiness*.[37] We list Seligman's key points below and encourage you to use this series of steps as often as you can.

- Select one important person from your past who has made a major positive difference in your life and to whom you have never fully expressed your thanks.
- Do not confound this selection with newfound romantic love, or with the possibility of future gain.
- Write a testimonial just long enough to cover one page.
- Take your time composing this: It may take several weeks; e.g., composing on a bus or as you fall asleep at night.
- Invite that person to your home, or travel to that person's home.
- It is important you do this face-to-face, not just in writing or on the phone.
- Do not tell the person the purpose of the visit in advance; a simple "I just want to see you" will suffice.
- Wine and cheese do not matter, but bring a laminated version of your testimonial with you as a gift.
- When all settles down, read your testimonial aloud slowly, with expression, and with eye contact.
- Then let the other person react unhurriedly.
- Reminisce together about the concrete events that make this person so important to you.

Signature Strengths

In his book, *Who You Are When No One's Looking*,[38] Bill Hybels lists character traits that belong on the endangered species list of our culture. These traits include courage, discipline, vision, endurance, and love.

Rapids, MI: Zondervan.

37 Seligman, M. E. P. (2004). Authentic happiness: Using the new positive psychology to realize your potential for lasting fulfillment. New York: Free Press.

38 Hybels, B. (1987). *Who you are when no one's looking*. Urbana, IL: InterVarsity.

Psychology echoes this concern. In 1998, Dr. Seligman helped begin a project called Values in Action (VIA) to identify scientifically determined human character strengths. The project members set out to find what wise people had to say about character traits from the beginning of recorded history. Their research found that across time and all cultures, all philosophies and all religions, people agree that human character can be summed up in six general categories: Wisdom, Courage, Justice, Humanity, Temperance, and Spirituality. These six character traits—often called virtues or moral traits—appear to be almost universal. The researchers found that all cultures value them for their own sake—from the Inuit to the Masai to the American to the Iranian.

As work continued on this project, the researchers subdivided these six broad categories into twenty-four "strengths" of character. The goal of the project is to show people how to enhance these human qualities in daily living. Here is a list of the twenty-four signature strengths.[39]

- Curiosity/Interest in the World
- Love of Learning
- Judgment/Critical Thinking/Open-Mindedness
- Ingenuity/Originality/Practical Intelligence/Street Smarts
- Social Intelligence/Personal Intelligence/Emotional Intelligence
- Perspective
- Valor and Bravery
- Perseverance/Industry/Diligence
- Integrity/Genuineness/Honesty
- Kindness and Generosity
- Loving and Allowing Oneself to Be Loved
- Citizenship/Duty/Teamwork/Loyalty
- Fairness and Equity
- Leadership
- Self-Control
- Prudence/Discretion/Caution
- Humility and Modesty
- Appreciation of Beauty and Excellence

---

39 If you are interested in exploring your personal strengths further you can complete the 240-item VIA Inventory of Strengths (VIA-IS) at http://www.viastrengths.org/index.aspx?ContentID=34.

- Gratitude
- Hope/Optimism/Future-Mindedness
- Spirituality/Sense of Purpose/Faith/Religiousness
  Forgiveness and Mercy
- Playfulness and Humor
- Zest/Passion/Enthusiasm

Chris Peterson, psychology professor at the University of Michigan, developed a questionnaire for discovering your signature strengths. More than a quarter of a million people from two hundred nations have completed it. By taking this questionnaire[40], you have the benefit of being able to compare yourself with other people like you around the world. Once you have the results, you will know your top five character strengths. These are called your Signature Strengths. Dr. Martin Seligman describes a signature strength as having the following criteria:

- A sense of ownership and authenticity ("This is the real me").
- A feeling of excitement while displaying it, particularly at first.
- A rapid learning curve as the strength is first practiced.
- A sense of yearning to find new ways to use it.
- A feeling of inevitability in using the strength ("Try and stop me").
- Invigoration rather than exhaustion after using the strength.
- Creation and pursuit of personal projects that revolve around it.
- Joy, zest, enthusiasm, even ecstasy while using it.

The twist is that once you have identified your Signature Strengths, you need to use them as much as possible. Rather than try to improve your lower ranked strengths you want to practice one or more of your Signature Strengths every day. The more you engage in those character traits that are meaningful to you, the more meaningful life will be to you. Max Lucado, pastor of Oak Hills Church in San Antonio, Texas, supports this emphasis when he encourages people to find their strengths as a way to trust God.[41] All people have strengths, and using them is one of the best ways to honor God's presence in your life.

---

40 You can take the VIA Signature Strengths Questionnaire by going to http://www.authentichappiness.sas.upenn.edu/questionnaires.aspx
41 Lucado, M. (2006). *The cure for the common life*. Nashville: W Publishing Group.

Summary

Happiness (of the Big "H" variety) has many elements: psychological wellbeing, emotional intelligence, strong emotional connections, hope, gratitude, and signature strengths. These are all part of becoming whole. Christians hear a lot about growing in their faith and becoming more spiritually mature, yet are seldom shown how to move along this path. Hopefully, this chapter has given you some tools from both the Bible and psychological research to enhance your lifelong faith journey.

Your growth and maturity in Christ have no limits. God has put no boundaries on far you can travel on your Christian journey. As you continue to use these skills, you will become more absorbed and engaged with life; you will have a more intimate sense of God in your life; and you will move to new heights you never expected to reach. Using these skills as often as possible will make them stronger and more pleasing at a very profound level in your soul.

Assignment

Make a worksheet like the following one and use such a worksheet each week. You will want to work on practicing one or more of these components of happiness every day. Some people start with the one they need to master the most. Others do just the opposite and refine the skills at which they are already quite good.

After you have chosen the skill or skills you want to practice, think of ways to do this during the day. You may want to improve your sense of autonomy by uncovering some religious rules that may be hindering your walk with God. Through prayer and study, you can move beyond these barriers into a more vibrant life of faith.

The same goes for each of the other five factors. This is an exercise that you may want to make part of your lifestyle. By monitoring, evaluating, and upgrading these parts of Christian Wellbeing, you can be actively moving to parts of your faith you never thought possible.

Worksheets may appear overwhelming at first. Rather than throw yourself full force into using them, go at your own pace and get used to only one or even just a part of one. Our students and readers tell us worksheets help them to focus in an otherwise busy world.

After you use them and understand the value of the worksheet concept, feel free to make your own. The research is adamant in showing that good record keeping is one of the keys to successful personal progress. Whatever you can do to enhance your Christian growth is always done to the glory of God.

Table 11-C: Psychological Wellbeing

	INCREASE AUTONOMY	ENVIRONMENTAL MASTERY	PERSONAL GROWTH	POSITIVE RELATIONS	PURPOSE IN LIFE	SELF ACCEPTANCE
Sunday						
Monday						
Tuesday						
Wednesday						
Thursday						
Friday						
Saturday						

Writing Tip #1

You can take Satisfaction With Life Scale (SWLS) as often as you like. It can be a good indicator for how well your new skills are working. Before beginning a new self-enhancement procedure, complete the SWLS and record your score. A month or two later, take it again and compare the results.

Writing Tip #2

When completing the Christian Wellbeing Worksheet, you can choose which ingredients you plan to work on. Decide each week which items you want to emphasize. Depending on how the week progresses you may decide to make changes before the week is out. Be creative in using this worksheet. Use it any way that is beneficial for you.

Writing Tip #3

You can make and use an Emotional Intelligence Worksheet for yourself similar to the above worksheet. This chapter has much material, so feel free to work at your own pace. You can work through the skills sequentially or decide what order is best for you. Although we did not provide a worksheet for improving your Emotional Intelligence, by now you can create your own.

Writing Tip #4

Improving your social network is done in two parts. First, take time to describe your current relationships using Table 11A entitled My Social Network. Do this in several sittings. When you have completed it to your satisfaction, pick one person and develop an Interpersonal Action Plan to help you decide how to improve the relationship.

Writing Tip #5

If you decide to use the Gratitude Visit (and we hope you do), be prepared for an emotional experience like few others. This is an exercise you can use often in your lifetime.

Writing Tip #6

Finally, discover as much as you can about the new Positive Psychology. If you are in therapy, ask your therapist to teach you these skills as you near the place in therapy where you are decreasing the emotional pain. Browse the Internet for continuing findings on the subject. Check the books in our Reference section. This is an exploding field. What we have presented has been merely an introduction to the subject. By the time you read this book, the field of Positive Psychology will have grown immensely.

Appendix One
Worry and Concern

Many people think worry is "just a part of life." After all, everyone worries. However, worry is a human activity which is destructive, worthless, and always counterproductive. It is most often a mental habit—a habit is something you do, that when you do it, you don't know you are doing it.

Some people think that the opposite of worry is apathy. This is not so. The flip side of worry is concern. This can be confusing to some people because it seems these two are really the same thing. Our culture is often quite supportive of worry because of the inappropriate connection with caring. Often, if you tell someone you do not worry about an issue, they may wonder if it is because you do not care. Worry is not a sign of caring; concern is the real companion of caring.

Unfortunately, some people are such chronic worriers that when they find themselves not worrying, they worry that something is wrong. These "worry warts" think that if they did not worry, life around them would fall apart. As strange as it seems, worry is viewed as a glue that holds life together.

One of your goals is to know the difference and to be able to discriminate between the two. This can be difficult at first because worry and concern have some similarities. They both...

- are mental activities
- can take a lot of effort and energy
- have the potential for focusing on important issues

In spite of these parallels, there are some important differences between worry and concern.

Running in circles. Worry seldom takes us to a place that is growth producing. Worry tends to be repetitive in a way that never helps us to resolve our problems. Concern, on the other hand, is more linear. Concern is characterized by forward movement. It advances us in our life's journey towards growth and maturation.

Destructive behavior. Since our thought processes eventually lead us to action, we see that worry often gets us to behave in ways that are not in our best interest. After we have done something counterproductive as a result of worry, we then have something else to worry about (see Running in circles above). Concern is a thought style that promotes constructive and healthy behavior.

Control. One of the important pieces of being human is our need to have a sense that we are in control of our destiny. We are at our most miserable when we sense that our life is out of control. Worry is a type of mental activity that focuses on those things in life that we have no control over. Human nature is strange — people spend so much of their time trying to control the very things that are out of their control. Concern only expends energy on dealing with those issues which are within our control: our behavior, our emotions, and our sensations.

Some people think that worry is important because it shows they care about what they are worrying about. This connection between caring and worry is a cultural myth. The true sign of caring about something or someone is concern. *Remember: worry is never effective nor necessary!*

Your goal is not to stop worrying. This does not make sense. If worry is a brain activity and you could stop it, then you would be brain dead. This is not a reasonable goal for your life. You want to learn how to *replace* worry with concern.

Appendix Two
Truth Statements

Should

1. I am going to substitute the words "will" or "choose" for the word "should".
2. I am an adult and can decide for myself what is right and wrong.
3. I now realize that I only feel guilty when you try to confuse fantasy and reality.
4. Guilt is one of your tricks to keep me dependent upon the unrealistic expectations of other people.
5. Even though I might wish that things were different, I can now recognize that I need to accept reality as it is.
6. I am not responsible for the feelings of other people.
7. I refuse to allow either you, Voice, or other people to guilt load me.
8. If I have really objectively hurt another person, I will apologize; otherwise I will not accept that responsibility.
9. I can only overcome guilt by actively fighting you, Voice—even though you tell me I can't win.
10. If I don't want to feel guilty, I don't have to—all I need to do is fight back against you, Voice.

Scripture

And as far as sunrise is from sunset, he has separated us from our sins.

—Psalm 103:12 (MSG)

Once again you will have compassion on us. You will trample our sins under your feet and throw them into the depths of the ocean!
—Micah 7:19 (NLT)

For God made Christ, who never sinned, to be the offering for our sin, so
that we could be made right with God through Christ.
—2 Corinthians 5:21 (NLT)

The steps of the godly are directed by the LORD. He delights in every detail of their lives. Though they stumble, they will not fall, for the LORD holds them by the hand.
—Psalm 37:23-24 (NLT)

Help, GOD—the bottom has fallen out of my life! Master, hear my cry for help! Listen hard! Open your ears! Listen to my cries for mercy. If you, GOD, kept records on wrongdoings, who would stand a chance? As it turns out, forgiveness is your habit, and that's why you're worshiped. I pray to GOD – my life a prayer – and wait for what he'll say and do. My life's on the line before God, my Lord, waiting and watching till morning, waiting and watching till morning. O Israel, wait and watch for GOD – with GOD's arrival comes love, with God's arrival comes generous redemption. No doubt about it – he'll redeem Israel, buy back Israel from captivity to sin.
—Psalm 130 (MSG)

I've seen it all in my brief and pointless life—here a good person cut down in the middle of doing good, there a bad person living a long life of sheer evil. So don't knock yourself out being good, and don't go overboard being wise. Believe me, you won't get anything out of it. But don't press your luck by being bad, either. And don't be reckless. Why die needlessly? It's best to stay in touch with both sides of an issue. A person who fears God deals responsibly with all of reality, not just a piece of it.
—Ecclesiastes 7:15-18 (MSG)

All that passing laws against sin did was produce more lawbreakers. But sin didn't, and doesn't, have a chance in competition with the aggressive forgiveness we call grace. When it's sin versus grace, grace wins hands down.
—Romans 5:20 (MSG)

God put the world square with himself through the Messiah, giving the world a fresh start by offering forgiveness of sins. God has given us the task of telling everyone what he is doing.
—2 Corinthians 5:19 (MSG)

Worthless (them)

1. Other people are allowed to make mistakes.
2. No matter what a person does to me, they still have infinite worth.
3. Voice, you only want me to be resentful so that I will eventually cut off all human support and caring.
4. I can be angry without being resentful and full of hatred.
5. You lie when you tell me, Voice, that the way to get things done with other people is to retaliate so they won't hurt me again.
6. The more hatred you allow me to feel, the more self-destructive my own life becomes.
7. All of these resentful feelings are really making me weak and not strong as you would have me believe, Voice.
8. The only person I will allow myself to feel hatred towards is YOU!!
9. Voice, you are my worst enemy and the collection of all evil in the world.
10. Anger can be constructive and maturing if I learn how to handle it properly.

Scripture

Don't repay evil for evil. Don't retaliate when people say unkind things about you. Instead, pay them back with a blessing. That is what God wants you t do, and he will bless you for it.
—1 Peter 3:9 (NLT)

For God is pleased with you when, for the sake of your conscience, you patiently endure unfair treatment.
—1 Peter 2:19 (NLT)

Make a clean break with all cutting, backbiting, and profane talk. Be gentle with one another, sensitive. Forgive one another as quickly and thoroughly as God in Christ forgave you.
—Ephesians 4:31 (MSG)

GOD's now at my side and I'm not afraid; who would dare lay a hand on me? GOD's my strong champion; I flick off my enemies like flies.
—Psalm 118:6-7 (MSG)

Quick-tempered leaders are like mad dogs—cross them and they bite your head off. It's a mark of good character to avert quarrels, but fools love to pick fights.
—Proverbs 20:2-3 (MSG)

Don't let evil get the best of you, but conquer evil by doing good.
—Romans 12:21 (NLT)

If you set a trap for others, you will get caught in it yourself. If you roll a boulder down on others, it will roll back and crush you.
—Proverb 26:27 (NLT)

A stone is heavy and sand is weighty, but the resentment caused by a fool is heavier than both.
—Proverbs 27:3 (NLT)

There's far more to this life than trusting in Christ. There's also suffering for him. And the suffering is as much a gift as the trusting.
—Philippians 1:27-29 (MSG)

Go ahead and be angry. You do well to be angry—but don't use your anger as fuel for revenge. And don't stay angry. Don't go to bed angry. Don't give the Devil that kind of foothold in your life.
—Ephesians 4:26 (MSG)

Danger

1. Feelings cannot destroy anyone—especially me.
2. If I want to get rid of this irrational fear, all I have to do is to fight you.
3. One of your lies is that if I don't insulate myself, other people will just use me as a doormat.
4. If this fear is rational, then it is normal and appropriate.
5. I refuse to let you, Voice, get me so irrationally afraid that I cannot think.
6. You're the source of all my irrational fears, Voice, so I've decided to fight you with all of my strength.
7. I am stronger than you, Voice. I'm going to win—you're going to lose.
8. I am not responsible for this irrational fear—it comes from agreeing with you.

9. Without you around I would never have to be unreasonably afraid anymore.
10. I am tired of being afraid of things that cannot hurt me.

Scripture

The LORD is my light and my salvation—so why should I be afraid?
The LORD protects me from danger—so why should I tremble?
—Psalm 27:1 (NLT)

The LORD is my shepherd; I have everything I need. He lets me rest in green meadows; he leads me beside peaceful streams. He renews my strength. He guides me along right paths, bringing honor to his name. Even when I walk through the dark valley of death, I will not be afraid, for you are close beside me. Your rod and your staff protect and comfort me. You prepare a feast for me in the presence of my enemies. You welcome me as a guest, anointing my head with oil. My cup overflows with blessings. Surely your goodness and unfailing love will pursue me all the days of my life, and I will live in the house of the LORD forever.
—Psalm 23 (NLT)

The LORD's Covenant of Peace: "I will make a covenant of peace with them and drive away the dangerous animals from the land. Then my people will be able to camp safely in the wildest places and sleep in the woods without fear.
—Ezekiel 34:25 (NLT)

You will keep in perfect peace him whose mind is steadfast, because he trusts in you.
—Isaiah 26:3 (NLT)

The fruit of righteousness will be peace; the effect of righteousness will be quietness and confidence forever.
—Isaiah 32:17 (NLT)

"Do not fear, O Jacob my servant; do not be dismayed, O Israel. I will surely save you out of a distant place, your descendants from the land of their exile. Jacob will again have peace and security, and no one will make him afraid.
—Jeremiah 46:27 (NLT)

I will make a covenant of peace with them; it will be an everlasting covenant. I will establish them and increase their numbers, and I will put my sanctuary among them forever.
—Ezekiel 37:26 (NLT)

Such people will not be overcome by evil circumstances. Those who are righteous will be long remembered. They do not fear bad news; they confidently trust the LORD to care for them. They are confident and fearless and can face their foes triumphantly.
—Psalm 112:6-8 (NLT)

Do not fear anything except the LORD Almighty. He alone is the Holy One. If you fear him, you need fear nothing else.
—Isaiah 8:13 (NLT)

So do not fear, for I am with you; do not be dismayed, for I am your God. I will strengthen you and help you; I will uphold you with my righteous right hand.
—Isaiah 41:10 (NIV)

For I am the LORD, your God, who takes hold of your right hand and says to you, Do not fear; I will help you.
—Isaiah 41:13 (NIV)

Stand

1. I may not like it, but I can deal with it.
2. What's happening to me now cannot make me feel trapped—only giving in to you, Voice, can do that.
3. I am strong and can control myself in any situation.
4. I have handled myself well in situations like this before.
5. The reason I am not trapped and helpless is because I can leave this situation anytime I want to.
6. Agreeing with you, Voice, will only make me feel more powerless and miserable.
7. By allowing you to make me feel trapped, Voice, you deny me my freedom.
8. I refuse, Voice to allow you to convince me of something so stupid and absurd—namely, that I am a helpless victim.
9. Other people don't feel helpless because they don't agree with you, Voice.

10. If I run away from this situation now, things will only get worse and I will allow you, Voice to have more power over my life.

Scripture

Our ancestors trusted in you, and you rescued them. You heard their cries for help and saved them. They put their trust in you and were never disappointed. . . . Yet you brought me safely from my mother's womb and led me to trust you when I was a nursing infant. I was thrust upon you at my birth. You have been my God from the moment I was born.
—Psalm 22:4-10 (NLT)

Bless the LORD, who is my rock. He gives me strength for war and skill for battle.
—Psalm 144:1 (NLT)

We can rejoice, too, when we run into problems and trials, for we know that they are good for us—they help us learn to endure. And endurance develops strength of character in us, and character strengthens our confident expectation of salvation.
—Romans 5:3-4 (NLT)

They attacked me at a moment when I was weakest, but the LORD upheld me.
—Psalm 18:18 (NLT)

He lifted me out of the pit of despair, out of the mud and the mire. He set my feet on solid ground and steadied me as I walked along.
—Psalm 40:2 (NLT)

He gives power to those who are tired and worn out; he offers strength to the weak. Even youths will become exhausted, and young men will give up. But those who wait on the LORD will find new strength. They will fly high on wings like eagles. They will run and not grow weary. They will walk and not faint.
—Isaiah 40:29-30 (NLT)

For I can do everything with the help of Christ who gives me the strength I need.
—Philippians 4 (NLT)

But the people who know their God will be strong and will resist him.
—Daniel 11:32 (NLT)

Each time he said, "My gracious favor is all you need. My power works best in your weakness." So now I am glad to boast about my weaknesses, so that the power of Christ may work through me.
—2 Corinthians 12:9 (NLT)

So if you are suffering according to God's will, keep on doing what is right, and trust yourself to the God who made you, for he will never fail you. —1 Peter 4:19 (NLT)

By faith these people overthrew kingdoms, ruled with justice, and received what God had promised them. They shut the mouths of lions, quenched the flames of fire, and escaped death by the edge of the sword. Their weakness was turned to strength. They became strong in battle and put whole armies to flight.
—Hebrews 11:33-34 (NLT)

But you belong to God, my dear children. You have already won your fight with these false prophets, because the Spirit who lives in you is greater than the spirit who lives in the world.
—1 John 4:4 (NLT)

Worthless (me)

1. No one or nothing can make me feel depressed—only agreeing with you, Voice, can do that.
2. Depression can be totally controlled by what I say to you, Voice.
3. No matter what I do, I am still a worthwhile person.
4. I allow myself to feel depressed by agreeing with you, Voice, when you tell me that I am a no-good person.
5. I am a wonderful, delightful, and lovable person merely because I am alive.
6. If other people put me down I do not have to agree with their remarks.
7. Only you, Voice, can put me in the pit; only I can get myself out.
8. My depression will continue until I begin to vigorously fight you, Voice.
9. By keeping me depressed, you have total control over me—I refuse to allow this to happen!

10. It is okay for me to feel sad or discouraged without getting depressed.

Scripture

Why are you down in the dumps, dear soul? Why are you crying the blues? Fix my eyes on God—soon I'll be praising again. He puts a smile on my face. He's my God.
—Psalm 43:5 (MSG)

Therefore, since we have been made right in God's sight by faith, we have peace with God because of what Jesus Christ our Lord has done for us.
—Romans 5:1 (NLT)

My dear children, you come from God and belong to God. You have already won a big victory over those false teachers, for the Spirit in you is far stronger than anything in the world.
—1 John 4:4 (MSG)

But there's one other thing I remember, and remembering, I keep a grip on hope: GOD's loyal love couldn't have run out, his merciful love couldn't have dried up. They're created new every morning. How great your faithfulness! I'm sticking with GOD (I say it over and over). He's all I've got left.
—Lamentations 3:21-24 (MSG)

It stands to reason, doesn't it, that if the alive-and-present God who raised Jesus from the dead moves into your life, he'll do the same thing in you that he did in Jesus, bringing you alive to himself? When God lives and breathes in you (and he does, as surely as he did in Jesus), you are delivered from that dead life. With his Spirit living in you, your body will be as alive as Christ's!
—Romans 8:11 (MSG)

Christ redeemed us from that self-defeating, cursed life by absorbing it completely into himself. Do you remember the Scripture that says, "Cursed is everyone who hangs on a tree"? That is what happened when Jesus was nailed to the Cross: He became a curse, and at the same time dissolved the curse. And now, because of that, the air is cleared and we can see that Abraham's blessing is present and available for non-Jews, too. We are all able to receive God's life, his

Spirit, in and with us by believing—just the way Abraham received it.
—Galatians 3:13-14 (MSG)

And I am convinced that nothing can ever separate us from his love. Death can't, and life can't. The angels can't, and the demons can't. Our fears for today, our worries about tomorrow, and even the powers of hell can't keep God's love away.
—Romans 8:38 (NLT)

What can we say about such wonderful things as these? If God is for us, who can ever be against us?
—Romans 8:31 (NLT)

When I look at the night sky and see the work of your fingers—the moon and the stars you have set in place—what are mortals that you should think of us, mere humans that you should care for us? For you made us only a little lower than God, and you crowned us with glory and honor. You put us in charge of everything you made, giving us authority over all things.
—Psalm 8:3-6 (NLT)

But whoever did want him, who believed he was who he claimed and would do what he said, He made to be their true selves, their child-of-God selves.
—John 1:12 (MSG)

To the church of God which is at Corinth, to those who are sanctified in Christ Jesus, called to be saints, with all who in every place call on the name of Jesus Christ our Lord, both theirs and ours.
—1 Corinthians 1:2 (NKJV)

Tragedy

1. It is reasonable to say "what if"; it is not reasonable to anticipate a personal tragedy or catastrophe.
2. Nothing bad will happen if I will just stop agreeing with you, Voice.
3. Even if something bad does happen, I can still act as a mature, responsible adult.
4. The worry is always worse than the actual event.
5. I can choose to stop worrying if I want to because worry is merely agreement with you, Voice.

6. I am and always will be in control; it is only you telling me that I am going to lose control.
7. I have always performed well and always will perform well in a crisis.
8. I can develop a plan to deal with anything!
9. Voice, you keep trying to trick me by insisting that a low probability event has a very good chance of happening.
10. If I allow myself to agree with you, I will only increase my chances of feeling misery and unhappiness.

Scripture

And we know that God causes everything to work together for the good of those who love God and are called according to his purpose for them.
—Romans 8:28 (NLT)

Each one of you will put to flight a thousand of the voice, for the LORD your God fights for you, just as he has promised.
—Joshua 23:10 (NLT)

Though I am surrounded by troubles, you will preserve me against the anger of my enemies. You will clench your fist against my angry enemies! Your power will save me.
—Psalm 138:7 (NLT)

You both precede and follow me. You place your hand of blessing on my head. Such knowledge is too wonderful for me, too great for me to know!
—Psalm 139: 5-6 (NLT)

My child, don't lose sight of good planning and insight. Hang on to them.

—Proverbs 3 (NLT)

But no weapon that can hurt you has ever been forged. Any accuser who takes you to court will be dismissed as a liar. This is what GOD's servants can expect. I'll see to it that everything works out for the best." GOD's Decree.
—Isaiah 54 (MSG)

But I'll deliver you on that doomsday. You won't be handed over to those men whom you have good reason to fear.
—Jeremiah 39 (MSG)

The LORD is my shepherd; I have everything I need. He lets me rest in green meadows; he leads me beside peaceful streams. He renews my strength. He guides me along right paths, bringing honor to his name. Even when I walk through the dark valley of death, I will not be afraid, for you are close beside me. Your rod and your staff protect and comfort me. You prepare a feast for me in the presence of my enemies. You welcome me as a guest, anointing my head with oil. My cup overflows with blessings. Surely your goodness and unfailing love will pursue me all the days of my life, and I will live in the house of the LORD forever.
—Psalm 23 (NIV)

Do not fear people who can kill the body. They cannot kill the spirit. But fear the one who can destroy both spirit and body in hell.
—Matthew 10:28 (WE)

Who is going to harm you if you are eager to do good? But even if you should suffer for what is right, you are blessed. Do not fear what they fear; do not be frightened.
—1 Peter 3:13-14 (NIV)

GOD met me more than halfway; he freed me from my anxious fears.
—Psalm 34:4 (MSG)

Do not be anxious about anything, but in everything, by prayer and petition, with thanksgiving, present your requests to God.
—Philippians 4:6 (NIV)

Appendix Three
Voice Fighting Kit

General Instructions: Purchase a set of 3x5 wire-bound index cards. Make copies of each the pages in Appendix Three (pages 147-155) and put them in your Voice Fighting Kit.

Instructions for Keyword Chart: Put a copy of this chart on the first page of your Voice Fighting Kit. The blank, right hand column is for your personal keywords.

KEYWORD CHART	
GENERIC KEYWORD	**MY KEYWORD (S)**
Should	
Worthless (them)	
Danger	
Stand	
Worthless (me)	
Tragedy	

Voice Fighting Kit Road Map

The chart below has been designed to fit into your Voice Fighting Kit. You need to make a copy and cut it out to fit on the *inside front cover* of your wire-bound 3x5 index cards.

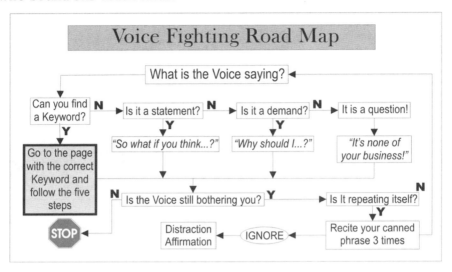

Make copies of the following six pages and paste them in your Voice Fighting Kit starting on the page immediately after the Keyword Chart. You will also find it helpful to tab the pages for each keyword (six tabs in all). That way you can quickly and easily find the pages you need. To see how this all might look, you can visit our web page at www.theworryfree-life.com.

Keyword: *Should*, Ought, Must, etc.
Source: *Mistake*

1. Voice, you're trying to make me feel **guilty**.
2. You want me to **punish** myself.
3. You lie when you tell me that I should (not) _____
4. The Truth is **I can make my own decisions because I am a responsible adult.**
5. Pick 3 arguments from the list below.

    (If the Voice repeats the Keyword, distract yourself and walk away.)

Truth Statements

1. I am going to substitute the words "will" or "choose" for the word "should."
2. I am an adult and can decide for myself what is right and wrong.
3. I now realize that I can only feel guilty when you try to confuse fantasy and reality.
4. Guilt is one of your tricks to keep me dependent upon the unrealistic expectations of other people.
5. Even though I might wish that things were different, I can now recognize that I need to accept reality as it is.
6. I am not responsible for the feelings of other people.
7. I refuse to allow either you, Voice, or other people to make me feel guilty.
8. If I have really objectively hurt another person, I will apologize; otherwise I will not accept that responsibility.
9. I can only overcome guilt by actively fighting you, Voice—even though you tell me I can't win.
10. If I don't want to feel guilty, I don't have to—all I need to do is fight back against you.

Scriptural Truth:

And you will know the truth, and the truth will make you free.
—John 8:32

Being made free from sin, you became servants of righteousness.
—Romans 6:18

Is not this the holy day for which I have given orders: to let loose those who have wrongly been made prisoners, to undo the bands of the yoke, and to let the crushed go free, and every yoke be broken?
—Isaiah 58:6

Blessed are those who do not condemn themselves by doing something they know is right. —Romans 14.22

As far as the east is from the west, so far has He removed our sins from us. —Psalm 103.12

Once again you will have compassion on us. You will trample our sins under your feet and throw them into the depths of the ocean.
—Micah 7:19

Keyword: *Worthless,* Rotten, No Good, etc. [THEM]
Source: *Violation*

1. Voice, you're trying to make me feel **resentful**.

2. You want me to **retaliate**.

3. You lie when you tell me that he or she is worthless because

4. The Truth is **that no matter what that person did to me they still have infinite worth.**

5. Pick 3 arguments from the list below.

   (If the Voice repeats the Keyword, distract yourself and walk away.)

Truth Statements

1. Other people are allowed to make mistakes.
2. No matter what a person does to me, they still have infinite worth.
3. Voice, you only want me to be resentful so that I will eventually cut off all human support and caring.
4. I can be angry without being resentful and full of hatred.
5. You lie when you tell me that the way to get things done with other people is to retaliate so they won't hurt me again.
6. The more hatred you allow me to feel, the more self-destructive my own life becomes.
7. All of these resentful feelings are really making me weak and not strong as you would have me believe.
8. The only person I will allow myself to feel hatred towards is YOU!!
9. You are my worst enemy and the collection of all evil in the world.
10. Anger can be constructive and maturing if I learn how to handle it properly.

Scriptural Truth:

But I tell you, love your enemies, bless those who curse you, do good to those who hate you, and pray for those who spitefully use you and persecute you. —Matthew 5: 44

A stone is heavy and sand is weighty, but the resentment caused by a fool is heavier than both. —Proverbs 27:3

Let all you do be done in love. —1 Corinthians 13:1

The LORD is with me; I will not be afraid. What can man do to me? The LORD is with me; he is my helper. I will look in triumph on my enemies. —Psalm 118: 6-7

Do not repay evil with evil or insult with insult, but with blessing, because to this you were called so that you may inherit a blessing. —1 Peter 3:9

Keyword: *Dangerous*, Scary, Frightening, etc.
Source: *Feelings*

1. You are Voice and you're trying to make me feel irrational fear.
2. You want me to insulate myself.
3. You lie when you tell me that these feelings are dangerous and can destroy me.
4. The Truth is even though these feelings are uncomfortable they can make me stronger.
5. Pick 3 arguments from the list below.

    (If the Voice repeats the Keyword, distract yourself and walk away.)

Truth Statements

1. Feelings cannot destroy anyone—especially me.
2. If I want to get rid of this irrational fear, all I have to do is to fight you.
3. One of your lies is that if I don't insulate myself, other people will just use me as a doormat.
4. If this fear is rational, then it is normal and appropriate.
5. I refuse to let you, Voice, get me so irrationally afraid that I cannot think.

6. You're the source of all my irrational fears, so I've decided to fight you with all of my strength.
7. I am stronger than you. I'm going to win—you're going to lose.
8. I am not responsible for this irrational fear—it comes from agreeing with you.
9. Without you around I would never have to be unreasonably afraid anymore.
10. I am tired of being afraid of things that cannot hurt me

Scriptural Truth:

The LORD is my light and my salvation—so why should I be afraid? The LORD protects me from danger—so why should I tremble? —Psalm 27:1

For God did not give us a spirit of timidity, but a spirit of power, of love and of self-discipline. —1 Timothy 1:7

You will keep in perfect peace him whose mind is steadfast, because he trusts in you." —Isaiah 26:3

So do not fear, for I am with you; do not be dismayed, for I am your God. I will strengthen you and help you; I will uphold you with my righteous right hand. —Isaiah 41:10

For I am the LORD, your God, who takes hold of your right hand and says to you, Do not fear; I will help you. —Isaiah 41:13

Keyword: Stand, Handle, Tolerate, etc.
Source: Conflict

1. Voice, you're trying to make me feel helpless.
2. You want me to run away.
3. You lie when you tell me that I can't stand_____
   .
4. The Truth is I have been standing it all my life.
5. Pick 3 arguments from the list below.

   (If the Voice repeats the Keyword, distract yourself and walk away.)

Truth Statements

1. I may not like it, but I can deal with it.
2. What's happening to me now cannot make me feel trapped—only

giving in to you, Voice, can do that.

3. I am strong and can control myself in any situation.
4. I have handled myself well in situations like this before.
5. The reason I am not trapped and helpless is because I can leave this situation anytime I want to.
6. Agreeing with you, Voice, will only make me to feel more powerless and miserable.
7. By allowing you to make me feel trapped, Voice, you deny me my freedom.
8. I refuse, Voice, to allow you to convince me of something so stupid and absurd—namely, that I am a helpless victim.
9. Other people don't feel helpless because they don't agree with you, Voice.
10. If I run away from this situation now, things will only get worse and I will allow you, Voice to have more power over my life.

Scriptural Truth:

Our ancestors trusted in you, and you rescued them. You heard their cries for help and saved them. They put their trust in you and were never disappointed . . . Yet you brought me safely from my mother's womb and led me to trust you when I was a nursing infant. I was thrust upon you at my birth. You have been my God from the moment I was born.
—Psalm 22:4-10

Bless the LORD, who is my rock. —Psalm 144:1

We can rejoice, too, when we run into problems and trials, for we know that they are good for us — they help us learn to endure. And endurance develops strength of character in us .—Romans 5:3-4

They attacked me at a moment when I was weakest, but the LORD upheld me. —Psalm 18:18

He gives power to those who are tired and worn out; he offers strength to the weak. —Isaiah 40:29-30

For I can do everything with the help of Christ who gives me the strength I need. —Philippians 4

Each time he said, "My gracious favor is all you need. My power works best in your weakness." So now I am glad to boast about my weaknesses, so that the power of Christ may work through me. —2 Corinthians 12:9

So if you are suffering according to God's will, keep on doing what is right, and trust yourself to the God who made you, for He will never fail you. —1 Peter 4:19 (NLT)

Keyword: *Worthless*, Rotten, No Good, etc. [ME]
Source: *Loss*

1. Voice, you're trying to make me feel depressed.
2. You want me to be lifeless.
3. You lie when you tell me that I'm worthless because _____
   .
4. The Truth is no matter what I do, I still have infinite worth.
5. Pick 3 arguments from the list below.

   (If the Voice repeats the Keyword, distract yourself and walk away.)

Truth Statements

1. No one or nothing can make me feel depressed—only agreeing with you, Voice, can do that.
2. Depression can be totally controlled by what I say to Voice who is you.
3. No matter what I do, I am still a worthwhile person.
4. I allow myself to feel depressed by agreeing with you, Voice, when you tell me that I am a no-good person.
5. I am a wonderful, delightful, and lovable person merely because I am alive.
6. If other people put me down I do not have to agree with their remarks.
7. Only you, Voice, can put me in the pit; only I can get myself out.
8. My depression will continue until I begin to vigorously fight you.
9. By keeping me depressed, you have total control over me—I refuse to allow this to happen!
10. It is okay for me to feel sad or discouraged without getting depressed.

Scriptural Truth:

And I am convinced that nothing can ever separate us from His love.
—Romans 8:38

He lifted me out of the ditch, pulled me from deep mud. He stood me
up on a solid rock to make sure I wouldn't slip. He taught me how to
sing the latest God-song, a praise song to our God. More and more
people are seeing this: they enter the mystery, abandoning themselves
to God.
—Psalm 40:2-3

Christ redeemed us from that self-defeating, cursed life by absorbing
it completely into himself. —Galatians 3:13

God created man in his own image. —Genesis 1:26

Are you not conscious that your body is a house for the Holy Spirit
which is in you, and which has been given to you by God? —1
Corinthians 3:17

You, dear children, are from God and have overcome them, because
the one who is in you is greater than the one who is in the world.
—1 John 4:4

Keyword: *Tragedy*, Catastrophe, Awful, etc.
Source: *Threat*

1. Voice, you're trying to make me feel unhealthy anxiety.
2. You want me to avoid something.
3. You lie when you tell me that something bad is going to happen
    and that would be a tragedy.
4. The Truth is nothing can happen to me which will keep me from
    making choices.
5. Pick 3 arguments from the list below.

    (If the Voice repeats the Keyword, distract yourself and walk away.)

Truth Statements

1. It is reasonable to say "what if"; it is not reasonable to anticipate a
    personal tragedy or catastrophe.
2. Nothing bad will happen if I will just stop agreeing with you.

3. Even if something bad does happen, I can still act as a mature, responsible adult.
4. The worry is always worse than the actual event.
5. I can choose to stop worrying if I want to because worry is merely agreement with you, Voice.
6. I am and always will be in control; it is only you telling me that I am going to lose control.
7. I have always performed well and always will perform well in a crisis.
8. I can develop a plan to deal with anything!
9. Voice, you keep trying to trick me by insisting that a low probability event has a very good chance of happening.
10. If I allow myself to agree with you, I will only increase my chances of feeling misery and unhappiness.

Scriptural Truth:

My child, don't lose sight of good planning and insight. Hang on to them. — Proverbs 3:21

God met me more than halfway, he freed me from my anxious fears. — Psalm 34:4

Do not be anxious about anything, but in everything, by prayer and petition, with thanksgiving, present your requests to God. — Philippians 4:6

Cast all your anxiety on him because he cares for you. 1 Peter 5:7

Don't fret or worry. Instead of worrying, pray. Let petitions and praises shape your worries into prayers, letting God know your concerns. — Philippians 4:6

No, in all these things we are more than conquerors through him who loved us. — Romans 8:37

Appendix Four
Satisfaction with Life Scale

Below are five statements that you may agree or disagree with. Using the 1 - 7 scale below indicate your agreement with each item by placing the appropriate number on the line preceding that item. Please be open and honest in your responding.

7 - Strongly agree
6 - Agree
5 - Slightly agree
4 - Neither agree nor disagree

3 - Slightly disagree
2 - Disagree
1 - Strongly disagree

_____ In most ways my life is close to my ideal.

_____ The conditions of my life are excellent.

_____ I am satisfied with my life.

_____ So far I have gotten the important things I want in life.

_____ If I could live my life over, I would change almost nothing.

30-35   Extremely satisfied, much above average
25-29   Very satisfied, above average
20-24   Somewhat satisfied, average for American adults
15-19   Slightly dissatisfied, a bit below average
10-14   Dissatisfied, clearly below average
5-9   Very dissatisfied, much below average

Tens of thousands of individuals across several cultures have taken this test. Here are some representative norms:

- Among older American adults, men score 28 on average and women score 26

- The average North American college student scores between 23 and 25

247

- Eastern European and Chinese students on average score between 16 and 19
- Male prison inmates score about 12 on average, as do hospital inpatients
- Psychological outpatients score between 14 and 18 on average
- Among older American adults, men score 28 on average and women score 26
- The average North American college student scores between 23 and 25
- Eastern European and Chinese students on average score between 16 and 19
- Male prison inmates score about 12 on average, as do hospital inpatients
- Psychological outpatients score between 14 and 18 on average

Glossary

Affirmations - Phrases that are used to replace the destructive messages from the Voice (worry) are called affirmations. The most striking aspect of affirmations is their unbelievability. They need to be used as replacement thoughts because you don't believe them. Affirmations are often used prematurely—before minimizing the influence of the Voice. They have little effect for people who live with a strong, demanding Voice.

Automatic Thinking - The thoughts we have just below the level of awareness. Many years ago, psychologists referred to these thoughts as the unconscious or subconscious. It was believed that these thoughts were unchangeable and inaccessible to us even while affecting us. With the new tools of cognitive psychology, people now have access to, and can modify, these subterranean thoughts.

Cognitive Behavioral Therapy (CBT) - CBT is one of a handful of therapy approaches with a solid scientific foundation. Begun in the 1950's CBT has as its basis the recognition that our emotions are the results of our thoughts. By changing our thoughts we can change our emotions. For example, once a person changes their belief that they are bad and worthless to a new belief in their infinite worthfulness, they no longer have to live with depression.

Conditioned Response - This is a behavior which has been learned so well that it has become automatic. It seems to happen without any effort or willfulness on our part. People who continue to pull slot machine levers even though they only get paid off now and then have been conditioned to do so.

Deficit Behavior - Things we don't do very often but need to more often are called deficit behaviors.

Domino Effect - The domino effect is a description of the relationship between our thoughts, sensations, emotions and behavior. This bundle is often preceded by a triggering event outside us and followed by a consequence outside of us. The first domino is a life event, followed by a thought (whether we are aware of it or not), which generates an emotion, that leads to a behavior, possible bringing about a change in our immediate environment.

Excessive Behavior - The opposite of a deficit behavior. It refers to something we do too much or too often that needs to happen less often.

Feelings - Feelings refer to our internal comfort state. Feelings are generally of two types: emotions and sensations. Both can be preceded by thoughts and followed by behaviors. The difference between emotions and sensations is often confusing. Examples of emotions include happiness, sadness, anxiety and fear. Sensations are physical feelings: urges, appetites, pains, muscular tensions, fatigue

Flow - Flow refers to an internal experience that occurs when we are intensely focused on an activity. It often occurs during a time of heightened concentration, serenity, a distorted sense of time, and a strong feeling of being in personal control. Only about 15% of all people never experience it.

Grace - Although grace can refer to a complex theological idea, we use the word in this book to refer to a state of existence provided by God that helps us to be all that he wants us to be.

Grace Partner - Someone you can trust to interact with you as you learn the skills in this book. Many people find that growth and maturity is greatly increased in the presence of other people.

Gratitude Visit - A specific exercise in chapter 11 of this book. It is one of the many specific skills that help people move from "zero to plus seven."

Healthy Emotional Pain - Not all pain and discomfort is bad for you. In fact, all emotions, with the exception of six emotions, are normal and healthy. Maturity skills help us to accept and then use these emotions to help us build Christian character.

Keywords - Keywords are words that identify the six core lies that the Voice uses to destroy you and run your life. Each keyword represents a specific Voice lie that destroys your ability to lead a healthy and authentic life.

Metaphor - A metaphor is a comparison showing how two unlike things are similar in a significant way. The Voice is a metaphor for worry (see Pests Metaphor).

Mindfulness - A life-building skill that helps you become acutely aware of your emotions and sensations. It helps you to accept healthy, painful emotions so that you let them make you stronger.

Motivator (reinforcer) - A motivator is any consequence that increases the behavior that preceded the consequence. A motivator does not have to be pleasant to be effective. Motivators are use to increase deficit behaviors.

Operational Definition - An objective way of defining something. Operational definitions are clear, measurable, specific, and unambiguous.

Pest Control Kit - Another title for the Voice Fighting Kit. This equipment is designed to help you cheat when dealing with the Voice. It minimizes the need for memorizing the steps for taking your life back. The more you use it, the stronger you will become.

Pests Metaphor (see metaphor) - The pests are destructive thoughts and beliefs that damage your ability to see the real world and to understand yourself clearly.

Positive Psychology - A new branch of psychology begun at the end of the twentieth century. This science for this new psychology began in the latter half of the twentieth century. Positive psychology mainly focuses on people's strengths and virtues and attempts to help people learn new skills for increasing happiness and well-being. Positive psychology emphasizes positive emotions, positive individual traits, and positive institutions.

Reducer - Since the word "punishment" is so emotionally loaded we have used the term "reducer" to indicate a consequence designed to reduce the frequency of a behavior.

Reinforcer - See motivator (reinforcer).

Replacement Behaviors - When people reduce or eliminate excessive behaviors, they need to replace them with behaviors that make it difficult for the excessive behaviors to return.

Replacement Truths - Similar to replacement behaviors. Once the Voice is weakened and minimized people need to replace the old thought processes with new, healthy replacement thoughts. The truths are often the opposite of the Voice's lies.

Resiliency - Resiliency is a person's ability to cope with, and bounce back from, trauma. Psychologists are finding that most people have more resiliency that previously thought. Most people can learn how to become more resilient.

Silent Assumptions - This is a phrase that identifies our thoughts that are beyond our awareness. The Voice likes hiding them so that we cannot change them but are still affected by them.

Unhealthy Emotional Pain - This is the type of emotional pain caused by the six lies from the Voice. Since there are only six of these, people can focus on decreasing them. Removing them from one's life makes it easier to work on replacement behaviors, increasing resiliency and experiencing Christian well-being.

Vermin Metaphor - The vermin seriously affect the garden of our mind. They stand for the six core lies from the Voice (see keywords).

Voice, the - Dealing with the "Voice" instead of "worry" is a powerful technique for managing habitual, destructive thoughts and beliefs. Putting the Voice outside of you allows you to give up responsibility for worry — negative thinking, destructive thoughts, etc. — and makes you *more* able to take responsibility for doing something about it.

Worry (destructive thinking styles) - Many people think of worry as ruminating about the future—about what will happen. We define worry as destructive thoughts not only about the future but also the past and present.

References

Books

Bell, R. (2005). Velvet Elvis: Repainting the Christian faith. Grand Rapids, MI: Zondervan.

Blanchard, K. (2006). Lead like Jesus: Lessons from the greatest leadership role model of all time. Nashville: W Publishing Group.

Brickman, P. & Coates, D. (Eds.). (1987). Commitment and mental health. Englewood Cliffs, NJ: Prentice-Hall.

Burka, J. B. & Yuen, L. M. (1983). Procrastination: Why you do it. What you can to about it. Menlo Park, CA: Addison-Wesley.

Campbell, A. (1981). The sense of well-being in America. New York: McGraw-Hill.

Campolo, T. (1995). Carpe Diem. Nashville: W Publishing Group.

Carnell, E. J. (1959). The case for orthodox theology. Philadelphia: Westminster Press.

Cloud, H. & Townsend, J. (2002). Boundaries. Grand Rapids, MI: Zondervan.

Cloud, H. (2006). Integrity: The courage to meet the demands of reality. New York: Collins.

Diener, E. & Lucas, R. (1999). Personality and subjective well-being. New York: Russell Sage.

Dryden, W. (1999). Overcoming jealousy. London: Sheldon Press.

Eisner, D. A. (2000). The death of psychotherapy: From Freud to alien abductions. Westport, CT: Praeger Publishers.

Eldredge, J. (2000). The journey of desire: Searching for the life we only dreamed of. Nashville: Nelson Books.

Ellis, A. & Yeager, R. J. (1989). Why some therapies don't work: The dangers of transpersonal psychology. Buffalo, NY: Prometheus Books.

Emde, R. N., Hewitt, J. K. & Kagan, J. (Eds.). (2001). Infancy to early childhood; Genetic and environmental influences on developmental change. Oxford: Oxford University Press.

Enright, R. D. (2001). Forgiveness is a choice: A step-by-step process for resolving anger and restoring hope. Washington, D.C.: American Psychological Association.

Enright, R. D. & Fitzgibbons, R. P. (2002). Helping clients forgive: An empirical guide for resolving anger and restoring hope. Washington, D.C.: American Psychological Association.

Flanigan, B. (1992). Forgiving the unforgivable. New York: Wiley.

Fromm, E. (1941). Escape from freedom. New York: Rinehart.

Gatchel, R. J. (2004). Clinical essentials of pain management. Washington, D.C.: American Psychological Assocation.

Goleman, D. (1995). Emotional intelligence: Why it can matter more than IQ. New York: Bantam Books.

Hindy, C. G. & Schwarz, J. C. (1990). If this is love why do I feel so insecure? New York: Fawcett.

Hodgson, R. & Miller, P. (1982). Self watching: Addictions, habits, compulsions: What to do about them. New York: Facts On File, Inc.

Hybels, B. (1987). Who you are when no one's looking. Urbana, IL: InterVarsity.

Hybels, B. & Nystrom, C. (1998). Too busy not to pray journal. Downers Grove, IL: InterVarsity Press.

Kabat-Zinn, J. (1990). Full catastrophe living: Using the wisdom of your body. New York: Dell Publishing.

Kagan, J. (2005). Young mind in a growing brain. Mahwah, NJ: Lawrence Erlbaum.

Kagan, J. (1998). Three seductive ideas. Cambridge, MA: Harvard University Press.

Kagan, J. (2004). The long shadow of temperament. Cambridge, MA: Belknap Press.

Kagan, J. & Lamb, S. (Eds.). (1990). The emergence of morality in young children. Chicago: University of Chicago Press.

Lamott, A. (2005). Plan B: Further thoughts on faith. New York: Penguin Books.

Langer, E. J. (1998). Mindfulness. Reading, MA: Addison-Wesley.

LeDoux, J. (2003). Synaptic self: How our brains become who we are. New York: Penguin Books.

Lewis, C. S. (2001). The problem of pain. San Francisco: HarperSanFrancisco.

Linder, S. (1970). The harried leisure class. New York: Columbia University Press.

Linley, P. A. & Joseph, S. (Eds.). (2004). Positive psychology in practice. New York: Wiley.

Lucado, M. (2006). The cure for the common life. Nashville: W Publishing Group.

McLaren, B. (2006). The secret message of Jesus: Uncovering the truth that could change everything. Nashville: W Publishing Group.

Meyer, J. (2002). Battlefield of the mind: Winning the battle in your mind. Joyce Meyer Trade.

Myers, D. (1987). Psychology through the eyes of faith. San Francisco: HarperSanFrancisco.

Myers, D. (1992). The pursuit of happiness: Who is happy and why. New York: William Morrow.

Myers, D. & Scanzoni, L. (2005). What God has joined together?: A Christian case for gay marriage. San Francisco: HarperSanFrancisco.

Nezu, A. M., Nezu, C. M. & Perri, M. G. (1989). Problem-solving therapy for depression: Theory, research and clinical guidelines. New York: Wiley.

Nezu, C. M. & Nezu, A. M. (2003). Awakening self-esteem: Spiritual and psychological techniques to enhance your well-being. Oakland, CA: New Harbinger.

Noll, M. (1994). The scandal of the Evangelical Mind. Grand Rapids, MI: William B. Eerdmans.

Ortberg, J. (2004). Living the God life. Grand Rapids, MI: Inspirio.

Ortberg, J. (2005). God is closer than you think: This can be the greatest moment of your life because this moment is the place where you can meet God. Grand Rapids, MI: Zondervan.

Ortberg, J. (2001). If you want to walk on water, you've got to get out of the boat. Grand Rapids, MI: Zondervan.

Ortberg, J. (2002). The life you've always wanted. (Expanded E edition ed.). Grand Rapids, MI: Zondervan.

Ortberg, J. (2003). Everybody's normal till you get to know them. Grand Rapids, MI: Zondervan.

Osteen, J. (2004). Your best life now: 7 steps to living at your full potential. Lebanon, IN: Warner Faith.

Phillips, J. B. (1960). Your God is too small. New York: Macmillan.

Pines, A. . M. (1998). Romantic jealousy: Causes, symptoms, cures. Oxford: Routledge.

Prochaska, J. O., Norcross, J. C. & DiClemente, C. C. (1994). Changing for good. New York: Harper-Collins.

Ruge, K. C. & Lenson, B. (2003). The Othello response: Dealing with jealousy, suspicion and rage in your relationship. London: Marlowe & Company.

Sandbek, T. J. (1993). The deadly diet: Recovering from anorexia and bulimia. Oakland, CA: New Harbinger.

Seabury, D. (1990). The art of selfishness. New York: Pocket Books. Reprint Edition

Seligman, M. E. P. (1995). What you can change and what you can't: The complete guide to successful self-improvement. New York: Ballantine Books.

Seligman, M. E. P. (1996). The optimistic child: Proven program to safeguard children from depression & build lifelong resilience. New York: Harper Paperbacks.

Seligman, M. E. P. (2004). Authentic happiness: Using the new positive psychology to realize your potential for lasting fulfillment. New York: Free Press.

Seligman, M. E. P. (1998). Learned optimism: How to change your mind and your life. New York: Free Press.

Shatte, A. & Reivich, K. (2002). The resilience factor: 7 essential skills for overcoming life's inevitable obstacles. New York: Broadway.

Siegel, D. J. (2001). The developing mind: How relationships and the brain interact to shape who we are. New York: Guilford Press.

Smedes, L. B. (1997). Art of forgiving. New York: Ballantine Books.

Spong, J. S. (2002). A new Christianity for a new world. San Francisco: HarperSanFrancisco.

Stanley, C. F. (2004). When the enemy strikes: The keys to winning your spiritual battles. Nashville: Nelson Books.

Staudacher, C. (1987). Beyond grief: A guide for recovering from the death of a loved one. Oakland, CA: New Harbinger.

Sulloway, F. J. (1996). Born to rebel: Birth order; family dynamics, and creative lives. New York: Pantheon Books.

Sweet, L. (2006). The three hardest words in the world to get right. Colorado Springs, CO: WaterBrook Press.

Swindoll, C. (2004). Getting through the tough stuff: It's always something. Nashville: W Publishing Group.

Sykes, C. J. (1993). A nation of victims: The decay of the American character. New York: St. Martins Griffin.

Tavris, C. (1989). Anger: The misunderstood emotion. Carmichael, CA: Touchstone Books.

Tillich, P. (1967). Systematic Theology. (Vol. 2). Chicago: University of Chicago Press.

Townsend, J. (2004). Who's pushing your buttons? Handling the difficult people in your life. Franklin, TN: Integrity Publishers.

Wallis, J. (2005). God's politics: Why the right gets it wrong and the left doesn't get it. San Francisco: HarperSanFrancisco.

Warren, R. (2002). The purpose-driven life: What on earth am I here for? Grand Rapids, MI: Zondervan.

Watson, D. & Tharp, R. (2001). Self-directed behavior: Self-modification for personal adjustment (6th edition). Pacific Grove, CA: Brooks/Cole.

Wilkinson, B. (2003). The dream giver. Sisters, OR: Multnomah Publishers.

Yancey, P. (2005). Finding God in unexpected places. Vine Books.

Articles

Pay nags at workers' job views. (1987), Chicago Tribune.

Curry, L. A., Snyder, C. R., Cook, D. L., Ruby, B. C. & Rehm, M. (1973). Role of hope in academic and sport achievement. Journal of Personality & Social Psychology 73(6), 1257-1267.

Diener, E., Horowitz, M. J. & Emmons, R. A. (1985). Happiness of the very wealthy. Social Indicators 16 262-274.

Diener, E. & Seligman, M. (2002). Very happy people. Psychological Science 13 80-83.

Diener, E. & Suh, E. (1998). Subjective well-being and age: An international analysis. Annual Review of Gerontology and Geriatrics 17 304-324.

Diener, E., Suh, E. & Oishi, S. (1997). Recent findings on subjective well-being. Indian Journal of Clinical Psychology.

Frisch, M. B. (1998). Quality of life therapy and assessment in health care. Clinical Psychology: Science & Practice 5(1), 19-40.

George, M. S., Ketter, T. A., Parekh, P. I. & Horwitz, B. (1995). Brain activity during transient sadness and happiness in healthy women. American Journal of Psychiatry 152(3), 341-351.

Horton, T. V. & Wallander, J. L. (2001). Hope and social support as resilience factors against psychological distress of mothers who care for children with chronic physical conditions. Rehabilitation Psychology 46(4), 382-399.

Ingram, R. E., P., Smith, T. W., Donnel, C. & Ronan, K. (1987). Cognitive specificity in emotional distress. Journal of Personality and Social Psychology 53(4), 734-742.

Myers, D. G. & Diener, E. (1996). The pursuit of happiness: New research uncovers some anti-intuitive insights into how many people are happy and why. Scientific American 70-72.

Parr, G., Haberstroh, S. & Kottler, J. (2000). Interactive journal writing as an adjunct in group work. Journal for Specialists in Group Work 25(3), 229-242.

Pavot, W. & Diener, E. (1993). Review of the Satisfaction With Life Scale. Psychological Assessment 5(2), 164-172.

Rafanelli, C., Park, S. K., Ruini, C., Ottolini, F., Cazzaro, M. & Fava, G. A. (2000). Rating well-being and distress. Stress Medicine 16(1), 55-61.

Ryff, C. D. (1989). Happiness is everything, or is it? Explorations on the meaning of psychological well-being. Journal of Personality and Social Psychology 57(6), 1069-1081.

Salovey, P. & Mayer, J. D. (1990). Emotional intelligence. Imagination, Cognition & Personality 185-211.

Schneider, S. L. (2001). In search of realistic optimism: Meaning, knowledge, and warm fuzziness. American Psychologist 56(3), 250-263.

Snyder, C. R., Harris, C., Anderson, J. R., Holleran, S. A., Irving, L. M. & Sigmon, S. T., et al. (1991). The will and the ways: Development and validation of an individual-differences measure of hope. Journal of Personality and Social Psychology 60(4), 570-585.

Snyder, C. R., Shorey, H. S., Cheavens, J., Pulvers, K. M., Adams, V. H. I. & Wiklund, C. (1994). Hope and academic success in college. Journal of Educational Psychology 94(4), 820-826.

Waterman, A. S. (1993). Two conceptions of happiness: Contrasts of personal expressiveness (eudaimonia) and hedonic enjoyment. Journal of Personality and Social Psychology 64(4), 678-691.

Yancey, P. (2005). Finding God in unexpected places. Vine Books.

More on *The Worry Free Life*

Congratulations! You are well on your way to living the worry free life God intended for you.

Your mind's "garden" can be free of unhealthy, worrisome thoughts—you just need to prune it regularly.

Authors Dr. Terry Sandbek and Patrick W. Philbrick provide further tools to attack the "weeds" that try to grow back while nurturing the positive growth that has already begun.

1. Visit **www.TheWorryFreeLife.com**

2. Subscribe to *The Worry Free Life* monthly newsletter by emailing **Suscribe@TheWorryFreeLife.com**

3. Request class materials to start your own small group or life skill class at **www.TheWorryFreeLife.com**

4. Receive updates on the latest related publications: books, CDs, sermon ideas, and more by emailing **Inquiry@TheWorryFreeLife.com**

Or, contact the publisher with requests, comments, questions or further information:

Green Valley Publishing LLC
4300 Auburn Bl, Ste 206
Sacramento, Ca 95841
(530) 621-3098

You really can live a life free from worry!